CONDOR CHRONICLES

AN ANGUS AIR STATION

A PICTORIAL AND ANECDOTAL STORY OF R.N.A.S. H.M.S. CONDOR

Compiled and edited by Ken Smith

Finavon Print & Design

First Published in Great Britain in 1998
by Finavon Print & Design
3 Cadgers Path, Finavon.
Angus. DD8 3QB

Typesetting & Design by Finavon Print & Design

ISBN 0 - 9528813 - 3 - 0

To Margaret

ACKNOWLEDGEMENTS

Air Britain (Historians) Ltd.
Angus Council.
A.R.N.O.
Condor Photographic Section.
F.A.A. Officers Association.
Imperial War Museum.
Naval Historical Collectors
and Research Association.
Naval Historical Society.
Royal Marines (Condor Barracks).
Tayside Police.

Angus Archivists.
Angus Tourist Board.
Commonwealth War Graves Commission.
Fleet Air Arm Museum.
Globe and Laurel.
Museum of Flight (Scotland).
Public Records Office.
Signal Tower Museum.
The Journal of the R.N. Medical Service.
The Wren (Association of Wrens).

Ian Archer.
Miss I.M. Austen M.B.E.
Derek Bates.
Don Crocker.
Muriel C. Currie M.B.E.
R.J. Dunn.
Mrs C. Fraser.
Eddy Griffiths.
J.J. Halley M.B.E.
T.C. Hollands.
E. Irwin.
Janet Langmaid.
Tom McKay B.E.M.
Alex Muir.
Bill Parker.
Tony Perrett.
Colin Price.
Adam Smith.
Alan Sturgeon.
Richard Taylor.
Tony Withers.
Muriel Woods.

Mrs L. Atkinson.
Peter Bing O.B.E.
Grenville Cooper.
Bill Clark.
Collin Davis.
W.D. Damiens.
Joy Freeman.
K Garry.
Brian Horton.
L.W. Hawkins.
Betty Kremis.
J.R.P. Lansdown.
A.S. McLean.
F.W.May.
John Platt.
Ted Phillips.
Ken Pryce.
Brian Sutherland.
Patricia Stanton.
Margaret Taylor.
Charles Wyatt.

J.F. Allen.
Peggy Blackburn.
D.J. Collingwood B.A.
G.J. Carter.
Alistair Donald.
Peter Dallosso.
Joan Fiddler.
A.J. Griffith.
Madge Helm.
Wendy Hogarth.
Colin Linington.
Peter Moody.
Julie Meyler.
Jo Nelmes.
C.T. Parsons.
George Parker.
Joe Riley O.B.E.
M.F. Simpson.
E.J. Sayce.
Jon Veale.
Tug Wilson.

My thanks to anyone I may have inadvertently overlooked, the help and support I have received from all sources has been greatly appreciated.

Ken Smith.

PROLOGUE

Only memories remain - now is the time to record the story of Condor - not just another history book but a way of life for many thousands of personnel, men, service and civilian. It was a happy station for most, for many it was their first time away from home, a big adventure. Some were married here, their children born here - some died here.

The men and women who made up the Ship's Company or Squadrons of Condor, those that settled here in Arbroath, or moved to the corners of the earth - these are the characters of this book, this is their story.

For those that attended the '96 Reunion, I hope it brings back happy memories. For those who, for various reasons, could not attend maybe it could renew old acquaintances, that lost oppo........

Unfortunately there is no chapter on civilian workers. They were there in abundance, boilermen, drivers, cobblers, barbers, storemen, and many others, not forgetting the ladies of the NAAFI. Apart from a few photographs of MT staff there is little to record..........

CONTENTS

Chapter 1

History and Construction

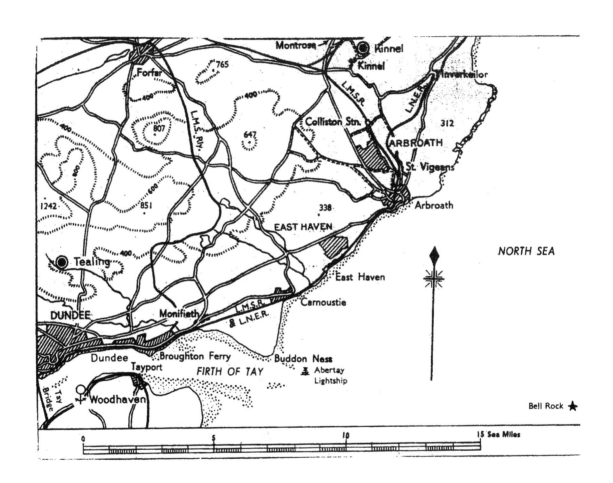

NORTH SEA

Montrose
Kinnel
Kinnel
Inverkeilor
Forfar
765
L.M.S.R.
L.N.E.R.
312
Colliston Stn.
807
L.M.S. Rly.
647
ARBROATH
St. Vigeans
1242
851
338
Arbroath
400
EAST HAVEN
600
600
Tealing
400
East Haven
DUNDEE
Monifieth
Carnoustie
L.M.S.R. & L.N.E.R.
Broughton Ferry
Buddon Ness
Dundee
Tayport
FIRTH OF TAY
Abertay Lightship
Tay Bridge
Woodhaven

Bell Rock ★

0   5   10   15 Sea Miles

Ship's Name.	H. M. S. CONDOR.
Approx. Area.	504 acres.
Tenure.	Purchased by Admiralty.
Date of Occupation or Acquisition.	1st July, 1940.
Date of Commissioning.	
Particulars of Encroachments.	
Reference to letters under which Establishment has been transferred on loan.	

Particulars of additional accommodation held on Lease or Requisition.

Description.	User Prior to Requisition.	Naval User.
A site 30' x 30'0" between Ashbrooke and Woodside House.	Farming.	H/F D/F Site.
Cromarty, Bank Street. 49'8". x 35'0". 49'8" x 33'6".	Business Premises.	Stores Dispersed and Aircraft.
Indoor Riding School, Chauffour's House, Carpenter's Shop and Saw Mill. The Old Forge, open Hay Shed. Stable and Coachhouse. Hay Loft and 6 Stall Stable.	Private and Estate.	Dispersal of Stores.
Pool Mill, Hume St., 70' x 40'.	Wholesale Fruiterers.	Aircraft repair shop extension.
Pool Mill Warehouse, Hume.	Wholesale Fruiterers.	Aircraft Repair Shop.
The Garage, Gravesend. 2,000 sq. ft.	Garage and Store.	Alternative accommodation for Messrs. Stephens (Fruiterers).
A site and strip of land on Paradiso Farm. 24' x 24'. Access strip 12' wide.	Farming.	Gun site for Defence of Airfield.
Area of land, Leysmill Station.	Rough grazing.	Landmark, Beacon Site.
Two areas of Land, Kits Den. 20 x 18.	Farming.	Rifle Range.
An area of land Kits Den. 2½ acres.	Farming.	Rifle Range.
An area of land East Seaton Farm. Approx. an acre.	Farming.	720 Housing Beacon Site.
Area of land Colliston Farm. acre.	Farming.	Aircraft Dispersal.
... of land	... ...	... ...

Description.	User Prior to Requisition.	Naval User.
Area of land, West Kirton Farm. 100 x 50.	Farming.	Aircraft Dispersal.
Area of land near Freserfield Farm. 66' x 50'	Farming.	Dispersed Aircraft.
Area of land near Boysackhill. 80 x 50.	Farming.	Dispersed Aircraft.
Area of land near Firthfield. 75 x 50.	Farming.	Dispersed Aircraft.
Two areas of land, Woodville Kennels. (a) 140 x 80 (b) 120 x 70.	Farming.	Dispersed Aircraft.
Mid Peebles Farm. 16 acres.	Farming.	Dispersed Aircraft.
Two areas of land, Woodville Kennels. (a) 66 x 50 (b) 75 x 50.	Farming.	Dispersed Aircraft.
Area of land at Little Denmark. 80 x 40.	Farming.	Aircraft Dispersal.
Area of land Boysackhill Farm. 200 x 120.	Farming.	Dispersed Aircraft.
Area of land Boysackhill Farm. 110 x 70.	Farming.	Dispersed Aircraft.
Area of land Firthfield Farm. 80 x 40.	Farming.	Dispersed Aircraft.
Area of land, East Mains Colliston Farm. ⅓ acre.	Farming.	Dispersed Aircraft.
Area of land, Cotton of Colliston. ½ acre.	Farming.	Dispersed Aircraft.
Area of land, Peebles Farm. 140 x 60. 120 x 50.	Farming.	Dispersed Aircraft.
Area of land, Muirheads Farm. 110 x 60.	Farming.	Dispersed Aircraft.
Area of land, Donside Colliston Farm. 140 x 120.	Farming.	Dispersed Aircraft.
Area of land Colliston Farm. 21 acres.	Farming.	Dispersed Aircraft.
Area of land Muirhead Farm. 20½ acres.	Farming.	Dispersed Aircraft.
Area of land Mid Peebles Farm. 16½ acres.	Farming.	Dispersed Aircraft.
Area of land, Peebles Farm, 42 acres.	Farming.	Dispersed Aircraft.
Area of land, Freserfield Farm. 120 x 30.	Farming.	Dispersed Aircraft.

Description.	User Prior to Requisition.	Naval User.
Area of Land, Leonhead of Colliston. 120 x 60.	Farming.	Dispersed Aircraft.
Area of land, Leonhead of Colliston. 80 x 50.	Farming.	Dispersed Aircraft.
Area of land, Denside. ½ acre.	Farming.	Dispersed Aircraft.
The Remainder Ashbrooke House.	Private Dwelling.	Security reasons.
Ashbrooke House.	Private Residence.	Offices for Air Signal School.
Woodside House.	Private Residence.	Accommodation for Defence Personnel.
Transfer from W.D. 16/12/41. 5001/4405/1A.		
* Woodville House.	Private Residence.	Sleeping accommodation for W.R.N.S.
Gynd House.	Private Residence.	Accommodation for W.R.N.S.
The Remainder of Letham Grange.	Private Residence.	Accommodation for W.R.N.S.
Letham Grange Mansion House.	Private Residence.	Dispersal of Personnel outside Arbroath R.N.A. Station.
Kelly Castle.	Private Residence.	Dispersed Sick Quarters.
Area of land Cotton of Colliston. 80 x 80.	Farming.	VH/F Receiver.
Area of land North Mains Farm.	Farming.	Quadrant Hut Site.
Three sites Letham Grange for Electric Light Poles.		Electric Lighting Installation.
Area of land Derfield Farm. 20 x 20.	Farming.	VH/F and D/F Sites.
A site for Manhole, Peebles Farm. 5'6" x 4'6".		Drainage of Aircraft Dispersal Field.
Area of land, Derfield Farm. 30'0" x 30'0".	Farming.	Rest Hut for VH/F D/F.

① Free for early release. — RARA 031154/2.46

15

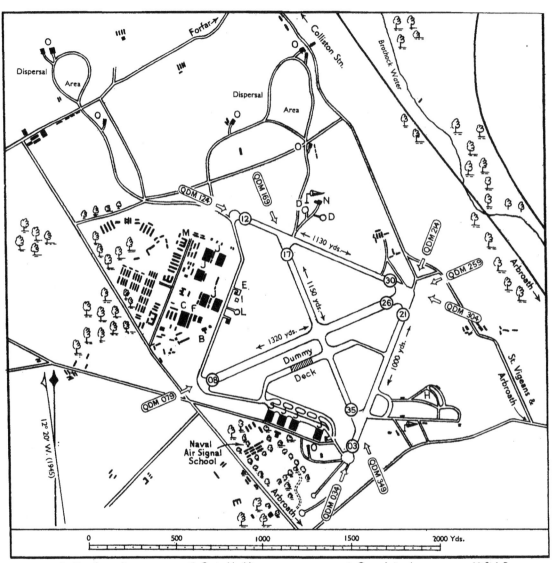

A. Aircraft standings
B. Armoury
C. A.R.S. hangar
D. Compass base

E. Control building
F. E.R.S. hangar
G. Equip: & Erect: hangar
H. Explosives area

I. Ground signals
J. Hangars
K. Pens
L. Radar test base

M. Sick Bay
N. Test butt
O. Workshop
P. Apron

HISTORY OF H.M.S. CONDOR

The Royal Naval Air Station, Arbroath, is the fourth ship to bear the name H.M.S. Condor. The first "Condor" was a gun vessel of 780 tons built in 1876. She had a complement of 100 and an armament of rifled muzzle loaders, the largest being a four and a half ton 7 inch gun. She took part in the bombardment of Alexandria in 1882 and saw action in the Sudan in 1884-85. She was eventually paid off in 1887.

The second "Condor" was a steel sloop of 980 tons which was commissioned in 1900 with a complement of 130 and an armament of six 4 inch quick firing guns. She was intended for service in the Pacific but whilst on passage between Esquimalt and Honolulu she encountered a violent gale and sank with all hands on 3rd December, 1901.

A hired trawler of 227 tons was the third ship to bear the name "Condor". She was commissioned for patrol service in 1914 but was wrecked off Lowestoft on 22nd November of the same year.

In April 1939, the Board of Admiralty announced their decision to build an airfield near Arbroath in the County of Angus. Rather more than a year later, with a displacement and complement somewhat larger than her predecessors, the Royal Naval Air Station, Arbroath was commissioned on 5th July, 1940, under the command of Captain E.M. Connolly Abel Smith, Royal Navy. On 6th July, 1940, 778 Squadron arrived only fourteen months after building had started on the airfield. Four days later, 763 Squadron arrived from the south of France. They were renumbered 767 Squadron and were employed on deck landing training.

August, 1940 saw the start of one of Condor's major wartime tasks, the Part II training of Observers. Until that time their training had been split between R.N.A.S. Yeovilton and R.N.A.S. Ford. The new scheme provided for Part I training at Ford and Part II training at Arbroath. The Observers School moved up with 751 and 753 Squadrons from Ford and 754 Squadron from Lee-on-Solent on 19th August and commenced flying on the 26th of that month. The training of Observers took 22 months from entry to being fully qualified and ready for the field.

By October, 1940 , the station supported 751, 753, 754, 758, 767 and 778 Squadrons with 791 Squadron forming. 778 Squadron was made up of several aircraft types and was employed on trials and testing experimental equipment. The squadrons consisted of up to 25 aircraft each and operated many types including Albacores, Swordfish, Walrus, Fulmars, Sharks and Proctors.

On 25th. October at 1845 the station was attacked by enemy aircraft. An estimated 12 bombs and 100 incendiaries were dropped from two Heinkel 111's and one Dornier 115. Of the bombs dropped, two failed to explode and four only partially exploded. A squadron office was demolished and two other buildings had their roofs blown off. Otherwise the damage was of a minor nature and the total cost of repairs was only four thousand pounds. The station air defence consisted chiefly of Lewis guns manned by the Army, who unfortunately, thinking that the enemy aircraft were friendly and about to land, didn't fire a single shot until it was too late.

In December, 1940, 791 Squadron was affiliated to 758 Squadron for deck landing practice, the flying task having increased with the training of air gunners here.

The year 1941 saw the already intensive flying task built up even further. In January, 880, 768 and 783 Squadrons started forming up as a station worked up to its peak and the final stages of the building programme were completed. There were as this time some R.A.F. personnel on the station who were lent for administration and maintenance duties.

On 8th March, 1941, King George VI visited the station and planted a tree just inside the main gate to mark his visit.

June 1939 - Mr C.F. Armstrong was called to the Admiralty - promoted to Superintending Civil Engineer to organise construction of R.N. Air Station as from 1st July 1939.

When he arrived the place was still under crops, but the "displenishment sale" had been held. This meant that a quantity of agricultural equipment was awaiting removal, the fields were mostly under crops which still had to be sold, gathered and removed.

For the first week or so he was alone on the site, making his office in a farmhouse of Beechwood Farm whilst his office was being built. Staff slowly arrived and surveys were made to enable planning in detail to proceed.

August - contractors arrive to deal with airfield and accommodation area as and when crops were lifted. The living accommodation was originally planned to be of timber construction. The outbreak of war caused an immediate shortage of timber, and it was decided to use brick in "rat trap" bond.

Work advanced steadily until January 1940 when appalling weather started, hard frost and snow for about six weeks, virtually stopping all work. However, by early March things were progressing well.

The first naval officer arrived, Paymaster Commander Eric Churcher. About mid-April, Rear Admiral Naval Air Training wanted to see how the station was progressing and could he fly in. On receiving a satisfactory answer Admiral Bell-Davis flew in, lunched at the Seaforth Hotel, and flew out again, the first aircraft to land at Arbroath.

The station was commissioned on 19th June 1940, under the command of Commander "Tom" Sawyer, pending the arrival of a captain. The first Captain was E.M.C. Abel-Smith.

About the middle of August, the Observer School at Ford was knocked out by raids. Arbroath was asked to re-accommodate the School. The buildings were not completed, no paths and gumboots rig of the day, but the School was accommodated.

Early October saw the first raid with bombing of the airfield. The most spectacular happening was a bomb which hit the first hut of the Petty Officers Mess, burst through it and the side wall, passed through both walls of the second hut, bruising one man from shoulder to elbow while he lay on his bunk reading the evening newspaper, knocked a hole in the wall of the third hut and fell back on the ground outside. It was defused safely next morning.

Naval airstations differ from R.A.F. stations in that they have four runways - one for dummy deck landings - they also normally have three storey air control towers instead of two - Arbroath (Condor) along with Henstridge (Heron) were exceptions in that they had five runways.

Within one year of the station commissioning, aircraft operating from Condor were flying 2000 hours per month, the record occurring in June when a total of 2230 hours 45 minutes flying time was achieved. In August, 1941, 751 Walrus Squadron was moved to Dundee to operate from the small Air Station, Stannergate. The reason for the move was that the aircrafts' undercarriages were being damaged on the runways at Condor and it was found to be more satisfactory to land them on the River Tay and taxi them to sheds by the waters edge.

At the end of the year three air firing ranges were started, these were in Lunan Bay, off Stonehaven and off Arbroath. The R.A.F. were given permission to use Stonehaven and Lunan Bay but not Arbroath as there had been several near-misses in the local area due to misunderstandings in air movements. These ranges were used until 1943.

The satellite airfield at Easthaven was used for the first time in early 1942 when 767 and 769 Squadrons moved there. Easthaven, commissioned as H.M.S. Peewit , was to be used for flying operations up to the end of the war. In February, 1942, the Signals School started at Arbroath and at the same time several front-line squadrons visited the station for short periods of rest.

During the year, a new system of maintenance organisation called Centralised Maintenance, was started. This entailed the heavy maintenance and repair jobs on aircraft being done by the stations and not by the squadrons. Squadrons had, at this time, been moved to various sites around the airfield, with the aircraft being housed in Dutch barns. This was done to cut down the possible damage from future attacks. Fortunately, there were no further raids.

During the years 1942 and 1943, the flying continued as in the previous year , a very large variety of aircraft being used. These included, in addition to the types already mentioned, Lysanders, Barracudas, Seafires, Hurricanes , Rocs and Skuas. As the end of the war approached the flying training commitment decreased. 1944 saw the departure of many of Condors' squadrons though a great deal of bombing practice was still carried out. The Observers' School left and Easthaven was virtually closed for flying. Quite a large number of aircraft still remained but Condor's future hung in the balance.

In 1945, R.A.R.A. or Rear Admiral (E) in charge of Reserve Aircraft Maintenance and Technical Training stations moved to Condor from Lee-on-Solent. The first R.A.R.A., Rear Admiral (E) Bedale, took up his appointment with no disciplinary powers and yet had charge of the aircraft and training in sixteen different air stations or establishments. This was to be changed later, in 1952, as was his title, to Rear Admiral (E) Reserve Aircraft.

By the end of 1945, Condors' new role had been decided and an advance party of officers and ratings from Newcastle-under-Lyme, the Aircraft Apprentices Training Establishment. With the advent of the jet age, the stations' operational flying days came to an end and Condor assumed her present important role of technical and new entry training.

The main body of Artificer Apprentices joined on 2nd January, 1946, some of whom were initially accommodated at Easthaven. Eventually there was a total of approximately 1500 trainees. Apprentices stayed at Easthaven until 1948, when the station was converted to temporary married quarters. It was finally closed in 1949.

In January, 1949, courses were started for Aircraft Mechanician. From 1950 until 1958 there were various conversion courses held for E.R.A. to A.A. During this period many nationalities including Canadians, Australians, Indians and Pakistanis could be seen attending instruction.

In 1958, the Leading Air Mechanics courses moved up from Yeovilton and when , in the same year, the Royal Naval Air Station at Bramcote closed, the Air Mechanic Training was transferred to Condor. During the two years, 1957 and 1958, Condor started courses for Naval Air Mechanics, Leading Air Mechanics, Short Aircraft Maintenance and Instructional Technique.

Virtually the whole of Fleet Air Arm ratings , A/E and O was taken over from 1958 and has remained here ever since. As the training task built up the flying task decreased and in 1959 the Flag Officer reserve Aircraft, the erstwhile R.A.R.A. left Condor to return to Lee-on-Solent.

In 1961, after a long and amicable association, and on her 21st birthday, the freedom of the Royal Burgh of Arbroath was conferred on H.M.S. Condor.

Condor consisted of the airfield and adjacent buildings and two large houses, Ashbrooke and Woodville. The ship's company included trainees some 1200 strong, about 100 of whom were W.R.N.S.

Long courses were held for Naval Air mechanic (A/E and O), Leading Air Mechanic (A/E and O), Aircraft Artificer Apprentice and Aircraft Artificer 3rd Class. Short courses include Electrical Officers Cross Training, Short Aircraft Maintenance, Air Armaments, Fleet Air Arm acquaintance for Sea Cadets and Instructional Technique.

Apart from the training of technical ratings, Condor's airfield was still open for communicating aircraft and for the training of Naval and R.A.F. personnel in gliding.

Whilst Condor remained the centre of technical training for the Fleet Air Arm she catered for those who lived up to her motto -

SORS VARIA OPUS IDEM.

Condor, Arbroath, Royal Naval Air Station commissioned 19th June 1940 (advance offices opened May

1940)- paid off 1st April 1971 (became Royal Marine barracks).

Included Royal Naval Air Station, Dundee (Condor II) (Which was also a Royal Naval Seaplane site 1912 - WW1) and Easthaven (later H.M.S. Peewit).

Condor II, Dundee, Royal Naval Air Station. Commissioned 15th July 1941 - paid off 15th June 1944.

Easthaven (later H.M.S. Peewit).

Commissioned as Landing Training School, later Naval Air Signals School - accommodated up to 200 aircraft - housed office of Commodore Flying Training, later R.A.R.A. (FORA) - flying ceased 1954, continued for ground training - paid off and taken over by Royal Marines as Condor Barracks.

Condor was granted the Freedom of Arbroath in October 1961 - Guard Commander Lt. A.E. Sturgeon (now Captain) with S/Lt. Brian Putlock as second in command. The Commander was Steve Sampson, he was relieved by Cdr. Lewes-Jones. Captain Illingworth's tour of duty was cut short as he was appointed to **M.O.D. and was relieved by Captain K.R. Hickson.**

The Queen Mother visited the Condor in September 1961.

02/02/40 at 1130hrs. - Two Dornier 17's pursued by Spitfire turned inland, chased out again low enough to just miss the spire of Ladyloan High Church.

Saturday 17/08/40.- Detachment from Condor attended funeral of two crew members of Heinkel 115 in Eastern Cemetery with **full military honours.**

Condor was one of the Navy's most active stations during WWII. Its first task, in '39 - '40 was as an observer training school and training of pilots for deck landing. In those roles Swordfish, Albacores, Walrus and Blackburn Sharks were used. Those aircraft, although of biplane configuration, served well in their training role.

Condor's workload was greatly increased as the war progressed, with target towing, radar instruction, practice dive bombing and a service trials unit. All this activity made the base very overcrowded, and it remained so until the opening of R.N.A.S. Easthaven,H.M.S. Peewit, just south of Arbroath, in mid 1943, when some of the deck landing units were transferred there. Both aerodromes saw many and varied aircraft, some of the more notable being the American-built Vought Chesapeake dive bomber, the mid-engined Bell Airacobra, Martlets and Avengers.

The Service Trials Unit was to evaluate some prototype and development aircraft, and February '43 saw the arrival of the large Blackburn Firebrand, and the very noisy Fairey Barracuda II, the Fairey Firefly and the legendary Supermarine Spitfire in Mark 12 configuration, the navy name for the last mentioned being

Seafire. It was extensively tested at Condor and Easthaven by Supermarine and RN test pilots. Another famous R.A.F. fighter modified for naval service was the Hawker Hurricane Mk 2. With all the test flying and training flights, many accidents happened, some with fatal results.

From late '44 all future aerial activity in the remaining war years would be of a friendly nature, with the pilots being those from Condor and Easthaven. They came from far and near, and some would lose their lives in accidents, many miles from home, without even taking part in the war. More than one of them had cause, however, to be grateful to the grieve of Parkhill farm, for on no less than three occasions he rescued crews from their crashed aircraft. For this he received the B.E.M.

Training continued at Condor and Easthaven , and on 23rd June 1944, a spectacular accident occurred in the early hours of the morning. A F.A.A. Barracuda crashed on Victoria Street, burst into flames, set fire to a house and damaged another with no injuries. The pilot baled out. He landed by parachute at Keptie pond, the pilotless
machine just missed a roof in Victoria Street, but part of it struck a chimney. The roof was holed and the 'plane then nose-dived into the garden at the front of the house, somersaulted and broke in two pieces across the street. It exploded on contact and burning fuel shot into the air. The road became a blazing inferno, flares from the 'plane exploded in all directions. Residents, using stirrup pumps and buckets, fought the fire until the Naval fire brigade and NFS took control.

1845hrs - 25th October 1940 - Attack by two Heinkel III's and one Dornier - dropped 12 bombs and 100 incendiaries - Two bombs failed to detonate and four only partially exploded. The following morning a mine was found suspended by it's parachute from a tree, later made safe. These aircraft were chased by a Hurricane of 111 Squadron R.A.F., piloted by S/Lt. Worral R.N., but failed to make contact and crashed on landing at Montrose airfield at 2000 hrs , fortunately without injury. It appears the raiders started a fire at Cellardyke, near Crail, in Fife, worked up to St. Andrews, H.M.S. Condor, Montrose and finished up at Wick and Lossiemouth. It is believed that the aircraft belonged to :-

> KAMPFGESCHWADER 26 (Bomber Group 26)
> 1 GRUPPE   (1 Wing).

consisting of :-

> STAB   (HQ Staff Flight).
> STAFFEL 1,2 or 3 (Squadron 1,2 or 3).

This was known as the 'LION' Bomber Group - on either side of the fuselage was painted the profile of a lion with the words 'VESTIGIUM

LEONIS' (The Sign of the Lion). The Squadron was based in Norway.

This raid also sank the 'DUTHIES' (F.A.A. tender) by a near-miss alongside the jetty at Montrose.

Types of bombs usually carried by Heinkels were :-

SC250 - SC for Sprengbombe Cylindrisch (Explosive Bomb Cylindrical) 250 Kilos (550 lbs)

Flammenbombe (Oil Bomb). Flamm C250 containing a lethal oil incendiary mixture plus H.E. bursting charge.

Parachute mines were principally :-

L.M.A. or L.M.B. (Luff - Mine A or B) - 500 Kg (1100 lbs) or 1000 Kg (2200 lbs).

Incendiary Bombs and BSK container - Container BSK36 with 36x1Kg magnesium bombs.

EXTRACTS FROM ARBROATH COUNCIL MINUTES.

08/05/39 - Naval Aerodrome.
From civil engineer to Admiralty, have decided to acquisition of land near Arbroath.

28/05/39 - Reference above.
Water supply required 100,000 gallons per day by March 1940 latest - letter dated 25th August from Messrs. A.G. Rennie and Sons, builders, Brechin, applying for supply in connection with contract work for new aerodrome.

28/11/40 - War Graves.
Captain Abel Smith requested reservation of 48 graves in the compartment of 'D' block north for R.N. personnel.

11/02/41 - Complaints.
Mr. Munro, hall keeper, reported to town council unsatisfactory conduct of F.A.A. ratings when attending dances in hall. Copy of letter to C.O. R.N.A.S.

01/05/41 - Reference above.
Letter sent to Captain Abel Smith, the chief constable could not corroborate with hall keeper's complaint, apologies for the tone of their letter to him.

18/05/41 - Swimming.
Captain Abel Smith requested solo use of swimming pool for one hour for four or five days a week. Instruction to be given by naval instructor.

Convenor gave permission for Thursday evenings at swimming club rate. If bathing slips required an offer was made by A.K. Adamson to supply "Beatrice Twill Slips" at 20/- per dozen, coupons required. Captain Abel Smith undertook to provide necessary priority certificates.

28/10/43 - War Graves.

50 extra lairs in Western Cemetery requested by Captain R.N.A.S. Cost three pounds per lair plus 7/6 registration fee, trees to be removed at Admiralty expense.

02/03/44 - Reference above.

Senior surveyor of lands, Rosyth, requested Council for reduction to Two pounds and ten shillings per layer at cemetery because Admiralty were clearing trees at a cost of Fifty pounds.

21/03/46 - Housing.

Request by Captain R.N.A.S. stating that accommodation for married personnel was under consideration. Town replied it was not possible to provide houses for naval personnel.

30/05/46 - Souvenir.

Mr.J.B. Simpson, 78 St. Vigeans Road, offered the town a souvenir of the"Graf Spee". Namely, a steam valve. Offer accepted.

29/08/46 - War Graves.

Council undertook maintenance of War Graves for all time at no cost.

23/01/47 - Compensation.

Claim against Admiralty for compensation on conclusion of hostilities for removal of trees at Muirheads reservoir to improve visibility of airfield at H.M.S. Condor.

20/03 & 24/04/47 - Compensation.

Discussion of compensation to salvage dredgers crew for salvage of "plane?" in June 1947, majority of crew members refused compensation offer.

30/06/47 - Housing.

Admiralty housing programme proposed naval housing estate of Lochlands for personnel of R.N.A.S.

17/04/50 - Signposting.

C.O. Condor requested signposting directing traffic through burgh to H.M.S. Condor, lorries having difficulty finding aerodrome.

11/10/51 - Memorial.

Erection of Cross of Sacrifice by War Graves Commission at service plots in Western Cemetery.

08/02/52 - Proclamation.

Council declared proclamation of Queen Elizabeth II.

27/04/53 - Memorial.

Unveiling of Cross of Sacrifice on 31st May 1953 by Vice Admiral Abel Smith.

02/06/53 - Coronation.

Parade of services. P.T. display by Condor, fire fighting display in conjunction with Angus Fire Service, fly past of Naval aircraft.

29/10/53 - Lifeboat.

Lifeboat 'Robert Lindsay' lost with six crew.

28/12/53 - Christmas.

Gifts from Condor to children in council care, party at R.N.A.S.

26/11/56 - Headstone.
Approval was given for erection of headstone in Western Cemetery for P.O.W.E. La Plant.

29/06/61 - Freedom.
Following 21st anniversary of Condor, freedom of burgh awarded. Celebration to be Saturday 14th October 1961.

08/03.65 - C.A.D.S.
Christopher Fry's "The Lady's Not For Burning" to be performed by Condor Amateur Dramatic Society in Condor cinema. Proceeds to Winston Churchill Memorial Appeal.

21/07/65 - Silver Jubilee.
March past and presentation, fireworks and entertainments. Entry half price to service personnel in uniform. Presentation of caldelabra to Captain R.H. Weber.

19/12/66 - Donation.
C.P.O. Mess donated gift of toys to needy kids.

29/02/68 -Future of Condor.
Forthcoming discussion with Captain Mott and Provost regarding government proposals as regards future of Condor.

26/12/68 - Removal.
First hints of Condor moving to Lee-on-Solent.

15/08/68 - Future of Condor.
First of several discussions on future of Condor though to 10/03/69.

28/08/69 - Donation.
A donation of Twenty-five pounds was offered to Condor subaqua club for voluntary assistance in clearing dock gates.

08/12/69 - 45 Commando.
Confirmation that 45 Commando R.M. taking over Condor in 1971.

16/02/70 - Freedom.
Freedom of Arbroath. Handing over ceremony for 22/07/70. Council extended hospitality to Condor, discussions with Captain Hardy.

31/03/71 - Housing.
Allocation of housing for Royal Marines prior to Allocation of married Quarters.

PROVOST's of ARBROATH during the period that H.M.S. CONDOR was commissioned.

1939 Sir Wm. Chapel.
1943 John Lamb.
1949 John Webster.
1952 J.K. Moir.
1957 D.A. Gardner.
1966 R.R. Spink

ABSTRACTS FROM NEWSPAPER CUTTINGS HELD IN ARBROATH LIBRARY.

19/05/56	Duke of Edinburgh at Condor.
13/10/56	Annual inspection, Rear Admiral R.L. Fisher Inspects Air Station and personnel, Superin tendent E.M. Hampson O.B.E. inspects Wrens.
01/11/57	H.M. The Queen lands at Condor.
21/05/58	Duchess of Kent visits Condor.
18/07/58	First Sea Lord, Earl Mountbatten visits Condor.
14/03/60	A First. Royal Marine Band based at Condor.
22/04/60.	New RC church opened by Bishop of Dunkeld , Rt. Rev. Dr. W.A. Hart.
23/12/60	Admiralty gives permission for Condor to be used as Dundee Airport.
27/01/61	Dan-Air and Admiralty officials meet.
24/02/61	Charlie Chester show at Condor.
20/05/61	Princess Marina, Duchess of Kent, inspects Wrens.
02/06/61	Dan-Air Dakota takes off for London.
21/07/61	Condor receives FREEDOM OF ARBROATH.
17/08/61	Queen Mother unveils stained glass windows in St. Christopher's church.
08/12/61	Dan-Air service discontinued due to lack of support.
19/01/62	St. Andrews makes gift to Condor church.
28/03/62	Dedication of Condor church.
04/08/62	History of Condor anchor furbished by J. Riley (now S/M J. Riley O.B.E.).
26/11/64	Rear Admiral J.K. Watkins congratulates volunteer band on winning Bambara Trophy.
26/03/65	C.A.D.S. perform "The Lady's Not for Burning" for Churchill Memorial Fund.
23/07/65	Presentation Ceremony for Condor semi-jubilee.
15/10/65	Vice Admiral Sir Richard M. Smeaton visits Condor.

18/03/66	Vice Admiral D.C.E.F. Gibson visits Condor.
09/12/66	Restored Walrus handed over to F.A.A. Museum.
01/03/68)	
19/07/68)	
16/08/68)	Concern over future of Condor, meetings,
23/08/68)	indecision. Provost puts case to Under-
13/12/68)	Secretary for Navy in London, more indecision,
03/0169)	rumours and conjecture, disaster for Arbroath,
17/01/69)	no reprieve , future still uncertain.
21/02/69)	
28/02/69)	
14/03/69)	
16/05/69)	
07/11/69)	
25/07/69	Freemen march through Arbroath, last Air day attended by Princess Alexandra and other distinguished guests.
12/12/69	Condor future settled, first Scottish Royal Marine Commando base.
08/05/70	Scottish Amateur Band Association Contest won by Condor Volunteer Band.
18/05/70	CPO Bob Criggie awarded BEM in Birthday Honours.
24/07/70	Freedom Scroll returned to Arbroath Council for safekeeping.
30/07/70	Last March Past for Freemen.
31/07/70	Government lifts axe on F.A.A. but Condor still closing.
14/08/70	Final Passing Out Parade after 30 years.
02/04/71	Commander D.H.D. Merrin hands over to Lt. Col. R.J. Ephraums , 45 Commando. Also musical spectacular in Webster Hall by R.M. Band as a farewell to Arbroath.

H.M.S. CONDOR

CAPTAIN G. W. TANNER, R.N.

Parade of the Queen's Colour
of the Fleet Air Arm

To celebrate the Birthday of
Her Majesty the Queen

●

Her Majesty the Queen will be represented by the Lord Lieutenant of Angus, the Rt. Hon. The Earl of Airlie, K.T., G.C.V.O., M.C., J.P.

The Parade will be inspected by Vice-Admiral Sir Deric Holland-Martin, K.C.B., D.S.O., D.S.C. and bar, the Flag Officer Air (Home)

●

Saturday, 11th June, 1960

Official Programme   **Sixpence**

PROGRAMME

EVENT	SPECTATORS	MUSIC
March on Markers (at 1025)	Remain seated	—
March on Platoons (at 1030)	Remain seated	*Colonel Bogey*
March on the Royal Guard and Colour (at 1040)	Stand. Gentlemen uncover	*Blue Devils*
Arrival of Inspecting Officer, the Flag Officer Air (Home) (at 1050)	Stand. Gentlemen uncover	*Iolanthe*
Inspection of Parade by Inspecting Officer	Remain seated	*Duke of York, Cavalry Brigade, Scipio, Berenice, I could have danced all night*
Arrival of the Lord Lieutenant of Angus, representing Her Majesty the Queen (at 1110)	Stand. Gentlemen uncover until completion of National Anthem	*National Anthem*
Inspection of Royal Guard	Remain seated	
Advance in Review Order	Stand. Gentlemen uncover until completion of National Anthem	*Nancy Lee, National Anthem*
"Q" Battery, 276 (Highland) Field Regiment, Royal Artillery (T.A.) fire Royal Salute Feu de Joie	Stand. Gentlemen uncover until completion of National Anthem	*National Anthem*
Three Cheers for Her Majesty the Queen	Stand. Spectators are invited to cheer with the Parade	
March past of Royal Guard, Colour and Parade, including 276 (Highland) Field Regiment, Royal Artillery (T.A.)	Stand. Gentlemen uncover as Queen's Colour passes	*Hearts of Oak, Thin Red Line, Our Director, Wings over the Navy*
Departure of the Lord Lieutenant of Angus and the Flag Officer Air (Home) (at 1150 approx.)	Stand. Gentlemen uncover	

OFFICERS OF THE PARADE

Parade Commander:
Commander T. S. Sampson, R.N.

Guard Commander:
Lieutenant Commander A. M. Keane, R.N.

Colour Officer:
Lieutenant P. J. Shaw, R.N.

Guard Second in Command:
Lieutenant E. O. Tonkin, R.N.

Parade Marshal:
Sub-Lieutenant J. A. Warner, R.N.

Platoon Commanders (in order of marching past):

Sub-Lieutenant R. T. James, R.N.
Lieutenant O. P. Verma, Indian Navy.
Lieutenant B. Shaw, R.N.
Lieutenant A. C. P. Spain, R.N.
Lieutenant E. J. Robinson, R.N.
Lieutenant J. H. Melvill, R.N.

Sub-Lieutenant C. P. H. Saunders, R.N.
Sub-Lieutenant W. F. S. Silverthorne, R.N.
Lieutenant D. E. Moore, R.N.
Sub-Lieutenant G. J. Carter, R.N.
Lieutenant Commander F. M. Meyler, R.N.
Sub-Lieutenant B. G. Puttock, R.N.

Third Officer P. M. A. Clarke, W.R.N.S.

Parade Chief Gunnery Instructor:
Chief Petty Officer L. S. G. Causon.

Colour Chief Petty Officer:
Chief Petty Officer A. W. H. Heald.

BANDS

The Royal Marine Band of the Scottish Command, conducted by Bandmaster H. C. Farlow, Royal Marines, will lead the Royal Guard in the March Past.

The Condor Brass Band, conducted by Band Sergeant F. Matthias, Royal Marines, will play during the March Past of unarmed platoons.

"Q" BATTERY, 276 (HIGHLAND) FIELD REGIMENT, ROYAL ARTILLERY (T.A.)

The Battery is commanded by Major J. G. Mathieson, R.A.

Captain N. M. Sharp, R.A., commands the detachment which is firing the salute.

The 21 gun Royal Salute is to be fired by 4 gun detachments from "Q" (Arbroath) Battery of 276 (Highland) Field Regiment, Royal Artillery (T.A.). All the men in the detachment are Territorial Volunteers from Arbroath, many of whom have come off work a few hours prior to taking part in the Parade. The Battery, which celebrated its centenary last year, has a strength of 80 men.

THE QUEEN'S COLOUR

The Colour which is being paraded on this occasion, is that which Her Majesty was graciously pleased to present in 1956 to the Fleet Air Arm, to honour its size and status.

The Colour is kept at the Royal Naval Air Station, Lee-on-Solent, which is the Headquarters of the Home Air Command.

The message which Her Majesty sent from Buckingham Palace on the occasion of the presentation is reproduced below.

The Queen's Colour may only be paraded by a Royal Guard of Honour mounted for a member of the Royal Family, a Foreign Sovereign, the President of a Republic, or at a Queen's Birthday Parade.

It is a White Ensign of Silk with Crown and Royal Cypher superimposed, and has blue and gold cord and tassels.

The Queen's Colour, when uncased, is at all times accorded the highest honours, and is guarded by a Royal Guard and Special Colour party.

BUCKINGHAM PALACE

Commodore Glenny, Officers and Ship's Company of the Royal Naval Barracks, Lee-on-Solent:

In 1924, my grandfather approved that eight King's Colours should be given to the Royal Navy to be kept at various stations at home and overseas. Two years ago I gave my approval to the addition of a further Queen's Colour to be given to the Royal Naval Barracks, Lee-on-Solent. I did so gladly, in order to recognise the part played by the Fleet Air Arm in the Royal Navy. Its speedy growth has been not merely in size, but in reputation and esteem. Its many gallant achievements constitute a record which is worthy of the glorious traditions of the Royal Navy, and of which the Royal Navy is justly proud. The Fleet Air Arm, in turn, is proud to be a part of the Royal Navy, which has now become equally at home in the air and at sea.

By its exploits in the Pacific and Atlantic Oceans, in the pursuit of the Bismark and at Taranto it has added to the long list of historic and decisive engagements fought over the centuries by British seamen; and it has a roll of honour of brave and resourceful men equal to that of any branch of the Fighting Services.

This Colour, which I give to you to-day as the representatives of the Fleet Air Arm, is the visual embodiment of the achievements of naval airmen since the Royal Naval Air Service was formed in 1914. Let it also be the symbol of your loyalty to your Sovereign and the inspiration of your devotion to your country. It has been fully earned by the service and sacrifce of your predecessors, and I am confident that you will uphold their reputation and add further glories to the Colour which their deeds and conduct have won for you.

Elizabeth R.

30th July, 1956.

MEETINGS WITH MINISTERS ON FUTURE OF RN
AIR STATION IN SCOTLAND

The Under Secretary of State for Defence (Navy), Dr. David Owen, and the Minister of State for Scotland, Dr. Dixon Mabon, met this morning at the Ministry of Defence Mr. John Bruce-Gardyne, M.P., Provost R.R. Spink, Provost of Arbroath, the Town Clerk of Arbroath (Mr. R. Robertson) and Mr. MacManus, Chairman of the Tayside Consultative Group. Mr. Bruce-Gardyne and Provost Spink had asked for the meeting to state fully to the Ministers their concern about the future of H.M.S. Condor at Arbroath.

Dr. Owen explained that the future of all the R.N. air stations was at present under consideration as part of the measures following the recent defence review. It was both necessary and right to look carefully at all the Fleet Air Arm shore establishments following a number of reductions in the Fleet Air Arm. He emphasised, however, that no decision had yet been made on the future of any of these establishments. The whole matter was still being examined by the Navy Department and a final decision would rest with the Government as a whole.

The local situation was one of the most important factors taken into account in any decision affecting reductions or closures of any M.O.D. establishment. Dr. Owen explained that before a final decision was taken on the future of any of the Fleet Air Arm establishments there would be full prior consultation with the Department of Employment and Productivity, the Department of Economic Affairs, the Board of Trade and, in the case of Scottish establishments, the Scottish Office. If any establishment was closed every effort would be made to interest one of the other Services or another government department to take it over.

Dr. Owen and Dr. Mabon thanked Mr. Bruce-Gardyne, Provost Spink and Mr. MacManus for their clear and cogent exposition of the importance of Condor to Arbroath, the county of Angus and the Tayside region. They had taken note of the points made and would certainly include them in any condition of the future of Condor.

Public Relations

((Royal Navy)

Ministry of Defence

Main Building, London, S.W.1

Trafalgar 8070 Extensions 7917/7918

Condor Chapel

Stained Glass window

Site of Admin. block

FIXED BAYONETS AND COLOURS FLYING The parade of personnel at H.M.S. Condor follow... ... ceremony, which granted them the privilege of marching with fixed bayonets, Colours fly... ...siting... the town. P.O. Apprentice H. V. Havnes carries the Freedom scroll, encased in... in front of the guard.

MONY : ARBROATH NSTRUMENTAL BAND

SIGNING THE BURGESS ROLL.—Captain P. H. C. Illingworth, officer commanding H.M.S. Condor, signs the roll of Burgesses of the Royal Burgh

PARADE MARCHES OFF.—The Band of the Royal Marines heads the parade which marches off from the Webster Hall after the Freedom ceremony.

INSPECTED.—Provost D. A. Gardner inspects the guard outside the Webster Hall, the personnel of H.M.S. Condor heard him publicly proclaim the Freedom

TOASTING THE TOWN.—Wrens and other personnel toasted the town in beer and lemonade when they were the guests of the Town Council.

PICTURES FROM FREEDOM DAY

The principals at the ceremony walking up High Street to the saluting base in front of the Town Hall.

RIGHT: The Provost reads the Burgess Ticket to H.M.S. Cavalier personnel drawn up outside the Winkster Hall.

The sailors exercise one of the rights conferred in the Freedom — firing bayonets for the March Past.

RIGHT: Rumour Quartett, accompanied by Provost and other distinguished guests, takes the salute at the ...

Arbroath Harbour

Arbroath Harbour

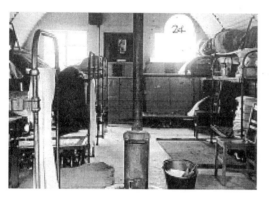

Home

Aerial View of Arbroath

Bell Rock

Arbroath Abbey

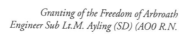

Granting of the Freedom of Arbroath
Engineer Sub Lt.M. Ayling (SD) (AOO R.N.

King George The Sixths Visit - March 8th 1941

H.M. lands at Condor on visit to Earl of Airlie c1956/57

H.M.S. Condor, Main Gate

Chapter 2

Royal Naval Air Station

Beech Expediter MkII

Seafire

Sea Hurricane

Faire y Fulmar

THE WORK OF H.M.S. CONDOR

The principal task of H.M.S. CONDOR is the training of the highest categories of air engineering ratings. The technical displays show you the scope of the work involved, and whereas a broken-down car may be pushed to the nearest garage, impending faults in an aircraft must be found and rectified before failure can occur.

Aircraft Artificer Apprentices come here after sixteen months at the general Artificer Apprentices' Establishment, H.M.S. FISGARD in CORNWALL, and all are volunteers for this branch of the service (the others may become Engine Room, Electrical, Ordnance or Shipwright Artificers). They spend two years and eight months in H.M.S. CONDOR, carrying out courses of instruction in the School, Factory and Technical Sections. When they leave they require only practical experience in the squadrons to become highly skilled and efficient in aircraft maintenance, and may eventually return

here to become instructors and so hand on their skill and knowledge.

Petty Officer Airmen Fitters arrive as Leading Airmen Mechanics, and spend six months acquiring skill of hand in Fitting and Turning or Sheetmetal work. In addition they carry out advanced maintenance work in their specialist trade—Airframes, Engines or Ordnance.

Other Leading Airmen Mechanics and Pilot's Mates carry out a two year course of instruction, first qualifying as Petty Officer Airmen Fitters in their own specialist trade. They then do a more advanced course and leave as Aircraft Mechanicians qualified in both engine and airframe maintenance or ordnance, and are interchangeable with Artificers in squadrons. A newcomer to H.M.S. CONDOR is the School of Aircraft Maintenance. Short courses are available to all air engineering officers and ratings on the latest types of aircraft and equipment, enabling them to keep up with modern advancements.

An instructor demonstrates to Aircraft Mechanicians a vertical milling machine

FACTORY AND WORKSHOPS

In this large and important section Apprentices, Mechanicians and Airmen Fitters are taught the basic skilled trades of air engineering. Sheetmetal work ranges from simple marking out, drilling and rivetting to the intricate examples you will see on display. Practical airframe repairs are carried out and the high standard of accuracy and finish required in such things as pressurised cockpit repairs should be noted. Similarly in fitting and turning the work extends from simple beginnings to advanced machining, milling and grinding, culminating in repairs to gas turbine components. Instruction is also given in coppersmithing and the various methods of welding. In addition to the more obvious aspects of the work, considerations such as identification of materials, correct heat treatment and anti-corrosion precautions are of vital importance.

THE MOUNTAIN RESCUE UNIT

The Mountain Rescue Unit is made up entirely of volunteers, the majority of whom are members of the CONDOR Mountain Club. The full complement is 40, and a nucleus of Chief Petty Officers and Petty Officers steadies the eager drive of the Apprentices who make up the major part of the unit.

Training takes place at week-ends, when the unit exercise in places such as Glen Nevis, Glen Clova, Cairngorms and Glen Esk. First aid training is essential and all members attend lectures given by the Unit doctor in this subject.

As the name implies, the main duty of the unit is Mountain Rescue, involving tasks that may vary from looking for crashed aircraft to searching for lost skiers and hikers.

When a search party is actually in progress, the unit is divided into teams of three, plus one fully experienced leader. Each team carries a wireless set, first aid kit, provisions and equipment necessary to ensure a comfortable night in the mountains. A base camp is set up, as near to the scene of the incident as possible. A doctor waits at this camp until the victim has been located. The search controller's camp, with the master radio set, is near the base camp and all teams make frequent progress reports by radio.

A type base camp can be seen demonstrated to-day at the Control Tower. The camp is staffed by members of the Mountain Rescue Unit, who will gladly answer any questions.

A member of the team "roping" down a rock face in Glen Mark.

THE CONTROL TOWER

Flying an aircraft from A to B is not as straight-forward as driving from Arbroath to Dundee. Even in the latter case there are rules to be obeyed, directions to be noted and forms of traffic control to be complied with. The Air Traffic Control Section is responsible for the safety of aircraft on the ground and in the air. You will see from the parked aircraft that the pilot has a very restricted view in some directions, that on the ground he may be unable to see straight ahead, and in cloud or bad weather he may be unable to see outside the cockpit. Air Traffic Control exists to help the pilot overcome these disabilities. Before leaving on a flight, the pilot is "briefed" on the weather conditions, radio communications and navigational aids available, alternative airfields for emergency use, prohibited areas to be avoided, and so on. Arriving aircraft may be "talked down" through cloud, and any aircraft given its position or any available information it may require.

At the end of the runway you will see the runway control van, which ensures that the runway is clear for landing and take off. The controller must even keep his eyes open for aircraft trying to land with undercarriage still retracted—a rare but expensive occurrence. The handling of aircraft on the ground, firefighting and the control of ground traffic and pedestrians are also the concern of Air Traffic Control. It is unfortunate that visitors cannot see the teams at work, for without the Control Tower the pilot's task would be much more difficult, if not impossible.

The control staff watch an aircraft land after a successful homing.

ELECTRICAL AND RADIO DISPLAY

The Electrical Branch is responsible for the maintenance of all the electrical and radio equipment fitted in aircraft, including navigational and other instruments.

The Electrical Display in B.3 Hangar shows the complete installation of electrical equipment fitted in the Firebrand aircraft (we leave you to guess what the electrical content of the Gannet would look like laid out in the same way), together with working assemblies of the latest navigational and flying control instruments. From these examples you can judge the increasing complexity of systems for accurate control of high speed aircraft, and the need for smaller components to reduce weight and size.

In the Radio Display, "miniature" equipment may be seen to advantage. Most of the modern radio equipment is of the Very High Frequency (V.H.F.) type similar to that which will be used by the new B.B.C. stations being built to improve radio reception throughout the British Isles. The elaborate test and repair equipment in the Radio Workshop is capable of servicing this and even more complicated equipment.

An Electrical Artificer carrying out tests on an aircraft radio set.

FLIGHT SERVICING

Training in the Flight Servicing Section is the practical consolidation of all technical training in H.M.S. CONDOR. In this department trainees work on Naval aircraft under conditions similar to those they will experience in squadrons afloat and ashore. The aircraft is dealt with as a whole, comprising the components and systems which have been learned separately in earlier training.

Power units of jet and piston engined aircraft are removed, replaced and fully ground tested, and the diagnosis and rectification of all types of faults must be learned. Routine inspections for serviceability are carried out and understanding of the function, application and maintenance of the wide range of ground equipment necessary to do this is essential. The complexity and diversity of modern aircraft, upon which skilled tradesmen of six different categories may be working at the same time, make essential ready appreciation of the relevant Air Publications and Maintenance Orders and the standard recording procedures for all repairs and inspection.

In addition to technical matters, the syllabus includes instruction on general matters of airmanship and safety precautions, and an acquaintance with the operation of aircraft from carriers and airfields, and routines and divisions of responsibility in the Fleet Air Arm. The wealth

An instructor points out a detail of the Sea Fury, while other members of the class watch below.

of experience of the instructors enables the trainee to settle down quickly in his maintenance work when he leaves H.M.S. CONDOR.

ENGINE DISPLAY

B.3 Hangar houses the Engine Training Section. Many different types of engine may be seen here, ranging from the simple designs of twenty years ago to the complex and powerful present-day piston and gas turbine units.

The equipment shown is used in the theoretical and practical training of the highly skilled ratings who must leave H.M.S. Condor with a comprehensive knowledge of the various engines. Classroom lectures are followed by practical work, which includes stripping and rebuilding the engines.

Instructors are present to explain the exhibits and to answer any questions. Do not be afraid to ask; they will be delighted to have a chance to air their knowledge.

Petty Officer Airmen Fitters study a Bristol Centaurus engine under the watchful eye of their instructor.

ORDNANCE DISPLAY

The Ordnance Section is responsible for all the armament used in aircraft, and also for equipment such as ejection seats, pyrotechnics and rocket assisted take off gear—in fact everything which goes off with a bang. Here you can see a varied selection of guns, bombs and torpedoes, and other stores fired or dropped from aircraft. Here too, you will at some future time find the guided missiles which will replace conventional armaments, although most people would no doubt prefer to admire atomic weapons from a distance.

MODEL AIRCRAFT DISPLAY

In C.2 Hangar is a selection of model aircraft built by members of the Angus and District Model Aircraft League. The League comprises clubs in Aberdeen, Arbroath, Carnoustie, Dundee, Forfar, Kirriemuir and Brechin, and exists to promote the study and practice of aeromodelling. Members design, construct and fly their own models, and compete each season for the Strathmore Trophy (for the best Club performance) and the Angus Cup (for the best individual). Most of the competitions are flown on this airfield. Several members are qualified pilots of full size aircraft and many members have entered the aircraft industry, the Fleet Air Arm and the Royal Air Force.

Although the airfield is unable to offer facilities for high speed jet aircraft, flying to and from the airfield is still carried out by aircraft as large and modern as the Gannet. Besides acting as a staging post, for example for rescue helicopters on their way to the North of Scotland, aircraft can be based here for Fleet exercises, and front-line squadrons have carried out their "working up" here. Scarcely a day passes without several aircraft coming and going, and while this does not compare with the intense activity at some Air Stations, it involves the provision of full flying facilities.

H.M.S. CONDOR is also the home of the Rear Admiral, Reserve Aircraft. His organisation is responsible for the supply of all naval aircraft. This involves the issue, storage and replacement of aircraft, and repair, conversion and modification work which is outside the capacity of squadron repair organisations.

The training activities of H.M.S. CONDOR require an immense supporting organisation behind the scenes. The Ship's Company must be housed, fed, paid and their other material needs supplied. The Supply Department is responsible for pay and victualling and the supply of every item from pins and buckets to wardrobes and aircraft components. It is in fact the equivalent of a large department store. The Sick Bay provides medical and dental attention, and the Education Department, which provides the school instruction necessary for the technical syllabuses, also caters for the educational aspects of advancement. The duties of the civil departments include maintenance of the

Cooks at work in the gleaming and spotless galley.

station and airfield, electrical and civil engineering. It will have been noticed that much care has been given to the lay out and development of the grounds.

There are two Chaplains who hold the usual Sunday services in their respective churches besides ministering to spiritual needs during the week. Members of the W.R.N.S. form an integral part of the Ship's Company and some are employed on technical work such as maintaining aircraft and radio equipment, and weather forecasting. Others are responsible for store keeping, clerical work, nursing, and operating the communications of the Station. The remainder perform domestic work including cooking. Several Wrens have also taken the course for Petty Officer Airman Fitter.

Many clubs and organisations cater for sporting and recreational activities ranging from handicrafts and music to gliding and skiing. These are well supported by both R.N. and W.R.N.S. personnel.

The Meteorological Officer and her assistants read the weather instruments.

ROYAL NAVAL AIR STATION - HMS CONDOR

After passing out as a Photo 'A' at the Royal Naval School of Photography at Bognor Regis a leave at Swindon, I travelled to Arbroath with my kitbag, hammock and suit case (do not remember a respirator). On the way I linked up with Ken Matthews at King's Cross Station in London. He was on the same course at Bognor. We reported to H.M.S. Condor on 5th December 1944. The Officer Commanding at the time was Captain Sherbrooke V.C. I believe that after the war he became Lord Lieutenant of Nottinghamshire. We were both allocated to the same hut - also 'Wally' Hammond , another member of the same course. The accommodation was typical barrack type with bunk beds with a Leading Hand in charge. This Killick was a MONAB wearing Army battledress but with a matelot's cap, jersey and naval insignia of rank and trade.

Billeted also in this hut was a wonderful character, an AB who had served his time before WWII (possibly served in WWI). Regret that I do not remember his name. He was released in the '30's, became a postman but recalled on the outbreak of hostilities. He was always up and about early in the morning. On his return from breakfast he would always bring back a jug of coffee - so Ken, Wally and I had coffee in bed. He would also let us know what was for breakfast. It was at this time that I first heard the term "herrins-in" which meant that breakfast was herrings in tomato sauce. I don't remember all the 'Old Salt's' duties, however, he was responsible for darkening ship at the Officers' quarters and mess - as I helped him on many occasions. He did advise me that should I see a cigarette box in any of the rooms not to be greedy, just take one cigarette only. He seemed always to wear a donkey jacket - I do not know how he got away with it. With hindsight, I believe that it could have been an ex-Post Office jacket. Most evenings he would stay in the bunk and make cigarette boxes out of perspex.

The Photographic Section comprised an OIC, Lieutenant Hedley Goodhall who, before the war, was an actor at the BBC in Bristol (have seen him since a couple of times on TV) a leading Photographer, and 6 Photographers (Photo A's). The other 3 being Scots - Jock Grimshaw, Jock O'Hare and another whose name eludes me. Grimshaw and O'Hare I had met before as they were at Bognor on a previous course prior to ours. Finally, but not least, there were 4 or 5 W.R.N.S. This was the first and only time that I was to serve with Photographic W.R.N.S. I often wondered where they were trained as I do not recall any being at Bognor.

Don't recall much about our Photographic Duties as I was only at Condor from December '44 until January '45 and a fortnight of this was taken up by overseas leave. I do remember spending a considerable amount of time clearing snow as the weather at the time was atrocious - heavy fall of snow and freezing conditions. Leading Hands i/c huts were ordered to remove icicles which were in danger of pulling the gutters down.

A number of firsts come to mind - seeing ratings with yellow faces. These were matelots who had returned from tropical climes and had been subjected to the daily dosage of mepacrine tablets to ward off malaria. and........

Issue of tobacco - tobacco was issued in three forms, cigarettes , pipe or leaf. I believe it was 1 lb. (2 x 1/2 lb. tins) per rating. "Wally" Hammond decided to take his ration in leaf form. He had arranged with our "Old Salt" to have it made into a prick of tobacco. No prizes for guessing how it got its name! This was used for chewing or smoking in a pipe - prior to the introduction of cigarettes. Although I saw it made up, it was very difficult to remember exactly how it was done. You can imagine what a pound of tobacco leaf looks like - quite a heap. This was placed on a piece of canvas. A length of twine was looped onto a hook in the wall, then attached to one end of the canvas leaving a few feet free. The loose end was bound around the canvas, continually being pulled tight enclosing the leaf. This procedure was carried out until all the leaf was enclosed in the canvas and twine. The prick ended up being about 8 inches long and 2 inches in diameter at the centre. All the length was covered in twine except the two tapered ends where the surplus canvas was cut away leaving about 1 inch proud. The twine to the hook was then also cut. Normally a tot of rum was poured over the leaf before commencement of the operation. Whether or not it was done on this occasion, I don't remember. The prick was then kept until the tobacco was mature. How long was that? - again , I don't know. When ready, the prick would be opened at one end and pieces of the black twist cut off , size depending on whether it was for smoking in a pipe or chewing.

Our OIC, Lieutenant Goodhall, was a grand chap. He took all the branch for a night out in Dundee, provided the gin and cigarettes which, were Wills "Three Castles" - of course , made in Bristol. I remember that H.M.S. Royal Sovereign was in harbour at the time which, I was given to understand, was given to the Russians and renamed "Archangel".

Lieutenant Goodhall produced a play at Condor during the time I was there. It was "Middle Watch" by Commander Stephen King Hall and Lieutenant Goodhall took the leading role.

At the end of January '45 I was posted to H.M.S. Waxwing in preparation for service at sea/abroad.

L.W. Hawkins. Photo 'A'.
FAA/MX 701478

Do you remember ....

"AULD BOB" R.N. H.M.S. CONDOR

Bob was originally a pup belonging to a Chief Petty Officer at "Condor". When the C.P.O. went on draft to Pompey he took Bob with him. However, the story goes that Bob was unhappy away from Arbroath so he decided to walk back. He completed about half the journey alone, then he was recognised by some "Condor" people who clubbed together and paid his train fare for the rest of the way.

He was adopted by the Petty Officer's Mess where he would entertain guests with tricks on visitors nights. He had many accomplishments which included going into Arbroath by himself on Pay Friday by bus (he was never charged), He would return on the last bus (never choosing the wrong one , altho' many stood

in the square). He had his own seat in the front, near the driver - no one else ever took his place.
He was a great sports fan, never missing a rugby of hockey match held on the camp.

Occasionally, he visited the camp cinema, and once barked in time to "The Queen" from start to finish, delighting the ship's company present.

He developed the bad habit of chasing vehicles and the Skipper had to intervene, he ordered Bob should be tied up during working hours, and the Q.M. would make the pipe "Ship's Company (and Bob) Secure" at 16.30.

Bob lived to a good age, and was, as you can see from this photograph, a very proud sailor.

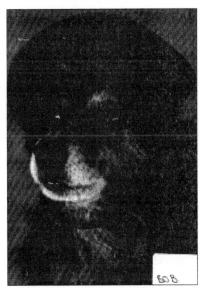

Auld Bob

'Guns' Have's Dog R.N.A.S. Arbroath, March 1943

CONDOR
April 1954 - March 1956.

I joined Condor as a Petty Officer for a 2 years Aircraft Mechanicians Course. The course included six Canadian Petty Officers. I believe that all but three of us passed the course.

One Englishman who persuaded his wife to stir things up with the authority with the result the first time he slipped up he was out. Another Englishman on his way to hospital to visit his pregnant wife on his motorcycle, was involved in an accident with a horse and was paralysed from the neck down. A Canadian from the class Ernie La Plant, a character, who had a speech impediment which didn't affect his drinking, finished up under a train in Waverley Station, Edinburgh, and now lies in Arbroath Cemetery.

As a bachelor, like myself, Ernie lived in the P.O.'s Mess. He always received Canadian Magazines. One day whilst sitting near me , he said "Say Nobby, take a look". Thinking he was going to show me a picture of a girl, I looked - it was a full page picture of a bottle of spirit with a glass half full. He then said "Nobby, that's the best godamn Rye you can buy".

During his first week in Arbroath he hired a car, and went out for a drive from Kirk Square to Guthrie Port. Unfortunately he hit a car parked on his right hand side of the road. His excuse to the police, the other chap wouldn't pull over. Of course Ernie didn't realise he was driving on the wrong side of the road, plus, of course, the other car was parked, with no driver. He lost his licence for a year. When he got his licence back he bought a motorcycle, a Norton Dominator, (a very popular bike at the time). He showed it to me after he'd collected it on a Saturday afternoon. I was quite envious. Ernie then said he was going onto the airfield to get the feel of it. An hour or so later he was back - what a state his bike was in. The ends of the rubbers of the handle grips and foot pedals were ripped off, dents on mud guards etc. "Whatever happened" I asked." It's O.K., Nobby, I've been practising falls". Evidently laying the bike over and letting it go its own way -good job he didn't do it on the runway!

The best fitter on our course was Dixie Lee, his use of file etc., were skillful to the extreme, always a perfect fit. Ernie's quite the opposite. One day Ernie looked skywards and said "Lord, why don't you help me for a change instead of Dixie Lee?"

"Bob" the collie. Yes, he was there during my time, One of the P.O.'s Mess members was primarily his keeper so when he was drafted down South it was suggested he took Bob. This he did but Bob, during the following months, found his way back to Arbroath. The story of his way back was told in an article in one of the comics of the day - the Eagle, I believe.

Bob would get on the bus for a trip to Arbroath getting off at Kirk Square - where he went to when there , who knows? Maybe he had a girl in town! I wouldn't say he rounded up the passengers but he certainly knew which bus to catch to' return to Condor. I'm not sure, but I believe he was still there when I returned to Condor in 1960 when I went back as a C.P.O. I know the last I saw of him he was a very old boy - grey more than black, and not too lively, spending most of his time lying in the P.O.'s Mess or on the grass between the Mess and the parade ground.

One chap at Condor who was always strutting around with his gaiters on, was a Warrant Gunnery Officer , Sammy "Fishy" Roe. He didn't like men lingering for a goodnight kiss with the Wrens on the wailing wall , so regularly did his night patrol moving chaps on. One night a colleague of mine, Steve Skelding, was kissing Molly, the stores Wren, goodnight. Along came Sammy "Say goodnight Petty Officer" Steve turned to him and said "Good night Sammy" - Sammy wasn't amused.

At Condor at this time we had quite a good crowd of potential performers who put on the Christmas shows etc. Our music always performed by the a P.O. Air Fitter Bob Gravestock , an excellent pianist. At one time he played a theatre organ professionally.

A number of us decided to put on a variety show to tour the area in addition to a Condor performance. "Out of the Navy Blue" (programme enclosed). I recall just before our first performance I was on Captain's report for using another chaps rail warrant to go on leave, for which I got 14 days stoppage of leave. Unfortunately our show was in Arbroath so I had to get special leave - see the Captain again - who asked what I did - " dance , sing, drama and comedy "" I replied - """ a key player " he said. " I look forward to seeing your performance". I never did hear what he thought of my dance i.e. a sand dance (Wilson Keppel and Betty type). Drama, I was the villain, top hat and cloak (Ah Ha me proud beauties), and the singing , a corruption of a radio song (copy enclosed), with derogatory words of life at Condor. Another sketch was the Can-Can, three lads and a young contortionist dancer, a Wren named Midge Timpson (later to have a large family and live in Arbroath). Our dresses, though home made followed the traditional style. The local chippie, I believe called "The Thistle" was off the main street Arbroath. The chap who owned it was named Joe. Instead of finishing the Can-Can by doing the splits we, in succession, turned our backs on the audience exposing our pants, on them were written Eat-At-Joes and when Midge did her flip over 2/6 !

The show was a great success , we performed at several places including Dundee, Montrose, Webster Hall Arbroath , and Condor for the Wrens RNBT. I often wonder where the players are now , I expect most are , or approaching , senior citizen status.

We were also involved in the station productions, which included pantomimes, one I remember was called Cinderella.

On the station working in the Hall, I'm not sure which department of the Admiralty it was, was a Rear Admiral Pratt. A jolly chap. He nominated himself as church choir master so if anyone, as I had, had a powerful voice, he didn't hesitate to press gang you into the church choir and subsequently at Christmas time into his carol singers. For the latter we did a round of several old people's homes. In the words of Admiral Pratt " the old dears are wetting their knickers with the excitement of knowing we are to visit". As he was convinced I could sing he told the Supply Commander , who was producing a Variety Show that he was to give me a solo singing spot. Needless to say I convinced the Commander that the only place I could sing was in the bath. The Commander, wasn't to be out done. I had to open the second half of the show. When the curtains opened there was I sitting in a bath of foam singing "Here in my bath I'm alone and so Lonely" i.e. bath instead of heart!!

GRAND OLD LADY GOES SOUTH

Walrus Restored at Condor for Fleet Air Arm Museum

Captain H. W. Sylvester, commanding officer of H.M.S. Condor, making his address at the handing-over ceremony of the Navy's last "Walrus."

Remains of Walrus - as it was found at Thame, near Oxford

What was described by Captain M. W. Sylvester, the commanding officer, as a unique and nostalgic ceremony, took place at the Royal Naval Engineering School, H.M.S. Condor, Arbroath, on Tuesday. It was the formal handing over, in one of the hangars, of the last Walrus amphibious plane in existence in this country to the Fleet Air Arm Museum at the Royal Naval Air Station, Yeovilton, Somerset.

The 27-year-old Walrus was found on a scrap dump at Thame, near Oxford, in 1963. It was purchased by the Historic Aircraft Preservation Society, and H.M.S. Condor undertook to restore the aircraft to its original state. This has just been completed after almost three years' work.

Some of the spare parts were obtained from as far away as Australia, and others, which could not be traced, had to be fabricated.

The Walrus was handed over by Captain Sylvester to Instructor Commander T. A. Marshall, curator of the Fleet Air Arm Museum.

Captain Sylvester in so doing recalled the time just prior to the Second World War, when the Fleet Air Arm was developing rapidly as an important part of the Navy's striking power.

It might seem surprising, he said, that when Schneider Trophy seaplanes were being produced, and aircraft like the Spitfire were being sketched, the Walrus was regarded as a major step forward in aviation.

"This aircraft, however, was built for hard work of a very diverse nature. It came at a time when aviation was spreading from aircraft carriers to cruisers, battle cruisers and battleships of the line, where gunnery spotting, reconnaissance and communications required an amphibious aircraft that could also be catapulted from a ship's deck.

"It proved a significant advance for flying boat construction and design for those days, and for many years, as a contemporary of the Swordfish, was a well-loved and well-used Fleet Air Arm aircraft, without which a vital part of naval strategy could not have been met."

Captain Sylvester continued:— "Our job here has been to restore the aircraft from the piece of iron-mongery that was found in a scrapyard to as near its original condition as possible. This we have done, and I would like you to know that over the past three years the small group of craft instructors, senior apprentices and Naval Air Mechanics, have found a great fascination and re-creation of forgotten skills in this work.

"It has been a significant objective for our young men here to see the sort of work of which they should be capable at the end of their training.

"We have received support for this venture from all over the Commonwealth, and Vickers and the Dunlop Rubber Company have supplied us with drawings and such spares as they have been able to find.

"The main plane and tail unit have been constructed virtually from nothing, and in over-all charge has been Mr W. S. Guild, the deputy workshop training officer, who designed the tail unit from photographs. When the drawings arrived, there was a very close correlation indeed to the correct structure.

"Chief Petty Officer Woods has been the senior craft instructor involved, and he and his team have, I think, done a remarkably fine job. The aircraft is complete except for some 'internals' in the engine and certain deviations from material specification which preclude it from flying.

"It is with great pleasure, but with a tinge of regret, that I now present to Commander Marshall Walrus No. L2301. Long may it be a reminder of stirring times in the Fleet Air Arm, and a memorial to the gallant aviators of those days."

In accepting the aircraft, Commander Marshall described it as a 'beauty,' and 'magnificent.'

He stated that ever since it was known that bits and pieces of the Walrus had been taken to Arbroath, the Museum had had a steady stream of inquiries from the general public both at home and abroad, asking how the work on its reconstruction was proceeding. This was indicative of the genuine interest that was being taken in the preservation of historic aircraft.

Commander Marshall mentioned that although the Fleet Air Arm Museum had only been in existence for three years, it already enjoyed a national and an international reputation. It had been visited by over 113,000 people. During the past year there had been a record attendance of 42,000. "I am sure this growth will continue, particularly when we can produce such exhibits as this."

The plane will be partly dismantled before being transported south.

HISTORY OF THE WALRUS

The Walrus, known universally as the 'Shagbat,' enjoyed a reputation in the Fleet Air Arm rivalled only by that of its contemporary, the Swordfish. Both these aircraft, biplanes in a monoplane age, attracted their share of ridicule from the less well-informed, who judged only by appearances and knew little of their solid virtues. Naval pilots, who knew better, sang their praises, and their loyalties remained unshaken. They had good reason to praise the Walrus, for it proved its dependability through 10 years of Fleet Air Arm service, flying in every imaginable climate, from the Arctic to the tropics, and performing a remarkable range of duties which on one occasion (during operations in the Red Sea) even included dive-bombing. Predominantly, however, the Walrus was a spotter-reconnaissance aircraft, and its first duty was to be 'the eyes of the Fleet.' Embarked as a catapult aircraft in warships and cruisers, the Walrus performed this role all over the world, from the Arctic to the Falkland Islands, from West Africa to Madagascar, and from Aden to Ceylon.

One of the functions of the Walrus was searching out commerce raiders and one squadron (No. 710)) was active on these duties only five days after the outbreak of war in 1939 from a base at Freetown, guarding the approaches to West Africa.

When the Walrus first appeared in 1933, it was known as the Seagull V, but it was a very different aircraft from the earlier Seagull amphibians of the 'twenties.

Whereas its Fleet Air Arm predecessor, the Seagull III, was a tractor amphibian of wholly wooden construction, the Seagull V had a pusher-engine, a metal hull, and offered enclosed accommodation for the pilot and navigator. Moreover, it was stressed for catapulting, and, in fact, became the first amphibian in the world to be catapulted from a warship with full military load. The prototype Seagull V was first flown on June 21, 1933, and was designed as a private venture by R. J. Mitchell, who later achieved fame for his creation of the Spitfire. First ordered by the Australian Government, who retained the name Seagull V, the type was adopted for the Fleet Air Arm under the name Walrus, after trials had taken place aboard H.M.S. Nelson in 1935. From July, 1936, Walruses served in battleships and cruisers as contemporaries of Swordfish and, later, of Seafox floatplanes.

CHEQUERED CAREER

How did L2301 get to Thame and what was its history before that?

The answer to this question reveals a curious and chequered career which began in 1939, when three Walrus 1s, originally part of a Fleet Air Arm order, were bought by the Irish Army Air Corps. One of the three was L2301, which was given the Air Corps number

N18. Early in March, 1939, the three aircraft took off from the Vickers-Supermarine works at Southampton for the Air Corps headquarters at Baldonnel, but none of them arrived at this destination. Heavy fog and general bad weather over the Irish Sea caused the formation to break up. One Walrus turned back and landed at Pembroke. N18, its engine giving trouble, put down on the sea off the Wexford coast; the third aircraft turned north and landed in Dublin Bay. A strong sea gave N18 difficulties and two local lifeboats were launched, but the crew successfully beached the aircraft.

In company with the Air Corps' Ansons, based mainly at Rineanna (Shannon), the three Walruses patrolled the south and west coasts of Ireland during the war on neutrality-protection and rescue operations. In 1942, N18 recrossed the Irish Sea in unusual circumstances. A young officer who was under open arrest flew it to Cornwall; his crew of two was unaware that the flight was unauthorised and the fuel barely sufficient to make a landfall. The aircraft and crew were returned and N18 continued in service until 1945, when it was sold to Aer Lingus as EI-ACC. Later it was sold for £150 to the Royal Auxiliary Air Force at Biggin Hill and gave flights to ground crews. There the Shag at entered the last phase of its active life, and after two years it passed into the hands of a scrap firm at Thame.

Perhaps the scrap yield of the Walrus was low, or perhaps its spirit of survival was high, because it somehow remained reasonably intact despite the wind and weather. The fact that it was a metal Mk. I and not a wooden hulled Mk. II no doubt had much to do with this.

In 1963 at Thame, it was found by the Historic Aircraft Preservation Society. The Curator of the Fleet Air Arm Museum was informed and arrangements were made for the hull, and all the bits and pieces of the aircraft which could be found, to be transported to R.N. Air Station, Arbroath, the R.N. Air Engineering School where all Fleet Air Arm maintenance ratings in the mechanical trade are trained. It arrived in January, 1964, and work has continued ever since to restore the aircraft to its original appearance. The mainplane and tail unit had been constructed virtually from nothing, and in overall charge had been Mr Guild, the H.M.S. Condor deputy training officer.

Captain Sylvester handed over the Walrus to Instructor-Commander T. A. Marshall, R.N., curator of the Fleet Air Arm Museum, Yeovilton, Somerset, to which it will be transported by road.

TO-DAY'S FREEDOM CEREMONY

Commander T. S Sampson Will Lead H.M.S. Condor Parade

Commander T. S. Sampson, executive officer of H.M.S. Condor, will lead the parade of almost 600 officers, Wrens and ratings of H.M.S. Condor through the streets of Arbroath to the Webster Hall to-day for the ceremony of conferring the Freedom of the Burgh on the Naval Air Station. Lieutenant-Commander P. Morris will be second in command.

Later he will lead the parade through the High Street past the Town House, where the salute will be taken by Provost D. A. Gardner, via Tower Nook, Abbey Pend, West Abbey Street, High Street, Ladybridge Street and Marketgate to the Drill Hall, where those on parade will be given hospitality by Arbroath Town Council.

The entire personnel of the Naval Air Station, except those needed to maintain the running of the camp and those engaged in sporting activities, will take part in the ceremony.

The Parade

The parade will have a Colour Party under Sub-Lieutenant Ayling and a guard under Lieutenant Sturgeon and Sub-Lieutenant Puttock. In charge of platoons in the parade will be Lieutenant-Commander Hall, Lieutenant-Commander Batchelor, and Lieutenant-Commander Tobinson, Lieutenant-Commander Currie, Lieutenant Dyer, Lieutenant Dulan, Lieutenant Torvell, Lieutenant A. F. Brown, Lieutenant Fitzpatrick, Sub-Lieutenant Murray, Lieutenant Harrison, Lieutenant Duddin, Sub-Lieutenant James, Third Officer Shaw and Third Officer Gray.

At the ceremony in the Webster Hall at 3 p.m. where the Burgess ticket will be presented to Captain P. H. C. Illingworth, commanding parade

officer of H.M.S. Condor, the platform party will include the Earl of Airlie, Lord Lieutenant of Angus and two Freeman of Arbroath, the Hon. John S. Maclay, Secretary of State for Scotland, and Mr Archibald S. Briggs, Pitlochry, as well as Provosts of other Angus towns. A large area of the hall will be occupied by Condor personnel, while in addition a hundred seats will be occupied by members of the public, who have previously made application for admission tickets to the Town House. Representatives of local organisations and others invited to the ceremony by the Town Council will also be seated in the hall.

Ceremony

After the National Anthem there will be a prayer by the Rev. T. Gemmell Campbell, Old Church, followed by Psalm 23. The minutes of the Town Council conferring the Freedom of H.M.S. Condor will be read by the Town Clerk before the Burgess register is signed by Provost D. A. Gardner, the Town Clerk and Captain Illingworth. The Burgess ticket will be presented to Captain Illingworth by the Provost and the proceedings within the hall close with hymn 626. Arbroath Instrumental Band will accompany the praise.

The Provost then inspects the guard of honour outside the hall and publicly proclaims the Freedom to the officers and ratings. The Provost will then present the freedom scroll to P.O. Apprentice Haynes.

The guard will then fix bayonets, and the parade will march past the Town House where the Provost will take the salute.

In event of bad weather the parade will be modified.

1960 - 1962.

Joined Condor in January 1960 to do an Instructional Technique Course (ITC), the small two rooms and an office at a remote part of the airfield being the school. The Instructor Officer Lieut. Morse, on hearing I came from North Walsham, Norfolk (I'd recently married a North Walsham girl) informed me he'd been educated at North Walsham's Paston Grammar School, a school a certain Admiral Lord Nelson had attended in his youth. Inst. Lieut. Morse suggested this being the only possible reason for his getting a commission.

It's quite amusing doing I.T. Courses where one of the class acts as the instructor. One Chief wasn't too well up on his subject, when asked a question Why? was so tied up in knots and at the end of his tether, he banged his notes down, and said " because it says so in the bloody book". At that point he closed his session , and we were only trying to help. At least he learned that before trying to teach you need to know your subject.

I was drafted to the Artificer Training A/E (Airframes Engine Section) mainly teaching airframe basic systems ... Theory of Flight, Fixed Wing and Helicopters.

With one class of Apprentices I was about to start a new phase on Helicopter theory. One normally attempted to get a good start by having an interesting introduction. I used a plastic toy from a cornflakes packet to zoom a rotor blade at the ceiling. The idea being to prove that in still air a rotating wing would go vertically up (the instruction to follow, under normal circumstances,to disprove it). At this point, by coincidence (most unusual at this time) I heard a helicopter. I therefore got everyone outside, where, lo and behold, we could watch a "Chopper" performing - I didn't disillusion the lads when they thought I had arranged it!

Going back into the classroom and extolling the virtues of the helicopter saying how it could hover, go backwards, forwards, up, down etc., outflying the potential of the birds, one Apprentice said - "that's all very clever Chief, but can it lay eggs?".

It was a pleasure to teach the Apprentices for they were relatively intelligent, with a fair amount of common sense and yet at the same time one had to be aware they were young lads who would, if given an inch, would take a mile.

I recall noticing one chap who regularly made a brief mark on his book as I was chalking and talking, my curiosity got the better of me so I challenged for an explanation. The one I got was that he was the scorer for the class as to the number of times I said "in fact" (and I believe they were having bets on it). I had to make a conscious effort to avoid using that phrase from then on. No doubt I adopted another to replace it.

As an instructor, I was brainwashed into the expression seeing is believing, or a picture is worth a thousand words, and certainly visual aids were great as learning aids.

I had it brought home to me when after a year of teaching I was given a group of Apprentices for revision pre exams. Thinking I would start on subjects I had taught three terms before I said " lets consider a particular aircraft's hydraulic system. The X pressure reduction valve , when in the system. is it fitted and what is its purpose Jones?. Jones seemed to go into trance as he closed his eyes and said "yes Chief, its on the left hand bottom corner of the board, going to the brakes its ...etc., etc.". I was pleased to realise he could picture the system as it had developed and put on the chalkboard 12 months earlier.

One of my colleagues, Air Artificer 1st Class Alf Stebbings B.E.M. was selected to teach a class of Indians, without doubt academically brilliant but practically they were hopeless. I hate to think what the servicing of their aircraft was like. Alf had a great rapport with them, so much so that one of the assured Alf that in the event of India being at war with us, they wouldn't kill him. I was asked to instruct them whilst Alf was away. Unfortunately my style of teaching included the odd joke, funny story, anecdote, etc., with the result these chaps , with their photographic memories, when it came to their exams, the answers they gave invariably included my odd jokes, etc.

During the late summer of 1961 I was called to the Training Commander's Office to be informed that I was to take a group of Apprentices to the Ben Nevis area on an expedition week. As I had no exped experience I attempted to make my excuses but was informed that my maturity was all the experience needed. I duly went as Safety Officer. Luckily our week coincided with an exped week by officers from the Officer Training School. We met up with them at the Y.M.C.A. Hostel in Glen Nevis. They were well equipped and well catered for. A British Rail cargo unit was waiting for them with an enormous quantity of kit and tinned food. It was decided by the Senior Officer that each Officer would be responsible for one or two Apprentices i.e. to test their leadership potential. Groups were formed. One pair of Apprentices had the misfortune to be joined by a Peruvian Officer who said he would select the victuals for the 24 hour walk they were to do. It wasn't until they got back to rendezvous the next day that we learnt the only thing they had had to eat was margarine. Their "leader" had decided it being the most suitable food to sustain them.

Whilst the exped was roughing it in their tents and off on their 24 hour walk, my time was spent in the Y.M.C.A. I preferred a bed to my sleeping bag. After a week of walks, including the Ben Nevis walk we returned to the Y.M.C.A. to say our farewells to the Officers. Our backpacks were full of excess victuals - the more you took , the more you had to carry. The remainder was given to the Y.M.C.A. We had to rendezvous the next day at a place about 12 miles away. The next night was spent in a cow shed. As I was in charge from then on, I found I had to cover twice the distance as I had to chivvy the stragglers then go forward to slow down the leaders..... Quite an experience, but not one I wish to repeat, I prefer a bed at night. A few weeks before joining Condor in 1960 I became a married man, the larger part of my time living in Married Quarters at 13 Camperdown Drive, Arbroath, having previously had a hiring in Sydney Street. My first daughter was born at the Arbroath Infirmary.

We certainly enjoyed our time at Arbroath, and in fact it so impressed us living in Scotland that very few years pass without us having a holiday there, but not necessarily in Angus.

Bill (Nobby) Clarke.

C.P.O. A.W. Collingwood B.E.M. was Chief Bosuns Mate at Condor throughout the war - he retired in 1934 after 24 years service but was recalled in 1939 for war service - drafted to Condor with Chief Gunner's Mate Bob Fletcher to "stand by" as the airfield and buildings were being constructed and to receive and train the first of the ship's company on completion.

He lived with his wife (now aged 100) on his second retirement in a house and land known as "Collindale", Cairnie Loan, Arbroath, and worked it as a small holding for many years.

He was awarded the B.E.M. in 1945 and died in 1976 and, by request, was buried amongst the war casualties in the Western Cemetery, attended by senior ratings from Condor.

Lt. Cdr. G.L. (Nick) Carter (retd). Drafted to CONDOR 1958 as Commissioned Air Engineer (Pre Sub Lt.) i/c station flight which included running RARA's barge (Percival Sea Prince) - RARA was Rear Admiral Tynedale-Biscoe, pilot was ledgendary Lt. Cdr. "Hookey" Walker. Station C.O. was Captain (E) 'Poppy' Tanner, exec. was Cdr. Bardber, Training Cdr. Goodchild. Approx ten Wren Air Mechanics helped to service "barge" with great pride - voluntarily they embroidered white head rest cloths for all aircraft seats with "R.A.R.A." intertwined letters in blue - a touch of "one upmanship" with FOAC's barge at Yeovilton.

One Wren on the filght - Doxberry - had several breaks in her service - subsequently discovered to be playing cricket for England.

Jimmy-the-one was Nigel Tetley who took part in the single handed "Round the World" race. Unfortunately he sank almost within sight of Lands End.

Halfway through the commision, he (Nick) was moved to the mechanics training scholl under Lt. Cdr. Peter Tisley.

Other personalities were Stewart Evans, a 'Schoolie' who went on to become quite a well known author. Also he wife, a Thrid Officer who went into T/V production.

Chief Officer McBride - later Director Wrens - was an excellent actress and took major parts in Arbroath's entry for Naval Air Command Drama competition and part in "All My Sons" for which Nick built the scenery and stage managed.

Station flight also had a Sea Baliol to enable RARA staff to fly to uphold their "hours".

The Captain at that time was concerned about some pornographic magazines being available to young recruits and took the NAAFI rep through the living accommodation saying "the sailors invariably stow this filthy literature under their matress or somewhere in their beds. Turn over any bed and you will find one or more of these disgusting magazines". He flicked over the pillow and exposed a Bible.

Nick's wife was a Wren Air Mechanic.

George Parker - general service telegraphist - was transferred to FAA to Arbroath - to us their knowledge of 'U' boat tracking in destroyers - to become a H/F D/F (huffduff) operator to enable aircraft to be guided back to base. In 1945, this was achieved by sending them out across the airfield with a walkie talkie on their backs to simulate aircraft whilst those in the D/F hut followed the signals - Unfortunately truding around the airfield in several feet of snow is not to be recommended. Needless to say there was much muttering. They also had flights doing much the same thing and on, at least, one occasion ditched and had to be rescued by fishers, making headlines in the Scottish Daily Express - the full facts of this were not made known to George until well after demob.

A second commission from 1953 to 1955 on Training staff as Apprentices D.O. and later Mechanicians D.O.

Captain after 1954, R.R. Shorto, had a much envied red drop-head Bentley.

Cdr(X) was A.G.Oliver , became parson on retirement.

RARA was Rear Admiral "Batchy" Rebbeck , married late, hence nickname.

Lt. Cdr. McLean 1947/48 recalls (as a schoolie) teaching mainly maths and theory of flight, also managing some twenty hours in mosquitoes of 772 Sqdn.. Also extramural activities such as wildfowling and fishing, Scottish dancing and amateur dramatics ("Quiet Wedding" and "Rope") - married L/Wren J Buchanan (aircraft checker) 1943/44, later 3/O Wrens 1946/48. Recalls editor of CONDOR magazine P.O. J. Evans. Also officer's mess dog "Guns":.

G.C. Fidler, now unfortunately deceased, log book reads " DLTS 15.3.43 - 7.4.43 and at 753 Sqdn. 27.4.43 - 24.5.43. Demobilised 1945 after a course at H.M.S. PEEWIT. Subsequently served on Mac Ships - qualified as solicitor - became Mayor of Burton-on-Trent - died January 1974. Wife Joan graduated from St. Andrews and joined Wrens serving at Chatham and Belfast.

Lt.Cdr. G.J.(Nick) Carter RN (retd). Drafted to CONDOR 1958 as Commissioned Air Engineer (Pre Sub Lt.) i/c station flight which included running RARA's barge (Percival Sea Prince) - RARA was Rear Admiral Tynedale-Biscoe, pilot was legendary Lt. Cdr. "Hookey" Walker. Station C.O. was Captain (E) "Poppy" Tanner, exec. was Cdr. Barber, Training Cdr. Goodchild. Approx ten Wren Air Mechanics helped to service "barge" with great pride - voluntarily they embroidered white head rest cloths for all aircraft seats with "R.A.R.A." intertwined letters in blue - a touch of "one-upmanship" with FOAC's barge at Yeovilton.

S & S Football Team H.M.S. Condor 1955

P.O. (S)	*CK (S)*	*CK*	*P.O.CK (S)*	*CK (S)*	*L/CK (S)*
Trainer	*Mooke*	*McQuarree*	*Cook*	*Conlon*	*Irvine*

L/CK (S)	*CK*	*CK*	*CK*	*CK*
McHardie	*Morrison*	*Colligan*	*Turbiton*	*Hutcheon*

Boxing Team

P.T. Staff

M.T. Section

Safe Driving Awards

M.T. Staff

Crash Crew

M.T. Drivers

M.T. Section

M.T. Section

M.T. Section

M.T. Section

Factory Training Aids Staff 1957

Civilian Messmen

Station Section - Summer 1945

Another Tot Perhaps!

P.O. John Evans & Photographer Neil Ker

Parachute Section - 1942

Electrical Section 754 S.U. 1944

Garden Party - Woodville 1942

Football Team 1943

Back row L-R   S. Stennett, K. Stevens, F. Dean, J. Cambell, G. West, D. Towns, S. Finnegan
Front row L-R   A. Prees, A. Griegson, P. Chapman, Paddy Brady, L. O'Connor, L. Jones

RNATE Military Band July 1946

Admiral inspecting Band July 1946

Divisions 1946

Vice Admiral Power - Summer 1946

Pussers "Tillies"

Royal Austrailian Navy - Fleet Air Arm
"Condor" 1948 - 1950
Conversion Course C4 - ERA's - M. Mechs To A.A.'s
Back row L-R R:. Roberts, J. Lamb, N. Hallas, A. Woods, H. Gibson, G. Cooker-Godson
Centre row: D. Eastrate, B. Gilroy, R. Smith, G. Foale, J. Sergeant, A. Sara, R. Higgins
Front row: C. Pripe, E. Barker, S. Cox, S. Paul

Excercise - Reserve Operation 1957

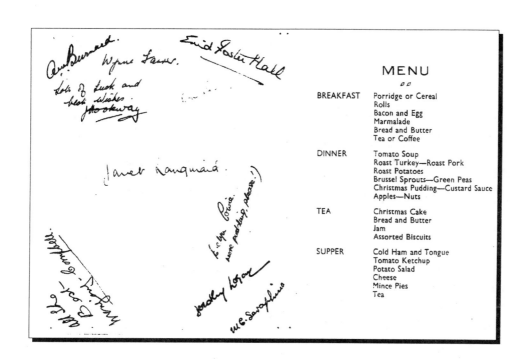

MENU

BREAKFAST	Porridge or Cereal
	Rolls
	Bacon and Egg
	Marmalade
	Bread and Butter
	Tea or Coffee
DINNER	Tomato Soup
	Roast Turkey—Roast Pork
	Roast Potatoes
	Brussel Sprouts—Green Peas
	Christmas Pudding—Custard Sauce
	Apples—Nuts
TEA	Christmas Cake
	Bread and Butter
	Jam
	Assorted Biscuits
SUPPER	Cold Ham and Tongue
	Tomato Ketchup
	Potato Salad
	Cheese
	Mince Pies
	Tea

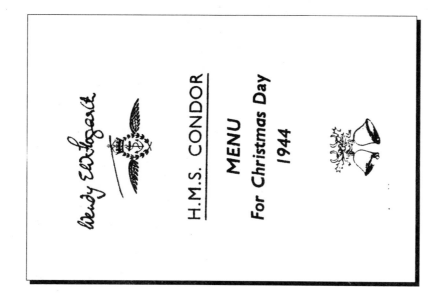

H.M.S. CONDOR

MENU
For Christmas Day
1944

Photographs of M.T. Section

Tempy. Lt. (A),   )(O) D.K. McIntosh
S.A.N.F.(V)   )
Headmaster Lt. .... S.W. Harman

July 1945

CONDOR

Commander .... J.W. Havers (act),
              (ret)
              (In Command)

Tempy. Lt.,   )
R.N.V.R.   ) F.J. Kippin (act)
Flight Lt.,   ) L.J. Cooke
R.A.F.   (For Administrative Duties)
Tempy. Com. (A),)(P) B.F. Cox (act)
R.N.V.R.   (And as Commander (Flying))
Lt.-Com. (A) .... W.J.H. Mills (act)
Tempy.,   ) A.L. Nunneley (act)
Lt.-Com. (A),   )(O) K. Hyde (act)
R.N.V.R.   )(P) R.P. Mason (act)
)(Lt.-Com. (Flying))
Lt. (A) .... J.E. Warren
Tempy.,   ) H.C. Howie (act)
Lt. (A),   ) J.S. Weaver (act)
R.N.V.R.   )(P) J.F. Urquhart
             A.W. Taylor
             M. Williams (act)
             F.C.K. Crowther
)(O) A. Carroll
Commander (E) .... G.L. Bailey
Tempy. Instr.Lt. ..... A.H. Fogg
Tempy. Chaplain, (Rev.T.L.F. Beattie
R.N.V.R.
Captain (S) .... K.U. White (act)
Tempy. Surg..,   )
Lt.-Com.,   ) J.M. McEwan, MB,
R.N.V.R.   ) chB (act)
Tempy. Surg.,   )
Lt.-Com. (D),   ) G.W. Hughes, LDS
R.N.V.R.   ) (act)
Lt.-Com. (S),   ) G.W. Kemp
R.N.V.R.   )
Tempy. Surg.Lt.,) M.C. Platten, MB,
R.N.V.R.   ) chB
Tempy. Surg. Lt.(D)) W.T. Moore, LDS
R.N.V.R.   )
Lt. (S) .... J.R. Watson
Tempy. Elect, Lt.,) R.L. Hughes
R.N.V.R.   )
Lt.-Com.(Sp.Br.),)(Met)E.P. West, MA (act)
R.N.V.R.   )
Tempy. Lt.-Com.,) T.C. Spurway (act)
(Sp.Br.),   )
R.N.V.R.   )
Tempy. Lt.,   ) G.F. Steel
(Sp.Br.),   ) F.G. Stanton (act)
R.N.V.R.   ) R.W. Wray
             J.S. Smith
             J.S. Atkinson

Instructional Staff

Tempy.,   )(O) G.C. Richardson
Lt. (A),   )(O) H.G. Wilks (act)
R.N.V.R.   )(And For Compass Duties)

Observer School

Commander .....(O) H..B Gardner (act)
              (Training Commander)
Lt.-Com. ......(O) J.W. Collett (act)
Lt. ....(P) D.A.E. Holbrook
            (O) F.L. Sherwin
               E.J. Treloar
Lt.-Com. (A)...(P) J.I. Baker
Tempy. Lt.-Com)
(A),   )(O) F.L. Page
R.N.V.R.   )
Tempy.,   )(O) N.H. Godwood
Lt. (A),   )(O) B.V. Doxat-Pratt
R.N.V.R.   )(O) K. Burt
           (O) D. Cunningham
           (O) R.B. Le Page
           (O) J.B. Mackay
           (O) J.D. Ridgeway
Tempy. Lt.(A),)
R.N.Z.N.V.R.)(O) M.B. Radford

Naval Air Signal School

Commander .....(O) T.W.B. Shaw, DSC (act)
              (Officer In Charge)
Lt.-Com. ......(O) C.C. Ennever, DSC
           (O) C.H. Pain (act)
      (And For R.N.A.S. Crail and Easthaven)
           (O) M.G. Chichester (act)
Tempy.,   )
Lt.-Com. (A),)(O) K. Hyde (act)
R.N.V.R.   )
Lt. (A). ......(O) R.V. Hinton
           (O) P.D. Lloyd
Tempy.,   )(O) J. Boyd
Lt. (A),   ) D.W.L. Farrall
R.N.V.R.   )(O) T.S. Hall
           (O) K.L. Jones
           (O) W.A. Forster
               V.E. Sills (act)
           (O) W.L. Orr
Tempy. Lt.(A),)
S.A.N.F.(V))(C) D.K. McIntosh
Headmaster Lt..... E. Reid, BSC

October 1945

CONDOR

Captain .... I. L. Porter
             (In Command)
Commander .... R.W. Keymer
Lt.-Com.,   ) I. Calvart-Jones
R.N.V.R.   )

The Church of S. Christopher.

H·M·S· "Condor."

Form of Service

ON THE OCCASION OF THE

UNVEILING AND DEDICATION

OF THE

EAST WINDOW.

Sunday, 19th November 1950.

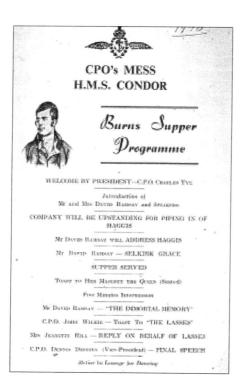

CPO's MESS
H.M.S. CONDOR

Burns Supper
Programme

WELCOME BY PRESIDENT—C.P.O. CHARLES TYE

Introduction of
Mr and Mrs DAVID RAMSAY and Speakers

COMPANY WILL BE UPSTANDING FOR PIPING IN OF
HAGGIS

Mr DAVID RAMSAY WILL ADDRESS HAGGIS

Mr DAVID RAMSAY — SELKIRK GRACE

SUPPER SERVED

TOAST TO HER MAJESTY THE QUEEN (Seated)

Five Minutes Intermission

Mr DAVID RAMSAY — "THE IMMORTAL MEMORY"

C.P.O. JOHN WILKIE — TOAST TO "THE LASSES"

Mrs JEANETTE HILL — REPLY ON BEHALF OF LASSES

C.P.O. DENNIS DEVEREAUX (Vice-President) — FINAL SPEECH

Retire To Lounge for Dancing

Falls 1500 Feet, Then Emergency 'Chute Opens

DR. CHARLES ROBERTSON, founder and chairman of the Scottish Parachute Club, yesterday retained the Scottish National Parachute Championship at H.M.S. Condor, Arbroath. Dr. Robertson was also runner-up in the open section.

While jumping yesterday Jim Knipe, of Bristol had to pull his reserve parachute at 1500 feet after his main parachute failed to open. Jim came down in a wood but escaped unhurt.

He had fallen 1500 feet after leaving the plane.

Among those who were present at the championships was Mr Yuri Dudin, an attache from the Russian Embassy in London. An invitation had gone to the Embassy but no reply was received. The first Condor knew of a representative being sent was when Mr Dudin called at the main gate.

Runner-up to Dr Robertson in the national championship was Robert Reid a member of the Scottish national team at present serving with the 16th Parachute Brigade. He was fourth in the open section.

Winner of the open section was Peter J. Wenk, of the Golden Arrows team from the 8th Infantry Division of the U.S. Army in Germany. Third in the open section was Peter Pagnanelli of the 63rd Parachute Company of the R.A.S.C.

The team event was won by the 2nd Battalion of the Parachute Regiment, represented by J. Baugham, W. Catt and D. McNaughton.

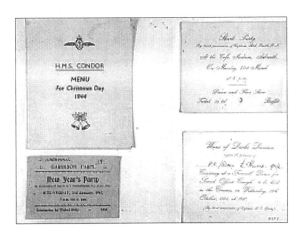

H.M.S. CONDOR

ANNUAL

ATHLETIC MEETING

by kind permission of
CAPTAIN L. E. PORTER, R.N.

SATURDAY, 28th JULY, 1945
at 1400

Station Sports Ground
R.N.A.S. ARBROATH

THIS year's Scottish Invitation Parachute Championships are being held to-day at the R.N.A.S., H.M.S. Condor, Arbroath, as part of the "Air Day" programme. The Naval Air Station will be open to the public from 11 a.m. and there will be a full programme of ground displays, flying events, and free-fall parachute jumping until the ceremony of Beating Retreat at 5.45 p.m.

Two young women will be among the 41 competitors taking part in the parachute championships. They are 21-year-old Mrs. Diane Knipe, a Bristol housewife, and Miss Helen Lambert (19), members of the British women's team at the world championships held earlier this year.

Entries for the championships have come from Scotland, England, Belgium, Australia and America.

With smoke bombs fixed to the heels of their boots, crack parachutists from all over Europe will give displays of sky-diving, with the thrilling formation drop and the passing of a baton as they hurtle downwards before opening their parachutes.

Winner of the national championship will receive the Chandy Trophy, which is at present held by C. A. Robertson, Glasgow. There will also be a cup for the winner of the open championship.

Failed To Open

Many of the competitors have been practising at Condor this week. Among them was Desmond Connelly, who made a jump for the first time since his parachute failed to open last year.

Desmond, a leading English parachutist, jumped in free fall with his son Tiggy from a plane flying at 2,500 feet over Condor. His last jump was made at Kiddlington, and on that occasion his parachute failed to open, and he crashed to the ground, breaking a leg.

The Russians have declined an invitation to take part in the championships, but there are Australians, Belgians and Americans from the U.S. forces in Germany, as well as British civilian and forces teams.

Three teams have come from the Parachute Regiment and all the members are skilled display divers who have been doing jumps at shows throughout England this summer.

Air Display

There will also be an air display in which Hunters, Scimitars and Buccaneers will take part.

An indication of the work of the naval air station will be given in the displays in hangars, and there will be an exhibition of silent drill and physical training.

The 4/5th The Black Watch will provide pipes and drums and a mountain rescue demonstration.

PARACHUTE WOMEN TRY FOR TROPHY

Express Staff Reporter

THE daring, nerve-tingling sport of parachute jumping is one not readily associated with the graces of the gentler sex.

But this week three young women will play a leading part in the Scottish Invitation Parachute Championships at H.M.S. Condor, the Royal Naval air station at Arbroath.

And on the ground a fourth, herself a parachutist with more than 50 jumps to her credit, will watch her husband compete for the main award, the Chandy Trophy.

Taking part in the competition are two members of this year's British Women's World Championship team, Diane Knipe, and Helen Flambert.

'Wonderful'

Flying one of the two aircraft from which the competitors make their jumps will be 28-year-old Mrs. Claire Roberts and watching the event, will be Mrs. Maureen Denley, whose husband Pete is leading the Scottish Parachute Club entry in the team event.

Diane said: "Parachuting is a sport we can both enjoy together and it is not a dangerous or death-defying hobby as so many people seem to think."

And Claire, who runs a commercial airline from Northampton with her husband and has logged more than 3,000 flying hours, said: "The parachutists are wonderful people to work with."

Taking part in the competitions will be about 40 of the world's top male parachutists, including Dr. Charles Robertson, chairman of the Scottish Parachute Club, captain of the Scottish national team, and holder of the Chandy Trophy.

Royal Naval Sick Quarters Kelly Castle

C. T. Parsons

DURING times of emergency a rapid increase in Royal Naval Medical Establishments is made possible by the creation of RN Auxiliary Hospitals and RN Sick Quarters: RN Auxiliary Hospitals by the requisition of Civilian Hospitals and large residential schools and RN Sick Quarters by the requisition of hotels, country houses and, in at least one case, a Scottish castle.

The history of the RN Auxiliary Hospitals has been fully documented in official War Histories, but not the RN Sick Quarters. This is the story of one such Sick Quarters, as recalled 45 years after the event.

In 1939, land and buildings near Arbroath were requisitioned for the construction of an airfield. On completion it was commissioned as HMS *Condor*, Royal Naval Air Station (RNAS) Arbroath; today it survives as RM Condor. At a later date provision was made for dispersed Sick Quarters at Kelly Castle.

Kelly Castle is situated near the village of Arbirlot, about three miles west of Arbroath and one mile inland from the North Sea. The castle stands in a wooded glen above the Elliot Water. The history of the site[1] can be traced back to 1208 and many famous Scots names are associated with it. The present structure dates from the 17th century and has been the historic seat of the Earls of Panmure, the Maule family and the Maule Ramsays. When Admiral George Ramsay became the 12th Earl of Dalhousie it became part of the Dalhousie estate. In 1939 it was the home of Captain Archibald Maule Ramsay MP who was an active supporter of Sir

Mr Parsons was formerly Librarian at RNH Halsar, and an ex-Sick Berth Attendant. He now lives in Market Drayton, Shropshire.

Oswald Mosely, leader of the British Fascist Party. This association led to the internment of Captain Maule Ramsay in Brixton Prison from May 1940 until September 1945, though during this time he remained an MP.

The castle opened as a Sick Quarters in May 1943 and closed in October 1945, a relatively short period, but a time of great activity in the training of aircrew. Eventually Kelly Castle served the needs of not only HMS *Condor* but also HMS *Peewit*, RNAS Easthaven, situated on the coast a few miles to the west.

The castle was approached from the west along a tree-lined avenue about a quarter of a mile long; at the end of this avenue the castle came into view (*Fig. 1*). Passing through the archway gave access to a courtyard about 100 feet square. Opening from this courtyard was the main entrance to the ground floor of the castle. On this floor was the galley, a large well lit room with coal fired ranges and a piano—it was almost certainly the only RN galley with such a piece of equipment. Next to the galley was the VADs' Mess and along the north wing, in the former domestic staff accommodation, were the dispensary, the WRNS Mess and WRNS Accommodation.

On leaving the ground floor by a fairly wide wooden staircase, one came to the first floor on which was the Nursing Sister's cabin and bathroom. Between these was the operating theatre, Sister's bathroom being used for 'scrubbing up' when the need arose. Also on this floor were three wards occupying the former lounge, dining room and library. These were Male Surgical with ten beds (*Fig. 2*), Officers with six beds and Female Surgical with five beds. Proceeding from the first floor up an extremely narrow spiral stone staircase (*Fig. 3*) one came to the Male Medical ward of ten beds,

Fig. 1. The approach to the Castle.

and also the Night Duty VAD's duty cabin. Continuing up the spiral staircase gave access to two rooms with very low ceilings, these were the accommodation for the VADs. An even narrower staircase led to a space where the Night Duty VAD slept, this was in the turret shown in Fig. 1.

Fig. 2. Male Surgical Ward in former dining room.

Fig. 3. The narrow spiral stone staircase.

Back on ground floor level and across the courtyard was a door that opened into a full sized billiard room. This area also contained the NAAFI; possibly the smallest in any shore establishment, it consisted of a cupboard approximately two feet high, one and a half feet deep and one foot wide. The Senior Sick Berth Rating was the honorary manager. Exiting from the billiard room brought one into the Sick Berth Staff mess, a small windowless room but with an anthracite stove. A third door from the courtyard led into the Administration Office, the window of which can be seen to the right of the archway in Fig. 1; here the duty Sick Berth

Rating slept. One of his duties was to close the archway doors at 2300 daily and open them at 0700.

Provision was made for the off-duty Sick Berth Ratings to sleep in what had originally been the castle stables and then the garages. This building was about 100 yards from the main building situated in the trees lining the approach drive. In what had been the harness room was a three-bedded dormitory; this also contained a large coal fired range (which was never seen lit by the author), a butler's sink with cold running water, and electric lighting.

The staff comprised one Nursing Sister (though accommodation was also provided for the Nursing Sister of HMS Condor), seven VADs (all Nursing Members), seven WRNS (one L/Cook, one Cook, one L/Steward, one Steward and three General Duties). These numbers remained constant throughout the commission of the Sick Quarters, however, for the Sick Berth Staff it was a different story. When the Sick Quarters opened there was one Sick Berth Petty Officer and two Sick Berth Attendants; by January 1944 with shore establishment complements being reduced to provide the necessary personnel for D Day, the figure was down to one Sick Berth Attendant (the author). This situation continued until July 1944 when the complement was increased to one Sick Berth Petty Officer and one Sick Berth Attendant, and so it remained until closure. Other staff comprised a civilian boilerman (a retired farmer) and a civilian handyman. The upkeep of the extensive gardens was the responsibility of the gardener who was still in the employ of Captain Maule Ramsay and who, from time to time, sent produce to the Captain in Brixton Prison; surplus produce, however, was donated to the galley. There was no resident Medical Officer, a daily visit being made by a Medical Officer from HMS *Condor* and also by a Medical Officer from HMS *Peewit* as the need arose.

Before requisition, the castle had been lit by electricity produced by damming the Elliot Water and the installation of a hydro-electric generator, but after requisition it was connected to the mains supply. The Navy Works department installed a sewage treatment plant in a distant part of the grounds, the treated effluent being discharged into the Elliot Water.

Routine was based loosely on that worked in RN Hospitals at that time with one major exception, all staff and patients, other than those on special diets, had the same meals. These were served pre-plated from the galley, the pre-plating being done by Sister, L/Cook and the Sick Berth Rating, then the trays with the meals were carried to the Wards by the VADs and WRNS.

The administration of the Sick Quarters was carried out by HMS *Condor* at a distance. Not once during the author's ten month stay were 'Rounds' carried out, other than Medical Rounds by the visiting Medical Officer, not even by the Senior Medical Officer of HMS *Condor*, although it must be admitted it was a time of extreme war effort. Patients were received from HMS *Condor*, HMS *Peewit* or Arbroath Infirmary after emergency treatment. Fresh cases were usually received about 1400 and, unless extremely ill, were required to walk up the stairs, as it was impossible to get a stretcher up the spiral staircase to the Male Medical Ward. Although the medical records of the establishment will not be released until the next century, it is known that in the early summer of 1945 there was an outbreak of industrial dermatitis among a section of Air-

craft Fitters at HMS *Condor* and so large was the number of cases received that a marquee was erected in the grounds of the castle as the wards were full.

Minor surgery was carried out as required and some simple procedures were carried out on the wards as this description by a former patient so aptly illustrates: "J . . . was brought in very ill with pleurisy. He never moved for two days, then they held him up in bed, stuck a long flat needle between the ribs in his back and from my bed opposite I saw them draw out a syringe full of brown fluid. From then on he steadily improved." Cold surgery cases were sent to the RN Auxiliary Hospital, north of Aberdeen, as were cases for specialist consultation. As this involved a round journey by train of 150 miles, patients for consultation had to take their kit with them in case they were admitted. Pathological specimens were sent to a hospital in Dundee. Stores, Medical, Victualling and Naval, were all obtained from HMS *Condor*, victuals being delivered each weekday afternoon with two days supply on Saturday mornings. Medical and Naval stores were delivered with the victuals as and when required.

The establishment of a small Naval community in the middle of a Scottish farming area was very well accepted and the staff were always welcome at village functions in Arbirlot, and in the autumn of 1945, when the Sick Quarters was closing, the villagers gave a party for the staff. Although the last patients left Kelly Castle in October 1945, it was not until January 1946 that the last stores were returned.

ACKNOWLEDGEMENT

I wish to acknowledge the assistance I have received from former members of staff and former patients of RN Sick Quarters Kelly Castle. Even all these years later it has been possible to trace many of the staff and draw on their knowledge. Kelly Castle is once again a private residence and I wish to thank the owner for his permission to describe this short chapter in the long history of his home.

REFERENCE

1. ANON. Kellie Castle, Angus. Derby. Pilgrim Press, 1975.
(NB: The current OS map shows KELLIE Castle whereas at the time of Naval occupation it was known as KELLY Castle. Both spellings are acceptable.)

Reproduced from Volume 75(1) of the Journal of the Royal Naval Medical Service, by kind permission of the Editor.

<u>December 1940</u>

CONDOR

Captain .........E.M.C. Abel-Smith
Commander....(O) J.H.F. Sawyer
Lt.-Com. ........J.W. Havers (ret)
                 T.A. Herriott (ret)
Lt. .............P.S.V. Smith (ret)
Lt.,   )
(Sp.Br.),   )(Met) E.P. West, BA
R.N.V.R.   )
Lt. (A).........G.A. Thomson
                 (For Technical duties)
                 (P) C.H. Ancil
                 (And for Technical duties)
Tempy.,   )
Lt. (A),   )   K.M. Fox
R.N.V.R.   )
Commander....(E) P. DuCane (act) (Emgcy)
Chaplain........ Rev.D.E. Jones, BA
Surg.,   )
Lt.-Com.,   ) C.A. Mathers, MB, chB
R.N.V.R.   )
Paym.,   )
Lt.-Com.,   ) E.G.S. Maclean
R.N.V.R.   )
Tempy.,   ) W.A. Robson, MB, chB
Surg. Lt.,   ) A.P. Curtin, MRCS, LRCP
R.N.V.R.   )
Surg. Lt. ...(D) W.I.N. Forrest, LDS
Tempy.,   )
Paym. Lt.,   )   F.S. Cooper
R.N.V.R.   )
Elect. Lt........F. Bolwell
Lt. R.M. ....W. Mitchell (ret)

For Special Duties.

Tempy.,   )
Lt. (A),   )   S.J. Cope
R.N.V.R.   )

Instructional Staff.

Commander ...(O) B.J.L. Rogers-
                 Tillstone (ret)
Lt. Com. ....(O) A.G. Rogers
             (O) R. Moore
             (O) N.G.R. Crawford
             (O) F.M. Griffiths
   (Al Fr.) (O) J.G. Hunt
             J.E. Smallwood
Lt. ....(O) J.S. Manning
             (O) J.A. Crawford
             (O) J.C.B. Boucher
             (O) A.W.N. Dayrell,DSC

<u>December 1941</u>

CONDOR

Captain. ......R.M.T. Taylor
Commander......F.M.R. Stephenson
Lt.-Com.......J.W. Havers (ret)
              (P) J.F. Nicholas (ret)
Lt. ..........E.G. Price (ret)
Tempy. Lt.,)
R.N.V.R.   )   J.M. Forster
Lt. (A) ......G.A. Thomson
                 (For Technical duties)
             (P) T.C. Brock
                 (For Armament duties)
Tempy.,   )   D.H. Hollins
Lt., (A),   )   (For Armament duties)
R.N.V.R.   )   K.M. Fox
                 J.K. Howitt
Commander (E) K.E. Smith
Lt. R.M. ......W. Mitchell (ret)
Tempy.,   )
Chaplain,   )Rev. J.J. Cowan, BA
R.N.V.R.   ) (proby)
Surg. Com. ....J. Wylie, OBE, MB, chB
Paym. Com.....E.D.T. Churcher
Surg.,   )
Lt.-Com.,   ) J.M. Banks, MB, chB
R.A.N.V.R.   )
Paym.,   )
Lt.-Com,   )   E.G.S. Maclean
Tempy.,   )   A.P. Curtin, MRCS, LRCP
Surg. Lt.,   )   S.M. Davidson, MB, Bch
R.N.V.R.   )
Tempy.,   )
Surg.,   )
Lt. (D),   )   J.M. Paterson, LDS
R.N.V.R.   )
Paym. Lt.......W.S.A. Lucas
Tempy.,   )
Paym. Lt.,   )   F.S. Cooper
R.N.V.R.   )
Elect. Lt. ....F. Bolwell
Flight Lt.,) J.F. Ward (act)
R.A.F.   )For Liaison and Welfare duties)
Lt.,   )
(Sp.Br.),)(Met) E.P. West, MA
R.N.V.R.   )
Tempy. Lt.,) T.S. Spurway
(Sp.Br.),) D.G. Huxley
R.N.V.R.   )

Instructional Staff.

Commander...(O) B.J.L.W. Rogers-
                Tillstone (ret)

```
Lt.-Com. .....(O) R. Moore              Tempy.,        )
             (O) B. Walford             Surg. ,        )
             (O) L. Hill                Lt. (D),       ) J.M. Paterson, LDS
Lt. .........(O) A.J.T. Roe             R.N.V.R.       )
             (O) A.W.F. Sutton,DSC      Paym. Lt. ......W.S.A. Lucus
             (O) W.H. Williams                          P.F. Gick
             (O) K.C. Grieve            Tempy.,        )
   *GC ...(O) P.N. Humphreys            Paym. Lt.,     ) F.S. Cooper
Lt. (A)......(O) P.B. Dawe              R.N.V.R.       ) E.L. Alexander
                                        Lt.,           )
June 1942                               (Sp. Br.),     )Med E.P. West, MA
                                        R.N.V.R.       )
CONDOR                                  Tempy. Lt.,    ) T.C. Spurway
                                        (Sp. Br.),     ) D.E. Huxley
Captain..........R.M.T. Taylor          R.N.V.R.       ) H. Swainsbury
Commander........Hon. R. Coke, AFC (ret)                 C. Albrecht
             R.M. Cobb (ret)
             (P) J.E. Fenton            Instructional Staff.
Lt.-Com. .........J.W. Havers (ret)
             (P) J.F. Nicholas (ret)    Commander....(O) B.J.L.W. Rogers-
             (P) S. Borrett                              Tillstone (ret)
Lt. .............E.G. Price (ret)       Lt.-Com. ....(O) R. Moore
Tempy. Lt.,    )                                     (O) F.D. Howie, DSC
R.N.V.R.       ) J.M. Forster                        (O) A.V. Lyle
Flight Lt.,    ) J.F. Ward (act)        Lt. .........(O) A.W.F. Sutton, DSC
R.A.F. (For Liaison and Welfare duties)              (O) C. Campbell-Meiklejohn
Tempy.        )   D.F. Hollins (act)                 (O) K.C. Grieve
Lt.-Com. (A),)(P) J.G. Crammond (act)      *GC...(O) P.N. Humphreys
R.N.V.R.      )                                      (O)J.R. Thomson (act)
Lt. (A).........G.A. Thomson            Lt. (A) .....(O) P.B. Dawe
             (For Technical duties)                  (O) H.E.H. Pain
             (P) A.S. Owensmith                          C.F.H. Joy
             R.J.T. Barrett                          (O) B.J. Longman
             (For Armament duties)      Lt. (A),      )
Tempy.        )   J.K. Howitt           R.N.V.R.      ) D.E. Moxey
Lt. (A),      )   R.H. Stewart
R.N.V.R.      )   W. Seivewright        December 1942
Commander (E).....F.V. Stopford
Lt.(E)...........W.P. Coghlan (ret)     CONDOR
Lt. R.M. .......W. Mitchell (ret)
Tempy. Lt.,   )                         Captain ........R.M.T. Taylor
R.N.V.R.      ) R.W. Wray (act)         Commander ......R.M. Cobb (ret)
Tempy.,       )                                    (P) J.E. Fenton, OBE
Chaplin,      )Rev. J.J. Cowan, BA                     A.F. Hall
R.N.V.R.      )                                        J.W. Havers (act) (ret)
Surg. Com. ......J. Whylie, OBE, MB, chB Lt.-Com. ....(P) J.F. Nicholas (ret)
Paym. Com. ......E.D.T. Churcher                    (O) D.G. Goodwin, DSC
Surg. Lt. .......R.T. Smith, MB, Bch               (S) A.T. Courtney
Surg. Lt.,    )                         Lt. .............E.G. Price (ret)
R.A.N.V.R.    ) R.E.S. Charlton, MB, BS Tempy. Lt.,   ) J.M. Forster
Tempy.,       )                         R.N.V.R.      ) R.W. Wray (act)
Surg., Lt.,   )R.H. Roberts, MB, chB    Flight Lt.,   ) J.F. Ward (act)
R.N.V.R.      )                         R.A.F. (For Liaison and Welfare duties)
                                        Tempy., Lt.-)(P) R.S. Maxwell, MC,DFC,
                                        Com. (A),     )   AFC
                                        R.N.V.R.      ) D.F. Hollins (act)
```

```
                    (P) J.G. Crammond (act)      Instructional Staff.
Lt.  (A) ....(P) A.S. Owensmith
                    R.J.T. Barrett              Commander   (O) B.E.W. Logan
                (O) A. Aitken                   Lt.-Com. ....(O) D.K. Buchanan-
Tempy.,    )        J.K. Howitt                                 Dunlop
Lt. (A),   )        R.H. Stewart                Lt. ........(O) A.W.F. Sutton,DSC
R.N.V.R.   )        K. Hyde                                 (O) D.J. Godden
                    P.R. Shackleford                        (O) A. Gregory
                    K.T. Hall                               (O) C.V.S. Malleson
                    H.M. Lowe                               (O) H.R.B. Janvrin,DSC
                    L.A. Webb                                   J. Bridgewater-Kitcat
Commander (E) ...F.V. Stopford              Lt. (A) .....(O) P.B. Dawe
Lt.  (E) .......W.P. Coghlan (ret)                         (O) H.E.H. Pain
Tempy.,    )                                Tempy.,    )       G.P.L. Bolt
Capt.,     ) J.W.H. Wylie                   Lt. (A),   )(O) W.A. Gillingham, DSC
R.M.       )                                R.N.V.R.   )
Lt.   R.M. .....W. Mitchell (ret)
Tempy. Lt.)     J.E.F. Codrington           June 1943
R.M.       )    W.L. Jeffrey
                W.P. Leitch                 CONDOR
                A.A.J. Foster
Tempy.,    )                                Captain ........R.M.T. Taylor
Chaplain,  )Rev. J.J. Cowan, BA             Commander ...(P) J.A.D. Wroughton, DSC
R.V.N.R.   )                                                 (act)
Surg. Com. ......J. Wylie, OBE, MB, chB                  J.W. Havers (act) (ret)
Paym. Com. ......E.D.T. Churcher                         T.S. Jackson (act) (ret)
Paym.,     )                                Lt.Com. .....(P) J.F. Nicholas (ret)
Lt. Com.   ) P.F. Gick (act)                            (O) D.G. Goodwin, DSC
Surg. Lt. .......R.T. Smith, MB, Bch        Lt. ........(S) J.R.G. Trechman
Tempy.,    )     D. McLean, MB, BS                      (O) P.B. Schondfeldt
Surg. Lt., )     R.A. Du Val, DSC, MB,                  (P) J.C.M. Harman
R.N.V.R.   )     BS                                         J.S.L. Crabb
                C.D. Coe, MB, chB                       (O) J.A.J. Smith-Shand, DSC
Tempy.,    )                                            (O) J.A. Shuttleworth
Surg.,     )     J.M. Paterson, LDS                     (O) C.G. Bush
Lt. (D),   )     W.T. Moore, LDS            Tempy. Lt.,)     J.M. Forster
R.N.V.R.   )                                R.N.V.R.   )     R.W. Wray (act)
Paym. Lt. .......W.S.A. Lucas                                J.W. Phippard (act)
                W.E.V. Woods (ret)          Flight Lt.,)     J.F. Ward (act)
Paym. Lt.,)                                 R.A.F.  (For Liaison and Welfare duties)
R.N.R.    ) V. Clarke                       Tempy. Lt.-) (P) R.S. Maxwell, MC,DFC,AFC
Tempy.,   )                                 Com. (A),  ) (P) J.D. Crammond (act)
Paym. Lt.,)     F.S. Cooper                 R.N.V.R.   )
R.N.V.R.  )     E.L. Alexander              Lt. (A) ........R.J.T. Barrett
Tempy.,   )     L.I. Loch                               (O) P.T. Lawman
Sub.Lt.(A))     J.W. Boote                             (O) A. Aitken
R.N.V.R.  ) (For Technical duties)                     (O) L.J. Smith
Lt.-Com., )                                            (P) C.J.I. Cunningham
(Sp.Br.), )(Met) E.P. West, MA (act)                   (O) P.J. Warrington
R.N.V.R.  )                                            (O) P.C. Brooker
Lt.,      )                                            (O) L.G. Wheeler
(Sp.Br.), )(Met) R.B. Pink                  Tempy.,    )     R.H. Stewart
R.N.V.R.  )                                 Lt. (A),   )     G. Hammonds
Tempy.Lt.,)     T.C. Spurway                R.N.V.R.   )     H.M. Lowe
(Sp. Br.),)     D.G. Huxley                                  L.A. Webb
R.N.V.R.  )     H. Swainsbury                                R.B. Horner
          (Met) W.G. Hewitt                                  C.H. Binden
                C. Albrecht                             (O) J.W.F. Jameson
                A. White                               (P) C.J. Mitchell
                G.F. Steel                                   L.R. Adams
                                                            A. White
                                                            M.G.F. Smith (proby)
```

Commander   (E) ... F.V. Stopford
Lt. (E) .... A.F. Turner
Tempy.,   )
Lt., (E),   ) .... I.M. Grant
R.N.V.R.   )
Tempy.,   ) .... J.W.H. Wylie
Capt.,   ) .... B.T.A. Grimshaw,
R.M.   )   (act)
Tempy. Lt.,   ) .... W.L. Jeffrey
R.M.   ) .... W.P. Leitch
                         H. Barnes
Tempy.,   )
2nd Lt.,   ) .... T.G. Garsed
R.M.   )
Tempy,   )
Chaplain,   ) Rev. A.D. Walmsley, MA
R.N.V.R.   )   (proby)
Surg. Com.,   ) .... E.I. Puddy, VD, MB,
R.N.V.R.   )   BS
Paym. Com. .... W.H. Bradby
Paym.,   )
Lt.-Com.   ) .... P.F. Gick (act)
Surg. Lt. .... R.T. Smith, MB, Bch
Tempy.,   ) .... G.A. Binns, MRCS, LRCP
Surg. Lt.,   )   (proby)
R.N.V.R.   ) .... K.W. Martin, MB, LS
                         C.R.G. Howard, MB, chB
                         A.G. Cummings, MB, chB
                         S. Dillon, MB, chB
                           (proby)
Tempy.Surg.,   ) .... J.M. Paterson, LDS
Lt., (D),   ) .... W.T. Moore, LDS
R.N.V.R.   )
Paym. Lt.,   )
R.N.R.   ) .... V. Clarke
:Tempy.,   ) .... H.F. Starling
Paym. Lt.,   ) .... E.L. Alexander
R.N.V.R.   )
Headmaster,   )
Lt.   ) .... S.W. Harman
Lt.-Com.,   ) (Met) E.P. West, MA (act)
(Sp. Br.),   )
R.N.V.R.   )
Tempy.Lt.-   )
Com.(Sp.Br.)   ) .... T.C. Spurway (act)
R.N.V.R.   )
Lt.,   )
(Sp.Br.),   ) (Met) R.B. Pink
R.N.V.R.   )
Tempy.,Lt.,   )   D.G. Huxley
(Sp. Br.)   )   C. Albrecht
R.N.V.R.   )   G.F. Steel
                         J.D. Moss
                    (Met) F.D. Ommanney

Commander ......   (O) B.E.W. Logan
Lt.-Com.   ...... (O) D.K. Buchanan-
                         Dunlop
                   (P) R.M. Everett (act)
Lt.   ...... (O) D.J. Godden
                   (O) H.R.B. Janvin, DSC
                   (O) J. Bridgewater-
                         Kitcat
                   (O) M.M. Dunlop, DSC (act)
                       E.G. Price (ret)
                   (O) Hon. W.A.C. Keppel,
                         DSC
                   (P) J.G. Baldwin
Lt. (A)   ...... (O) P.B. Dawe
                       M.J. Thomas
                       G.R. Woolston
Tempy.,   )... (O) N.E. Kindell
Lt., (A),   )... (O) M.A. Pears
R.N.V.R.   )... (O) J.H. Crole-Rees
                   (O) C.D. Haigh
                   (O) J.C.M. Paton
                   (O) K.G. Wallace (act)
                   (O) A.G.M. Wilson (act)
                   (P) K.L. Wood
                   (O) J.W.F. Jameson

December 1943

CONDOR

Captain   *VC ..... R. St. V. Sherbrooke,
                         DSC
                         (In Command)
Commander ......(P) J.A.D. Wroughton,
                         DSC (act)
                       J.W. Havers (act)(ret)
                   (O) D.G. Goodwin, DSC,
                         (act)
Lt.-Com.   .....   (P) J.F. Nicholas (ret)
                   (O) J.A.J. Smith-Shand,
                         DSC
                       P.C. Whitfield (act)
Lt.   .....   (O) P.B. Schondfeldt
                   (P) J.C.M. Harman
                   (O) J.A. Shuttleworth
                   (O) C.G. Bush
Tempy. Lt.,) ..... W.R. Wray (act)
R.N.V.R.   ) ..... J.W. Phippard (act)
Flight Lt.,) ..... J.F. Drysdale
R.A.F.   (For Liaison and Welfare Duties)
Tempy. Lt.-) (P) R.S. Maxwell, MC,
Com. (A),   )   DFC, AFC
R.N.V.R.   ) (P) G.H. Winn (act)
                   A.J. Bridges (act)
Lt. (A) ....(O) P.T. Lawman
                   (O) L.J. Smith

	(P) C.J.I. Cunningham
	(O) P.J. Warrington
	(O) P.C. Brooker
	(O) L.G. Wheeler
Tempy.,)	R.H. Stewart
Lt. (A),)	G. Hammonds
R.N.V.R.)	L.A. Webb
	R.B. Horner
	(O) J.W.F. Jameson, DSC
	(P) C.J. Mitchell
	(P) G.C.H. Last
	G.M. Robinson
	R.T. Bailey
Lt. (E)	A.F. Turner
Tempy.,)	
Lt. (E),)	I.M. Grant
R.N.V.R.)	
Tempy,	J.W.H. Wylie
Captain	B.T.A. Grimshaw (act)
R.M.)	W.P. Leitch
Tempy.,)	
2nd. Lt.,)	T.G. Garsed
R.M.)	
Tempy.,)	
Chaplain,)	Rev. A.D. Walmsley, MA
R.N.V.R.)	
Paym. Com.	W.H. Bradby
Paym.Lt.-)	
Com.)	P.F. Gick (act)
Surg. Lt.	R.T. Smith, MB, Bch
Tempy.,)	K.W. Martin, MB, LS
Surg. Lt.,)	A.G. Cumming, MB, chB
R.N.V.R.)	J.H. Foxton
Tempy.,)	
Surg.,)	W.T. Moore, LDS
Lt. (D),)	G.W. Hughes, LDS
: R.N.V.R.)	
Tempy.,)	H.F. Starling
Paym. Lt.,)	E.L. Alexander
R.N.V.R.)	G.H. Baker
Elect.,)	
Lt.-Com.)	J. Haigh (ret)
Headmaster)	
Lt.)	S.W. Harman
Lt.-Com.,)	
(Sp. Br.),)	
R.N.V.R.)	(Met) E.P. West, MA (act)
Tempy.,)	
Lt.-Com.,)	T.C. Spurway (act)
(Sp.Br.),)	
R.N.V.R.)	
Tempy. Lt.,)	D.G. Huxley
(Sp.Br.),)	C. Albrecht
R.N.V.R.)	G.F. Steel
	G.A. Lynch
	(Met) J.H. Hornbuckle
	F.G. Stanton (act)

Instructional Staff

Commander	(O) B.E.W. Logan
Lt.-Com.	(O) V.G.H. Ramsey-Fairfax, DSC
	(O) R.C. Sewell
	(P) R.N. Everett (act)
Lt.	E.G. Price (ret)
	(O) Hon. W.A.C. Kepple, DSC
	(O) J.S.L. Crabb
	(O) C.H. Jeffery
	(O) C.G. Bush
	(O) D.R. Bailey
	(S) C.R. James
Lt. (A)	(O) G.R. Woolston
	(O) H.E. Rumble
	(O) D.J. Cook
	(O) M.F.A. Regan
Tempy.,)	(O) N.E. Kindell
Lt. (A),)	(O) J.H. Crole-Rees
R.N.V.R.)	(O) K.G. Wallace (act)
	(O) A.G.M. Wilson (act)
	(P) K.L. Wood
	(O) J.W.F. Jameson
	(O) R.D. Pears
	(O) F. Hemmingway
	(O) R. Mellars
	(O) G. Barnwell
	(O) R.L.G. Cook
	(O) P.H. Woodham, DSC
	(O) F.S. Martin
	(O) A.W.R. McLean
	(O) J.F. Begley
	(O) S.L. Revett, DSC

February 1944

CONDOR

Captain	*VC R. St. V. Sherbrooke, DSC
	(In Command)
Commander	(P) J.A.D. Wroughton, DSC (act)
	J.W. Havers (act), (ret)
	(O) D.G. Goodwin, DSC (act)
	Hon. A.B. Carnegie (ret)
	(P) H.S. Cooper (act), (emgcy)
Lt.-Com.	(P) J.F. Nicholas (ret)
	(O) J.A.J. Smith-Shand, DSC
	P.C. Whitfield (act)
Lt.	(O) P.B. Schondfeldt
	(P) J.C.M. Harman
	(O) J.A. Shuttleworth
	(O) C.G. Bush
Tempy. Lt.,)	R.W. Wray (act)
R.N.V.R.)	J.W. Phippard (act)

Flight Lt.,)	J.F. Drysdale
R.A.F. (For Liaison and Welfare Duties)	
Tempy. Lt.-)	(P) G.H. Winn (act)
Com. (A),	A.J. Bridges (act)
R.N.V.R.	A.L. Nunneley (act)
Lt. (A) ....(O)	P.T. Lawman
(O)	L.J. Smith
(P)	C.J.I. Cunningham
(O)	P.J. Warrington
(O)	P.C. Brooker
(O)	L.G. Wheeler
(P)	W.H. Stevens
Tempy.,)	R.H. Stewart
Lt. (A),	R.B. Horner
R.N.V.R.	(P) C.J. Mitchell
(P)	G.C.H. Last
	G.M. Robinson
	R.T. Bailey
	J. Hall (act)
(O)	D.J. Price
	W.K. Cassels
Tempy,)	
Lt. (A),	E.F. Reay
R.N.Z.N.V.R.)	
Tempy. Lt.(E),)	
R.N.V.R.)	I.M. Grant
Tempy. Capt.,)	J.W.H. Wylie
R.M.)	B.T.A. Grimshaw (act)
Tempy. Lt.,)	
R.M.)	W.P. Leitch
Tempy.2nd Lt.,)	
R.M.)	W.C. Smith
Tempy,)	
Chaplain,)Rev. A.D. Walmsley, MA
R.N.V.R.)	
Paym. Com. .... W.H. Bradby
Tempy.Surg.,)	J.M. McEwen, MB, CHB,
Lt.-Com.,	(act)
R.N.V.R.	
Tempy.Paym.,)	
Lt.-Com.,	G.W.J. Pugh (act)
R.N.V.R.)	
Surg. Lt. .... R.T. Smith, MB, Bch
Tempy.Surg.Lt.)	A.S.L. Rae, MB, chB,
R.N.V.R.)	DPH
Tempy.Surg.,)	W.T. Moore, LDS
Lt. (D),	G.W. Hughes, LDS
R.N.V.R.)	
Tempy.,)	H.F. Starling
Paym. Lt.,	E.L. Alexander
R.N.V.R.)	G.H. Baker
Elect.Lt.-Com. .... J. Haigh (ret)
Headmaster,Lt. .... S.W. Harman
Lt.-Com.,	
(Sp.Br.),)(Met)E.P. West, MA (act)
R.N.V.R.	
Tempy.,)	
Lt.-Com.,	T.C. Spurway (act)
(Sp.Br.),	
R.N.V.R.)	

Tempy. Lt.,)	D.G. Huxley
(Sp.Br.),	C. Albrecht
R.N.V.R.)	G.F. Steel
	G.A. Lynch
(Met)J.H. Hornbuckle
	F.G. Stanton (act)
	P.H. Fowler

Instructional Staff

Commander. ....(O)	B.E.W. Logan
Lt.-Com. ......(O)	V.G.H. Ramsey-
	Fairfax, DSC
(O)	R.C. Sewell
(P)	R.N. Everett (act)
Lt.	E.G. Price (ret)
(O)	Hon. W.A.C. Kepple,
	DSC
(O)	J.S.L. Crabb
(O)	C.H. Jeffery
(O)	C.G. Bush
(O)	D.R. Bailey
(S)	C..A. James
Lt. (A) ...... (O)	G.R. Woolston
(O)	H.E. Rumble
(O)	D.J. Cook
(O)	M.F.A. Regan
Tempy.,) (O)	N.E. Kindell
Lt. (A),	(O) J.H. Crole-Rees
R.N.V.R.) (O)	K.G. Wallace (act)
(O)	A.G.M. Wilson (act)
(P)	K.L. Wood
(O)	J.W.F. Jameson, DSC
(O)	R.D. Pears
(O)	F. Hemingway
(O)	R. Mellars
(O)	G. Barnwell
(O)	R.L.G. Cook
(O)	P.H. Woodham, DSC
(O)	F.S. Martin
(O)	A.W.R. McLean
(O)	J.F. Begley
(O)	S.L. Revett, DSC

June 1944

CONDOR

Commander .... B.E.W. Logan
	(In Command)
(P)	J.A.D. Wroughton,
	DSC (act)
	J.W. Havers (act)(ret)
(O)	D.G. Goodwin, DSC(act)
	Hon. A.B. Carnegie (ret
Lt.-Com. ......(O)	J.A.J. Smith-Shand,
	DSC
(P)	H. Muir-Mackenzie (act)
(O)	K.W. Beard
Lt. ....(O)	P.B. Schondfeldt

(P) J.C.M. Harman
(O) J.A. Shuttleworth
(O) C.G. Bush

Lt., R.N.V.R. } J. Lewis

Tempy. Lt.) R.W. Wray (act)
R.N.V.R.) J.W. Phippard (act)
Flight Lt.) L.J. Cooke
R.A.F.)(For Administrative Duties)
Lt.-Com. (A) (O) P.C. Brooker (act)

Tempy.,)
Lt.-Com.(A) } A.L. Nunneley (act)
R.N.V.R.)

Lt. (A) .....(O) P.T. Lawman
(O) L,J, Smith
(P) C.J.I. Cunningham
(O) P.J. Warrington
(O) P.C. Brooker
(O) L.G. Wheeler

Tempy.,) R.H. Stewart
Lt. (A),) R.B. Horner
R.N.V.R.)(P) C.J. Mitchell
(P) G.C.H. Last
R.T. Bailey
W.K. Cassels
E.H. Pritchard
W.F. Walmsley
(O) R.A.R. Wilson

Tempy,)
Lt. (A), } E.F. Reay
R.N.Z.N.V.R.

Tempy. Capt.) B.T.A. Grimshaw (act)
R.M.) W.P. Leitch (act)
Tempy. Lt.,) W.C. Smith
R.M.) A.L. Hallam
(Part 11 "O" Cse)
H. Caldbeck

Tempy.,)
Chaplain,)Rev.A.D. Walmsley, MA
R.N.V.R.)

Paym. Capt. .... W.H. Bradley (act)
Paym. Com.,) I. Dummer
R.N.R.)

Tempy. Surg.)
Lt.-Com.,) J.M. McEwan, MB, chB,
R.N.V.R.) (act)

Tempy. Paym,)
Lt.-Com.,) G.W.J. Pugh (act)
R.N.V.R.)

Tempy.,)
Surg. Lt.,) A.S.L. Rae, MB, chB,
R.N.V.R.) DPH

Tempy. Surg,) W.T. Moore, LDS
Lt. (D),) G.W. Hughes, LDS
R.N.V.R.)

Paym. Lt. ..... J.B. Watson
Tempy,) H.F. Starling
Paym. Lt.,) E.L. Alexander
R.N.V.R.) G.H. Baker

Headmaster Lt. .... S.W. Harman

Tempy.,)
Elect. Lt., } R.L. Hughes
R.N.V.R.)

Tempy.,)
Elect. Lt., } J.M. Davison
R.C.N.V.R.)

Lt.-Com.,)(Met) E.P. West, MA (act)
(Sp.Br.),)
R.N.V.R.)

Tempy.,)
Lt.-Com., } T.C. Spurway (act)
(Sp.Br.),)
R.N.V.R.)

Tempy.,Lt.,) D.G. Huxley
(Sp.Br.),) C. Albrecht
R.N.V.R.) G.F. Steel
W.H.F. Ollis (act)
H.G.P. Skell (act)
G.F. Stanton (act)

Instructional Staff

Lt.-Com. ... (O) C.G. Bush (act)
(O) J.W. Collett (act)

Tempy. Lt.-)
Com. (A), } (O) C.G. Hide (act)
R.N.V.R.)

Lt. .... E.G. Price (ret)
(O) Hon.W.A.C. Keppel,DSC
(O) J.S.L. Crabb
(O) C.H. Jeffery
(O) D.R. Bailey
(S) C.A. James

Lt. (A) ....(O) G.R. Woolston
(O) M.F.A. Regan
(O) P.R. House
(O) R.V. Hinton
(O) D.L. Stirling

Tempy.,) (O) K.G. Wallace
Lt. (A), } (O) A.G.M. Wilson (act)
R.N.V.R.) (P) K.L. Wood
(O) R.D. Pears
(O) S.G. Green
(O) R. Mellars
(O) G. Barnwell

Tempy.,) (O) R.L.G. Cook
Lt. (A), } (O) P.H. Woodham, DSC
R.N.V.R.) (O) F.S. Martin
(O) A.W.R. McLean
(O) J.F. Begley
(O) S.L. Revett, DSC
(O) N.H. Godwood
G.W.D. Wright (act)

CONDOR

Commander ...... B.E.W. Logan
     (In Command)
    (P) J.A.D. Wroughton, DSC,
    (act)
    J.W. Havers (act)(ret)
    Hon. A.B. Carnegie (ret)
Lt.-Com. ....(O) J.A.J. Smith-Shand, DSC
    (O) C.C. Ennever, DSC (act)
Lt. ....(P) J.C.M. Harman
    (O) J.A. Shuttleworth
Tempy. Lt.,)   R.W. Wray (act)
R.N.V.R.)   J.W. Phippard (act)
    D.P. Ridgwell
    J. Lewis
Flight Lt.,)   L.J. Cooke
R.A.F.   )(For Administrative Duties)
Tempy.,   )
Com. (A),)(H) G.H. Winn (act)
R.N.V.R.)(Commander (Flying)
Tempy. Lt.-) A.L. Nunneley (act)
Com. (A),)(O) K. Hyde (act)
R.N.V.R.)(P) R.P. Mason (act)
    (Lt.-Com. (Flying)
    (O) W.A. Gillingham, DSC,
    (act)
Lt. (A). ...(O) P.T. Lawman
    (O) L.J. Smith
    (P) C.J.I. Cunningham
    (O) P.J. Warrington
    (O) L.G. Wheeler
Tempy.,   )   R.H. Stewart
Lt. (A),)   R.B. Horner
R.N.V.R.)(P) C.J. Mitchell
    R.T. Bailey
    W.K. Cassels
    (O) R.A.R. Wilson
    W.M. Laidlaw
    F.C.T. Wallington
Tempy.Lt.(A))
R.N.Z.N.V.R.)   E.F. Reay
Commander (E)... D.J. Hoare
Tempy. Capt.)   W.P. Leitch (act)
R.M.   )
Tempy. Lt.,)   W.C. Smith
R.M.   )   H. Caldbeck
Instr.Lt.Com. ...R.G. Cross, BA
Tempy.,   )
Chaplain,)Rev.A.D. Walmsley, MA
R.N.V.R.)
Paym. Capt. .... W.H. Bradley (act)
Tempy.Surg.,)   J.M. McEwan, MB, chB,(act)
Lt.-Com.,)   D.F. Heath, MRSC, LRCP,
R.N.V.R.)   (act)
Paym.Lt-Com.)   K.A.R. Clarke (act)
R.N.R.   )

Tempy.Paym.,)
Lt.-Com.,)   G.W. Pugh (act)
R.N.V.R.)
Tempy. Surg.,)   W.T. Moore, LDS
Lt. (D),)   G.W. Hughes, LDS
R.N.V.R.)
Paym. Lt. .... J.B. Watson
Tempy. Paym.Lt)   E.L. Alexander
R.N.V.R.)   G.H. Baker
Headmaster Lt. ... S.W. Harman
Tempy. Elect.,)
Lt.,   )   R.L. Hughes
R.N.V.R.)
Tempy. Elect.,)
Lt.,   )   J.M. Davison
R.C.N.V.R.)
Lt.-Com.,)Met)E.P. West, MA (act)
(Sp.Br.),)
R.N.V.R.)
Tempy.Lt.-Com,)   T.C. Spurway (act)
(Sp.Br.),)
R.N.V.R.)
Tempy. Lt.,)   D.G. Huxley
(Sp.Br.),)   C. Albrecht
R.N.V.R.)   G.F. Steel
    W.H.F. Ollis (act)
    H.G.P. Skell (act)
    F.G. Stanton (act)

Instructional Staff

Commander .....(O) D.G. Goodwin, DSC, (act)
Lt.-Com. ......(O) C.G. Bush (act)
    (O) J.W. Collett (act)
    A.J. Debenham, DSC
    (P) H. Muir-Mackenzie (act)
Lt.-Com.(A) ...(O) P.C. Brooker (act)
    (O) M.J. Thomas (act)
Tempy. Lt.-)
Com. (A),)(O) C.G. Hide (act)
R.N.V.R.)
Lt. ....(O) Hon. W.A.C. Keppel, DSC
    (O) D.R. Bailey
    (O) C.A. James
Lt. (A) ......(O) R.V. Hinton
Lt. (A),)(O) P.R. House
R.N.V.R.)
Tempy.,)(P) K.L. Wood
Lt. (A),)(O) S.G. Green
R.N.V.R.)(O) D.R.G. Cook
    (O) P.H. Woodham, DSC
    (O) F.S. Martin
    (O) A.W.R. McLean
    (O) S.L. Revett, DSC
    (O) N.H. Godwood
    G.W.D. Wright (act)
    (O) J.D. Ridgeway
    (O) J.B. Mackay
    (O) D. Cunningham

```
                (O) D.M. Andrew
                (O) J. Boyd ..
                (O) K. Burt
Tempy.Lt.(A), )(O) M.B. Radford
R.N.Z.N.V.R.  )
```

January 1945

CONDOR

```
Captain .....*VC R. St. V. Sherbrooke,
                DSC
                (In Command)
Commander ....(P) J.A.D. Wroughton, DSC (act)
                J.W. Havers (act)(ret)
Lt.-Com. .....(O) J.A.J. Smith-Shand, DSC
Lt. .........(P) J.C.M. Harman
             (O) J.A. Shuttleworth
Tempy. Lt.,  )   R.W. Wray (act)
R.N.V.R.     )   J.W. Phippard (act)
                 D.P. Ridgwell
Flight Lt.,  )   L.J. Cooke
R.A.F.       )(For Administrative Duties)
Lt.-Com. (A)..(O) P.C. Brooker (act)
             (P) J.I. Baker (act)
Tempy. Lt.-  )   A.L. Nunneley (act)
Com. (A),    )(O) K.Hyde (act)
R.N.V.R.     )(P) R.P. Mason (act)
             (Lt.-Com. (Flying)
Lt. (A) ......... W.J.H. Mills
Tempy.,      )   R.H. Stewart
Lt. (A),     )   R.B. Horner
R.N.V.R.     )(P) C.J. Mitchell
                 R.T. Bailey
                 W.K. Cassels
             (O) R.A.R. Wilson
                 H.C. Howie (act)
                 J.S. Weaver (act)
                 A.G. Coles
Commander (E) .. D.J. Hoare
Tempy. Instr.Lt.. J. Gregson, BSC
Tempy.,      )
Chaplain,    )Rev.A.D. Walmsley, MA
Captain (S) ..... W.H. Bradley (act)
Tempy. Surg.,)   J.M. McEwen, MB, chB,(act)
Lt.-Com.,    )   D.F. Heath, MRCS, LRCP,
R.N.V.R.     )   (act)
Tempy. Lt.-  )   G.W. Pugh (act)
Com. (S),    )   T.M. Purvis (act)
R.N.V.R.     )
Tempy. ,     )
Surg. Lt.,   )   R.H. Wesley, MD
R.C.N.V.R.   )
Tempy. Surg. )   W.T. Moore, LDS
Lt.(D),      )   G.W. Hughes, LDS
R.N.V.R.     )
Lt. (S) ......... J.B. Watson
```

```
Tempy.       )   E.L. Alexander
Lt. (S),     )   G.H. Baker
R.N.V.R.     )   A.R. Scott
Headmaster Lt. ..S.W. Harman
Tempy. ,     )
Elect. Lt.,  )   R.L. Hughes
R.N.V.R.     )
Lt.-Com.,    )Met) B.P. West, MA (act)
(Sp.Br.),    )
R.N.V.R.     )
Tempy.,      )
Lt.-Com.,    )   T.C. Spurway (act)
(Sp.Br.)     )
R.N.V.R.     )
Tempy.Lt.,   )   D.G. Huxley
(Sp.Br.),    )   C. Albrecht
R.N.V.R.     )   G.F. Steel
                 W.H.F. Ollis (act)
                 H.G.P. Skell (act)
                 F.G. Stanton (act)
```

Instructional Staff

```
Commander ...(O) T.W.B. Shaw, DSC (act)
   (In Charge, Naval Air Signal School)
             (O) H.H. Gardener (act)
                 (Training Commando)
Lt.-Com. ....(O) C.G. Bush (act)
             (O) J.W. Collett (act)
             (O) J. Wood, DSC (act)
Lt.-Com.(A)..(O) M.J. Thomas (act)
             (O) C.C. Ennever, DSC (act
Tempy. Lt.-) (O) C.G. Hide (act)
Com. (A),  ) (O) F.L. Page (act)
R.N.V.R.   )
Lt. ........(O) D.R. Bailey
             (O) F.L. Sherwin
             (P) D.A.E. Holbrook
Lt. (A),   ) (O) P.R. House
R.N.V.R.   )
Tempy.,    ) (P) K.L. Wood
Lt. (A),   ) (O) S.G. Green
R.N.V.R.   ) (O) N.H. Godwood
             (O) J.D. Ridgeway
             (O) J.B. Mackay
             (O) D. Cunningham
             (O) D.M. Andrew
             (O) J. Boyd
             (O) K. Burt
             (O) D.W.L. Farrall
             (O) B.V. Doxat-Pratt
             (O) R.B. Le-Page
                 R. Houghton (act)
        (Senior Air Radio Instr.)
Tempy.,    )
Lt. (A),   )(O) M.B. Radford
R.N.Z.N.V.R.)
```

April 1945

CONDOR

Captain ....*VC R. ST. V. Sherbrooke,
                 DSO
                 (In Command)
Commander .... J.W. Havers (act) (ret)
Tempy. Lt.,)   J.W. Phippard (act)
R.N.V.R.   )   D.P. Ridgwell
Flight Lt.,)   L.J. Cooke
R.A.F.   )(For Administrative Duties)
Tempy.,   )(P) B.F. Cox (act)
Com. (A),   )(And as Commander (Flying))
R.N.V.R.   )
Lt.-Com.(A)...... W.J.H. Mills (act)
Tempy.,   )   A.L. Nunneley (act)
Lt.-Com.(A)   )(O) K. Hyde (act)
R.N.V.R.   )(P) R.P. Mason (act)
)   (Lt.-Com. (Flying))
Tempy.,   )   R.T. Bailey
Lt. (A),   )   H.C. Howie (act)
R.N.V.R.   )   J.S. Weaver (act)
            (P) J.F. Urquhart
               A.W. Taylor
               M. Williams (act)
               E.C.K. Crowther
Commander ....(E) G.L. Bailey
Tempy.,   )   J. Gregson, BSC
Instr. Lt.)Met) W.H. Gillion, BA
Tempy.,   )
Chaplain,   )Rev. A.D. Walmsley, MA
R.N.V.R.   )
Captain (S) .... K.U. White (act)
Tempy. Surg.)   J.M. McEwan, MB, chB,
Lt.-Com,   )   (act)
R.N.V.R.   )   W.C. Sloan, MB, BCH,
Tempy. Surg.)   (act)
Lt.-Com.(D),)   G.W. Hughes, LDS (act)
R.N.V.R.   )
Tempy.,   )   G.W. Pugh (act)
Lt.-Com.(S),)   T.M. Purvis (act)
R.N.V.R.   )
Tempy.,   )
Surg. Lt.,)   R.H. Wesley, MD
R.C.N.V.R.)
Tempy. Surg.)
Lt. (D),   )   W.T. Moore, LDS
R.N.V.R.   )
Lt. (S) .... J.B. Watson
Tempy.Elect.)
Lt.,   )   R.L. Hughes
R.N.V.R.   )
Lt.-Com.,   )
(Sp.Br.),   )Met) E.P. West, MA (act)
R.N.V.R.   )
Tempy,   )
Lt.-Com.,   )   T.C. Spurway (act)
(Sp.Br.),   )
R.N.V.R.   )

Tempy. Lt.,)   C. Albrecht
(Sp. Br.),)   G.F. Steel
R.N.V.R.   )   W.H.F. Ollis (act)
)   F.G. Stanton (act)
                 R.W. Wray
                 J.S. Smith

Instructional Staff

Tempy.,   )
Lt. (A),   )(O) G.C. Richardson
R.N.V.R.   )

Observer School

Commander .....(O) H.H. Gardner (act)
                 (Training Commander)
Lt.-Com. ..... (O) J.W. Collett (act)
               (O) P.C. Brooker (act)
Lt. .... (P) D.A.E. Holbrook
               (O) D.R. Bailey
               (O) F.L. Sherwin
Lt.-Com. (A)...(P) J.I. Baker (act)
Tempy. Lt.-)
Com. (A),   )(O) F.L. Page (act)
R.N.V.R.   )
Tempy,   )   R.H. Graham
Lt. (A),   )(Acting Observer)
R.N.V.R.   )(O) N.H. Godwood
               (O) B.V. Doxat-Pratt
               (O) K. Burt
               (O) D. Cunningham
               (O) R.B. Le Page
               (O) J.B. Mackay
               (O) J.D. Ridgeway
Tempy.Lt.(A),)
R.N.Z.N.V.R.)(O) M.B. Radford

Naval Air Signal School

Commander .....(O) T.W.B. Shaw, DSC (act)
                 (Officer In Charge)
Lt.-Com. ......(O) C.C. Ennever, DSC
               (O) J. Wood, DSC (act)
Lt. .... (O) C.H. Pain (act)
Tempy.,   )
Lt.-Com. (A),)(O) K. Hyde (act)
R.N.V.R.   )
Lt. (A). ..... (O) R.V. Hinton
               (O) P.D. Lloyd
               (P) G.N.P. Hunt
Tempy.,   )(O) J. Boyd
Lt. (A),   )   D.W.L. Farrall
R.N.V.R.   )(O) R.A.R. Wilson
               (O) R.O. Bonnett
               (O) T.S. Hall
               (O) K.L. Jones
               (O) H. Taylor
               (O) T.A. Wilson
               (O) W.A. Forster
                   R. Houghton (act)
             (Senior Air Radio Instructor)

Tempy. Lt. (A),   )(O) D.K. McIntosh
S.A.N.F.(V)   )
Headmaster Lt. .... S.W. Harman

July 1945

CONDOR

Commander .... J.W. Havers (act),
               (ret)
               (In Command)

Tempy. Lt.,   )
R.N.V.R.   )   F.J. Kippin (act)
Flight Lt.,   )   L.J. Cooke
R.A.F.   (For Administrative Duties)
Tempy. Com. (A),   )(P) B.F. Cox (act)
R.N.V.R.   (And as Commander (Flying))
Lt.-Com. (A) .... W.J.H. Mills (act)
Tempy.,   )   A.L. Nunneley (act)
Lt.-Com. (A),   )(O) K. Hyde (act)
R.N.V.R.   )(P) R.P. Mason (act)
)(Lt.-Com. (Flying))
Lt. (A) .... J.E. Warren
Tempy.,   )   H.C. Howie (act)
Lt. (A),   )   J.S. Weaver (act)
R.N.V.R.   )(P) J.F. Urquhart
           A.W. Taylor
           M. Williams (act)
           F.C.K. Crowther
         (O) A. Carroll
Commander (E) .... G.L. Bailey
Tempy. Instr.Lt. ...... A.H. Fogg
Tempy. Chaplain,)Rev.T.L.F. Beattie
R.N.V.R.
Captain (S) .... K.U. White (act)
Tempy. Surg..,   )
Lt.-Com.,   )   J.M. McEwan, MB,
R.N.V.R.   )   chB (act)
Tempy. Surg.,   )
Lt.-Com. (D),   )   G.W. Hughes, LDS
R.N.V.R.   )   (act)
Lt.-Com. (S),   )   G.W. Kemp
R.N.V.R.   )
Tempy. Surg.Lt.,)   M.C. Platten, MB,
R.N.V.R.   )   chB
Tempy. Surg. Lt.(D))   W.T. Moore, LDS
R.N.V.R.   )
Lt. (S) .... J.B. Watson
Tempy. Elect. Lt.,)   R.L. Hughes
R.N.V.R.   )
Lt.-Com.(Sp.Br.),)Met)E.P. West, MA (act)
R.N.V.R.   )
Tempy. Lt.-Com.,)   T.C. Spurway (act)
(Sp.Br.),   )
R.N.V.R.   )
Tempy. Lt.,   )   G.F. Steel
(Sp.Br.),   )   F.G. Stanton (act)
R.N.V.R.   )   R.W. Wray
           J.S. Smith
           J.S. Atkinson

Instructional Staff

Tempy.,   )(O) G.C. Richardson
Lt. (A),   )(O) H.G. Wilks (act)
R.N.V.R.   )(And For Compass Duties)

Observer School

Commander .....(O) H..H Gardner (act)
         (Training Commander)
Lt.-Com. ......(O) J.W. Collett (act)
Lt. ....(P) D.A.E. Holbrook
        (O) F.L. Sherwin
           E.J. Treloar
Lt.-Com. (A)...(P) J.I. Baker
Tempy. Lt.-Com)
(A),   )(O) F.L. Page
R.N.V.R.   )
Tempy.,   )(O) N.H. Godwood
Lt. (A),   )(O) B.V. Doxat-Pratt
R.N.V.R.   )(O) K. Burt
        (O) D. Cunningham
        (O) R.B. Le Page
        (O) J.B. Mackay
        (O) J.D. Ridgeway
Tempy. Lt.(A),)
R.N.Z.N.V.R.)(O) M.B. Radford

Naval Air Signal School

Commander .....(O) T.W.B. Shaw, DSC (act)
         (Officer In Charge)
Lt.-Com. ......(O) C.C. Ennever, DSC
        (O) C.H. Pain (act)
  (And For R.N.A.S. Crail and Easthaven)
        (O) M.G. Chichester (act)
Tempy.,   )
Lt.-Com. (A),)(O) K. Hyde (act)
R.N.V.R.   )
Lt. (A). ......(O) R.V. Hinton
        (O) P.D. Lloyd
Tempy.,   )(O) J. Boyd
Lt. (A),   )   D.W.L. Farrall
R.N.V.R.   )(O) T.S. Hall
        (O) K.L. Jones
        (O) W.A. Forster
           V.E. Sills (act)
        (O) W.L. Orr
Tempy. Lt.(A),)
S.A.N.F.(V))(O) D.K. McIntosh
Headmaster Lt..... E. Reid, BSC

October 1945

CONDOR

Captain .... I. E. Porter
         (In Command)
Commander .... R.W. Keymer
Lt.-Com.,   )   I. Calvert-Jones
R.N.V.R.   )

Swordfish over Ark Royal

Harvard

Miles Martinet

Vought Sikorsky Sea Kingfisher

De-Haviland Mosquito

Westland Lysander

Percival Proctor

Tempy. Lt.,) J.C. McDowell
R.N.V.R.)
Tempy.,)(P) B.F. Cox (act)
Com. (A),)(And As Commander
R.N.V.R.)(Flying))
Lt.-Com. (A)....... W.J.H. Mills (act)
Tempy., A.L. Nunneley (act)
Lt.-Com. (A),)(O) K. Hyde (act)
R.N.V.R.)(P) E.L. Galley (act)
(Lt.-Com. (Flying)
Lt. (A). .... J.E. Warren
Tempy.,) H.C. Howie (act)
Lt. (A),) J.S. Weaver (act)
R.N.V.R.)(P) J.F. Urquhart
A.W. Taylor
M. Williams (act)
(O) A. Carroll
A. Norman
(Air Intelligence Duties)
Tempy.,)
Chaplain,)Rev.T.L.F. Beattie
R.N.V.R.)
Captain (S). ...... R.H. Rump (act)
Commander (S) ..(I. Du.) J.E. Langdon
Surg.Lt.-Com....... D. Ewart, MB, BS
Tempy. Surg.,) (emgcy)
Lt.-Com.,) J.M. McEwan, MB, chB,
R.N.V.R.) (act)
Tempy. Surg.,)
Lt.-Com. (D),) G.W. Hughes, LDS
R.N.V.R.) (act)
Lt.-Com. (S),) D.C. Cook
R.N.V.R.)
Tempy.,)
Lt.-Com. (S),) R.V. Ward (act)
R.N.V.R.)
Tempy.Surg.Lt.,)
R.N.V.R.) M.C. Platten, MB, chB
Tempy. Surg.,)
Lt. (D),) J. McC. Cringean, LDS,
R.N.V.R.) (proby)
Tempy. Elect.,)
Lt.,) E.W. Barton
R.N.V.R.)
Tempy. Lt.,) G.F. Steel
(Sp.Br.),) P.G. Stanton (act)
R.N.V.R.) R.W. Wray
J.S. Smith
J.S. Atkinson
F.J. Kippin

Instructional Staff

Lt.-Com. ...... (O) E.G. Brown (act)
(As Officer-In-Charge Ops. Officers'
Information Centre)
Tempy.,)(O) G.C. Richardson
Lt. (A),)(O) H.G. Wilks (act)
R.N.V.R.)(And For Compass duties)
(O) S.G. Strong
(O) C.G. Weir (act)

Observer School

Lt.-Com. ....(O) J.W. Collett (act)
(O) W.G. Leek (act)
Lt. .... (P) D.A.E. Holbrook
(O) F.L. Sherwin
E.J. Treloar
Lt.-Com. (A) (P) J.I. Baker (act)
Tempy.,)(O) N.J. Godwood
Lt.(A),)(O) B.V. Doxat-Pratt
R.N.V.R.)(O) K. Burt
(O) R.B. Le Page
(O) J.B. Mackay
(O) J.D. Ridgeway

Naval Air Signal School

Commander ...(O) T.W.B. Shaw, DSC (act)
(Officer In Charge)
Lt.-Com. ....(O) C.C. Ennever, DSC
(And For R.N.A.S. Crail and Easthaven)
(C) M.G. Chichester (act)
Lt.-Com.(A)..(O) J.W. Neale, DSC,
D.F.C. (act)
Tempy. Lt.-)
Com. (A),)(O) K. Hyde (act)
R.N.V.R.)
Lt. (A) .....(O) R.V. Hinton
(O) P.D. Lloyd
Tempy.,)(O) J. Boyd
Lt. (A),) D.W.L. Farrall
R.N.V.R.)(O) T.S. Hall
(O) K.L. Jones
(O) W.A. Forster
V.E. Sills (act
(O) W.L. Orr
Tempy.,)
Lt. (A),)(O) D.K. McIntosh
S.A.N.F.(V))
Headmaster)
Lt.) E. Reid, BSC
Captain........ E.W. Anstice
(Commodore 2nd Class Commodore Flying
Training)
Secretary,
Lt.-Com. (S).... C.F. Trythall (act)
Chief Staff Officer,
Captain .... C.J.M. Atkinson
Secretary,
Tempy.,
Lt. (S) .... A.G. Newell, RNVR
Commander ...(O) J.A. Crawford (act)
(As Deputy C.S.O. to Cdre. Flying
Training)

For duty in Commodores Office

Lt. (S).........A.R. Cole
(As Secretary to Maintenance Captain
to Cdre. Flying Training)
Tempy. Lt.(S),) E.A. Bramley
R.N.V.R.)

```
Captain......... A.G. Davidson (act)
Commander.....(P) H.S. Cooper (act)
Tempy. Lt.,  )    P.L. Masters (act)
R.N.V.R.     )
Lt.-Com. (A) .... W.J.H. Mills (act)
         (As Air Engineer Officer
             to C.F.T.)
Tempy. ,      )(P) J. Cooper, DSC (act)
Lt.-Com.(A)   )(P) W.J.S. Sheppard (act)
R.N.V.R.      )(P) M.J. Cox (act)
                 C.M. Stewart
```

July 1946

CONDOR

```
Lt. ............ P.D. Williams
Lt. (A) ........ W.F.H. Scott, MBE
            (O) M.V. Driver (emgcy)
            (Air Intelligence duties)
Commander (E) ... G.L. Baily
Lt.-Com. (E) .... G.A. Thompson (act)
Chaplain ....Rev. T.E. Gover
Tempy.,     )
Chaplain,   )Rev.G. Carse
C. of S.    )
Tempy.,     )
Chaplain,   )Rev.T.L.F. Beattie
R.N.V.R.    )
Commander (S) (I. Dir.) J.E. Langdon
Surg.Lt.-Com..... D. Ewart, MB, BS,
                 (emgcy)
Surg.,       )
Lt.-Com. (D) .... A. Simpson, LDS
Lt.-Com.(S) ..... J.F.W. Hastings (act)
Tempy.,       )
Surg. Lt.,    )   F.R. Aston, MRCS,LRCP
R.N.V.R.      )
Tempy.Lt.(S),)    J.T. Walker (act)
R.N.V.R.     )
Elect. Lt....... G.W. Cooper
                 T. Orr
Tempy.Lt.-Com)
(Sp.Br.),    )    P.H. Fowler
R.N.V.R.     )
Tempy. Lt.,  )    R.W. Wray
(Sp.Br.),    )
R.N.V.R.     )
```

Naval Air Signal School

```
Commander.... (O) T.W.B. Shaw, DSC (act)
            (Officer In Charge)
Lt. (A) .... .(O) P.D. Lloyd
Headmaster Lt. .. E. Reid, BSC
Captain ......... A.G. Davidson (act)
Lt.-Com. (A) .... J.F. Warren
         (As Air Engineer Officer
             to C.F.T.)
Lt. (E) ........ W.J. Spendlow (ret)
```

Miscellaneous

```
Commander ..... N.R. Courthorpe-
                Munroe
Lt. (A) ....... C.T.J. Ware
Tempy.,        ) D.G.P. Sheppard
Lt. (A),       ) C.M. Stewart
R.N.V.R.       ) M. Williams
Captain (E)      W.R. Axford
Commander (E)    G.L. Bailey
Commander (S)    R.H. Rump
Tempy. Lt.(S))   D.F. Buchanan
R.N.V.R.     )
Tempy. Elect.)
Lt.-Com.,    ) N.S. Goddard
R.N.V.R.     )
```

July 1947

```
Captain (E).... B.H. Cronk, DSC
            (In Command)
Commander ..... M. Cursham
Commander (E).. E.C. Senior
Lt.-Com. (E) .. A.L.S.S. Thackara
Lt. (L) ....... G.W. Cooper
                F.R. Tattersall
Instr. Lt. .... F.G. Fennell, BSC
                R.J. Thomas
                A.E.L. Smith
Chaplain ...Rev.T.E. Gover, MA
Chaplain,
(C. of S.)..Rev.D. Stewart
Commander (S) ..J.S.S. Smith
Surg. Lt.- ) A. Simpson, LDS
Com. (D),  )
Lt.-Com. (S) ...J.P. Parker
               (SO (S).)
Tempy.Surg.Lt)  A.J. Dinn, MS,BS (proby
R.N.V.R.     )  H. Revill,MB,chB (proby
Lt. (S) ........M.G. Slattery
                J.M. Donaldson
```

Naval Air Signal School

```
Instr. Lt. .... E. Reid, BSC
                P.W. Hunter
```

Miscellaneous

```
Commander ..... H. Duncan, DSC
Lt. (A) ....(P) L.W.A. Barrington
            (P) P. Carmicheal
            (P) T.J. Mahoney
            (P) T. McVey
Captain (E) ... W.B. Axford, OBE (act)
                G.L. Bailey
Lt. (E) ....... W.J. Spendlow, DSC (ret.
                T.P. Irwin
Commander (S) ..R.H. Rump
```

R.N.A.T.E. ARBROATH.

```
Commander (E) ... A.C. Mahony
Lt. ............. D.G. Smeeton
lt. (A) ........ J.H. Blackmore
                 E. Grocock
                 L.H. Weston
                 D.A. Lyn-Carlisle
Tempy. Lt. (A)... W.R. Bailey (act)
Lt. (E) ........ M.W.E. Parker
                 J.S.L. Steedman
                 R.W. Gillespie
                 J.R. Clarke
                 W.F. Galletly
Instr. Lt.-Com. .. H.C. Rice
Instr. Lt. ...... F. Crossley, BA
                 J.A. Bell, BA
                 B.F. Darbyshire
                 D.W. Trigg
                 H.G. Wood
```

R.N.A.S. ARBROATH.

```
Lt. .........(O) F.D. Kelly
Lt. (A). ....... B.J. Matthew
Commander (E) ... J.E. Esmonde, OBE,DSC.
Lt.-Com. (E) .... P.L. Cloete
                 N.S. McMath,MBE (ret)
Lt. (S) ....... A.C. Long
```

January 1948

R.N.A.S. ARBROATH

```
Captain (E) ..... B.H. Cronk, DSC
                 (In Command)
Secretary,
Lt. (S) ........ C.E. Powell
Lt. ............. D.G. Smeeton
Lt. (A) ......(P) A.W.S. Turney
                 E. Grocock, MBE
                 D.A. Lyn-Carlisle
                 L.H. Weston
                 B.J. Matthew
                 D.W. Wooler
Commander (E) ... J.W. Esmonde, OBE, DSC
                 (Executive Officer)
                 A.C. Mahony
                 (Training Commander)
                 P.L. Cloete
Lt. (E) ........ R.W.P. Gillespie
                 T.P. Irwin
                 J.S.H. Steedman
                 M.W.E. Parker
                 W.F. Galletly
                 J.B. Clarke
Lt. (L) ........ A.W. Cooper
Instr.- Com. .... H.A. Fowler
Instr. Lt.-Cm .. A.F. Howell
Instr. Lt. ...... F. Crossley
```

```
                 H.G. Wood
                 E.D. Simmons
                 J.K. Wallace
                 R.W. Lowe
                 C. Buckley
                 H.H. Glen
                 J.H. Baker, BSC
                 R.M. Horner
                 V.W.C. Price
Chaplain .....Rev. T.E. Gover
           Rev. C.W. Webster
Meth.Chaplain Rev. F. Street
Tempy ,
Chaplain,R.C. Rev. B. Curningham
Commander (S) .... A.C. Mathews, OBE
Surg. Lt.-Com. ... A.G.G. Toomey
Surg. Lt.-Com.(D). A. Simpson, LDS
Lt.-Com. (S) ..... J.P. Parker (S.O.(S) )
Tempy. Surg.Lt.,) H. Revill, MB, Bch (act)
R.N.V.R.        )
Surg. Lt. (D). ... I.S. Ferguson, LDS (act)
Lt. (S) ......... J.M. Donaldson
                 J. Richards
```

Naval Air Signal School

```
Instr. Lt. ....... P.W. Hunter
```

No. 4 Ferry Flight

```
Lt. (A) ......(P) L.W.A. Barrington
         (P) A.J. Standbridge
         (P) G.E. Legg
         (P) J.J.H. Ashworth
Surg. Lt. (D) .... I.S. Ferguson, LDS (act)
```

April 1948

```
Captain (E) ...... F.E. Clemitson
                 (In Command)
Secretary, Lt. (S) C.E. Powell
Lt. ............. D.G. Smeeton
Lt. (A) ......(P) A.W.S. Turney
                 D.A. Lyn-Carlisle
                 L.H. Weston
                 B.J. Mathew
                 D.W. Wooler
                 L.M. Whittingham (AED)
                 M.J. Conway (AED)
Commander (E) .... J.W. Esmonde, OBE, DSC
                 (Executive Officer)
                 A.C. Mahony
                 (Training Commander)
Lt.-Com. (E) ..... G.A. Thompson
                 R.E.H. Blanchflower
Lt. (E) ......... T.P. Irwin
                 J.S.H. Steedman
                 M.W.E. Parker
                 W.F. Galletly
                 J.B. Clarke
```

Mraching up West Port - September 1945

Volunteer Band - Spetember 1945

Piping in The Haggis

Trafalgar Ball 1950

P.T. Display & Staff

ROUTINE WILL BE USUAL,
AS USUAL.

- - - - - - - -

11... ....

DUTY WATCH. 2ND.PART.STBD.

STAND BY WATCH. 1ST.PART STBD.

DRESS OF THE DAY ..No.3's.

WELFARE ..... DAILY......

DETAILS:-

DUTY LIEUTENANT COMMANDER .... Lt. Commander DRUMMOND

OFFICER OF THE DAY .... Lieut. SEDGWICK

AIR WATCH OFFICER .... a/Sub Lt. CHAMBERS.

DUTY R.P.O. .... MANLEY, SAILMAKER.

DUTY C P.O. .... COVENEY, E.A.

DUTY P.O. .... RUFFLES, BOY.

I/C FIRE PARTY .... HAYNARD, S.P.O.

DUTY ARTISAN .... RAWLINGS, JNR.

- - - - - - - - -

INFORMATION:-

GUARD AND STEERING;   ALL AS USUAL.
                      SENTRIES.
                      LEWIS GUNNERS.
                      A/A LOOK-OUTS.

SENIOR LEADING HANDS OF LASSES ARE RESPONSIBLE THAT ONE
HAND IS DETAILED TO CLEAN OUT HIS OWN MESS AND FLATS.

BLOCKS ALL TO BE CLEARED BY AND RETURN BY 2030.

PORT.   WATCH FROM 1130 TILL 0700.
CHIEF AND P.O.s 1800 TILL 0730.
LEADERS 20, 2000.

```
                          P.L. Luby
                          M.W. Sylvester
                          D.D. Kennedy
Lt. (L) ........ A.L. Smith
Instr. Com. ...... H.A. Fowler
Instr. Lt.-Com. .. A.F. Howell                    L.H. Weston (AED)
Instr. Lt. ....... F. Crossley                    B.J. Mathew (AED)
                          H.G. Wood               L.M. Whittington
                          E.D. Simmons            (AED)
                          J.R. Wallace            M.J. Conway (AED)
                          R.W. Lowe       Lt. (A) ........ P.J. Carmichael
                          C. Buckley                      (SATCO)
                          H.H. Glenn              R.P. Sutherland
                          R.M. Horner             (AATCO)
                          V.W.C. Price            L.A. Holmes
                          P.J. Franklin           (AATCO)
                (Met). M.S. Withers, BA. (act)    E.T. Spratley (AED)
Chaplain .... Rev. T.E. Gover                     R.G. North (AED)
            Rev. C.W. Webster              (P) H. Cureton
Meth.Chaplain Rev. F. Street                      (L.T.I.D.)
Tempy.,                              Commander (E) ... J.W. Esmonde,OBE,DSC
Chaplain, R.C.Rev. B. Cunningham                  (Executive Officer)
Surg. Com. (D) ... H.V. Pell, LDS                 R.A. Lockley
Commander (S) .... A.C. Mathews, OBE              (Training Commander)
Surg. Lt.-Com. ... A.G.G. Toomey       Lt.-Com. (E) .... G.A. Thompson
Lt.-Com. (S) ..... R. Carter (act)                R.E.H. Blanchflower
           (S.O.(S) )               Lt. (E) ........ T.P. Irwin
Tempy. Surg. Lt.,                                 W.F. Galletly
R.N.V.R.        H. Revill, MB, Bch(act)           J.B. Clarke
Tempy.Surg.Lt.(D),                                D.J. Rowath
R.N.V.R.        K.C. Moxon, LDS                   M.J. Dutton
Lt. (S) ......... E.S. Irvine          Lt. (L) ........ A.L. Smith
                          J. Richards   Instr.-Com. ..... H.A. Fowler
                                        Instr. Lt.-Com. . A.F. Howell
                                        Instr. Lt. ...... A.E. Simmonds
      Naval Air Signal School                     E.D. Simmons
                                                  J.R. Wallace
        No. 4 Ferry Flight                        C. Buckley
                                                  H.H. Glenn
Lt. .........(F) I.J. Davis, DSC                  R.M. Horner
Lt. (A) ......(P) L.W.A. Barrington               V.W.C. Price
          (P) A.J. Standbridge                    P.J. Franklin
          (P) G.E. Legg                  (Met) M.S. Withers, BA
          (P) R.E. Dubber                         R. Heron, BA
          (P) H.R. Hunt                           A.M. Peduzzi, BSC
          (P) G.C.J. Knight             Tempy. Instr. Lt. P.J. Franklin
          (P) J.P. Keane                Chaplain .....Rev.T.E. Gover
          (P) A. Jones                          Rev. C.W. Webster
                                        Meth.Chaplain Rev. F. Street
                                        Tempy.,
     July 1948                          Chaplain R.C. Rev. B. Cunningham
                                        Surg. Com. (D) ... H.V. Pell, LDS
Captain (E) ..... F.E. Clemitson        Commander (S) .... A.C. Mathews, OBE
          (In Command)                  Lt.-Com. (S) ..... R. Carter (act)
Secretary. Lt.(S) C.E. Powell                    (S.O.(S) )
Lt.-Com. ........ D.G. Smeeton          Tempy. Surg. Lt.,) H. Revill, MB, Bch
Lt.-Com. (A) .(P) L.A. Cubitt           R.N.V.R.         ) R.S. Kagan, MRCS, LRCP
Lt. (A) ......(P) M.D. Campbell-Miller             (proby) (act)
          (P) J. Grieve                 Tempy.Surg.Lt.(D)) K.C. Moxon, LDS
          (P) N.E. Peniston-Bird        R.N.V.R.         )
          D.A. Lyn Carlisle             Lt. (S). ........ E.S. Irvine
          (AED)
```

October 1948

Captain (E) .... F.E. Clemitson
            (In Command)
Secretary,
Lt. (S). .... C.E. Powell
Lt. .... R.L. Hutton
            (P.T. & W. Duties)
Lt.-Com. (A).(P) L.A. Cubitt
Lt. (A) .....(P) M.D. Campbell-
            Miller
            D.A. Lyn Carlisle
            (AED)
            L.H. Weston
            (AED)
            B.J. Mathew
            (AED)
            L.M. Whittingham
            (AED)
            M.J. Conway
            (AED)
            P.J. Carmichael
            (SATCO)
            R.P. Sutherland
            (AATCO)
            L.A. Holmes
            (AATCO)
            E.T. Spratley
            (AED)
            R.G. North
            (AED)
        (P) H.Cureton
            (L.T.I.D.)
Commander (E) .. J.W. Esmonde,OBE, DSC
            (Executive Officer)
            R.A. Lockley
            (Training Commander)
Lt.-Com. (E) ... G.A. Thompson
            R.E.H. Blanchflower
Lt. (E) .... T.P. Irwin
            W.F. Galletly
            J.B. Clarke
            D.J. Rowath
            M.J. Dutton
Lt.-Com. (L) ... A.L. Smith
Instr.-Com...... H.A. Fowler
Instr.Lt.-Com. . A.F. Howell
Instr. Lt. ..... E.D. Simmons
            J.R. Wallace
            C. Buckley
            H.H. Glenn
            R.M. Horner
            V.W.C. Price
            P.J. Franklin
        (Met.) M.S. Withers, BA
            R. Heron, BA
            A.M. Peduzzi, BSC
Tempy.,   ) P.J. Franklin
Instr. Lt.) A.S. McLean, BA
Chaplain ...Rev. T.E. Gover
        Rev. D.J.W.L. Arter

Meth. Chaplain ...Rev. F. Street
Tempy. ,   )
Chaplain, R.C.) Rev. B. Cunningham
Surg. Com. (D) .... H.V. Pell, LDS
Commander (S) .... A.C. Mathews, OBE
Lt.-Com. (S) .... R. Carter
            (S.O.(S))
Tempy.,   ) H. Revill, MB, Bch
Surg. Lt.,   ) R.S. Kagan, MRCS,
R.N.V.R.   ) L.R.C.P.(proby)(act)
Lt. (S) .... E.S. Irvin

April 1949

Captain (E) .... F.E. Clemitson
            (In Command)
Secretary., Lt. (S). C.E. Powell
Lt.-Com. ....(P) L.A. Cubitt
Lt. .... R.L. Hutton
            (P.T. & W. Duties)
Lt................(P) M.D. Campbell-
            Miller
            R.P. Sutherland
            (AATCO)
            L.A. Holmes
            (AATCO)
Commander (E) .... J.W. Esmonde, OBE, DSC
            (Executive Officer)
            R.A. Lockley
            (Training Commander)
Lt.-Com. (E) .... G.A. Thompson
            R.E.H. Blanchflower
Lt. (E) .... T.P. Irwin
            W.F. Galletly
            D.J. Rowath
            M.J. Dutton
            J.G. Revolta
        (P) G.O.G. Weall
            (AED)
            D.A. Lyn Carlisle
            (AED)
            E.D. Crabb
            (AED)
            B.J. Mathew
            (AED)
            L.M. Whittingham
            (AED)
            M.J. Conway
            (AED)
            E.T. Spratley
            (AED)
            R.G. North
            (AED)
Lt.-Com. (L) .... A.L. Smith
Instr.-Com. .... E.I. Spinks, BA
Instr.Lt.-Com. .... A.F. Howell
Instr. Lt. .... J.R. Wallace
            R.M. Horner
            V.W.C. Price
            R. Heron, BA
            A.S. McLean, BA
            B.W. Seeley, BSC

J.A. Currie, MA
W.L. Wilkinson, BA
Chaplain ....Rev. D.J.W.L. Arter
Meth. Chaplain..Rev. F. Street
Tempy., ⎫
Chaplain, R.C.⎭ Rev. B. Cunningham
Commander (S) ...... C. Parsons
Lt.-Com. (S) .... M.A. Task
Tempy.Surg.Lt.⎫   R.S. Kagan, MRCS,LRCP
R.N.V.R.   ⎭   F.D. Edwards, MB,chB
                     (act)
Surg. Lt. (D). ..... W. Hall, LDS
Lt. (S). .... E.S. Irvine

October 1949

Captain (E) .... F.E. Clemitson
                    (In Command)
Secretary, Lt. (S).. C.E. Powell
Lt. .... R.L. Hutton
                    (P.T. & W. duties)
Surg. Com. .... W.A.S. Grant, MB, chB,
                    (S.M.O.)
Commander (S) ...... C.E.C. Tomkins, OBE
                    (S.S.O.)
Lt. (S). .... W.E. Pochon
                    J.M.S. Collins

July 1950

Captain (E) .... J.H. Illingworth
                    (In Command)
Secretary, Lt. (S). W.T. Kerr
Lt. .... R.L. Hutton
                    (P.T. & W. duties)
                    H.H. Simpson
                    (ATCO)
Commander (E) ...... M.H. Sayers, DSC
                    (Executive Officer)
                    J.F. Tucker
                    (Training Commander)
Lt.-Com. (E) .... D.G. Bourne
                    E.D. Crabb, MBE
                    (AED)
                    J. Milham
                    (AED)
                    S.N. Haigh
Lt. (E) .... D.J. Rowath
                    M.J. Dutton
                    C.D. Marsh
                    G.R. May
                    D.G. Rowies
                    (AED)
                    W.G. Lockhart
                    (AED)
Lt. (L) .... F.C.T. Wallington
Instr. Lt.-Com. .... S.M. Stock, BSC
                    D.E.A. Wiltshire

Instr. Lt. ...... J.A. Currie, MA
                  W.L. Wilkinson, BA
                  D.E. Harbour
                  G.L. Tomlinson, BSC
                  A.E. Collins, BSC
                  K.F. Tucker, BSC
                  D.E. Beynon, BSC
Chaplain .....Rev.D.J.W.L. Arter
Chaplain,   ⎫
(C. of S.)   ⎭Rev. C.R.M. Macleod
Commander (S) .... C. Parsons
Tempy. Surg.,⎫   J. Eyton-Jones, MB,
Lt.,   ⎬   chB, (act)
R.N.V.R.   ⎭   J. Symonds,MB,chB,(act)
Surg. Lt. (D) .... W. Hall, LDS
Lt. (S). .... R.V. Archard
                  W.C. Richards

July 1951

Captain (E) ...... J.H. Illingworth
                  (In Command)
Secretary, Lt. (S).W.T. Kerr
Lt. .... R.L. Hutton
                  (P.T. & W. duties)
Commander (E) .... M.H. Sayers, DSC
                  (Executive Officer)
                  J.F. Tucker, DSC,
                  MIMARE
                  (Training Commander)
Lt.-Com. (E) ..... D.G. Bourne
                  E.D. Crabb, MBE
                  (A.E.D.)
                  S.N. Haigh
                  T.M. Myles
                  (A.E.D.)
Lt. .... C.D. Marsh
                  G.R. May
                  D.G. Rowies
                  (A.E.D.)
                  M. Robertson
                  (A.E.D.)
                  G.W. Holroyd
                  (A.E.D.)
                  S.K. Sharrock
                  P.H. Wood
                  (A.E.D. 807 Squadron)
                  T.N. Chapman
                  (A.E.D. 810 Squadron)
                  R.H. Leeson
                  (A.E.D. 898 Squadron)
Lt.-Com. (L) ..... F.C.T. Wallington
Instr. Com. ...... S.M. Stock, BSC
Instr. Lt.-Com. .. D.E.A. Wiltshire
Instr. Lt. .... J.A. Currie, MA
                  D.E. Stevenson, MA
                  D.E. Harbour
                  A.E. Collins, BSC

Blackburn Shark MkII 821 Squadron

Firefly

Avenger

Sea Hornet

Baracuda

Sea Otter

Avro Anson

Firefly

Avenger

Sea Hornet

Baracuda

Sea Otter

Avro Anson

K.F. Tucker, BSC
D.E. Beynon, BSC
G.L. Tomlinson, BSC
Chaplain Rev. J.K. Boulton Jones, BA
Chaplain, Rev. C.R.M. Macleod
(C. of S.)
Commander (S)..D.V. Jesseman
Lt.-Com. (S) ..R.V. Archard (act)
Tempy.,   )
Surg. Lt.,   ) J. Eyton-Jones, MB,chB
R.N.V.R.   ) J. Symonds, MB,chB

October 1951

Captain (E) .. R.F. Storrs
            (In Command)
Secretary,   )
Lt. (S).   ) W.T. Kerr
Commander (E) D.J. Hoare
            (Executive Officer)
            J.F. Tucker, DSC
            MINarE
            (Training Commander)
Lt.-Com. (E).. D.G. Bourne
            F.A.J. Pilcher
            (A.E.D.)
            S.N. Haigh
            T.N. Myles
            (A.E.D.)
Lt. (E) ...... D.W.G. Robotham
            G.R. May
            D..G. Rowles
            (A.E.D.)
            M. Robertson
            (A.E.D.)
            G.W. Holroyd
            (A.E.D.)
Lt. (E) ...... S.K. Sharrock
            P.H. Wood
            (A.E.D. 807 Squadron)
            T.N. Chapman
            (A.E.D. 810 Squadron)
            R.H. Leeson
            (A.E.D. 898 Squadron)
Lt.-Com. (E).. F.C.T. Wallington
Instr. Com. .. S.M. Stock, BSC
Instr. Lt. ... J.A. Currie, MA
            D.E. Stevenson, MA
            D.E. Harbour
            A.E. Collins, BSC
            K.F. Tucker, BSC
            D.E. Beynon, BSC
            G.L. Tomlinson, BSC
            D.L. Jones, BSC
Chaplain Rev. J.K. Boulton Jones, BA
Chaplain,
(C.of S.) Rev. C.R.M. Macleod
Commander (S) D.V. Jesseman
Lt.-Com. (S) J.R. Tournay
Tempy.   )
Surg. Lt.,   ) J. Symonds, MB, chB
R.N.V.R.   )

Surg. Lt. (D) ... W. Hall, LDS (emgcy)
Lt. (S) .... F.G. Hogben

April 1952

Captain (E) ..... R.F. Storrs
            (In Command)
Secretary, Lt.(S) W.T. Kerr
Lt.-Com.   (P) J.M. Bruen, DSO, DSC
            (Lt.-Com.(Air))
Lt. ....(P) K. Holme
            (S.A.T.C.O.)
Commander (E)   D.J. Hoare
            (Executive Officer)
            J.F. Tucker, DSC,MIMarE
            (Training Commander)
Lt.-Com. (E) (P) R.C. Pearson
            F.A.J. Pilcher
            (A.E.D.)
            P.J. Nops
            T.M. Myles
            (A.E.D.)
Lt. (E) .... D.W.G. Robotham
            G.R. May
            D.G. Rowles
            (A.E.D.)
            M. Robertson
            (A.E.D.)
            G.W. Holroyd
            (A.E.D.)
            S.K. Sharrock
Lt.-Com. (L) .... F.C.T. Wallington
Instr. Com. ..... S.M. Stock, BSC
Instr. Lt. ...... J.A. Currie, MA
            D.E. Stevenson, MA
            D.E. Harbour
            K.F. Tucker, BSC
            D.E. Baynon, BSC
            G.L. Tomlinson, BSC
            D.L. Jones, BSC
            J.R. Hardy
Chaplain ....Rev. J.K. Boulton Jones, BA,
            BD, LLD(hon)
Chaplain,
(C. of S.).. Rev. C..R.M. Macleod
Commander (S) ... D.V. Jesseman
Surg.,
Lt.-Com. (D) .... W. Hall, LDS (act, int)
            (emgcy)
Lt.-Com. (S) .... J.R. Tournay
Tempy.,   )
Surg. Lt.,   ) W.C. Shepherd, Mb, chB
R.N.V.R.   ) (act)
Surg. Lt.   ) J.H. Wallington, MB, BS
R.N.V.R.   ) (act)
Lt. (S) .... F.G. Hogben

October 1952

Captain (E) ..... R.F. Storrs
            (In Command)

Secretary,
Lt.-Com. (S). .... A.E. Parsons
Lt.-Com.   (P) J.M. Bruen, DSO, DSC
              (Lt.-Com.(Air))
Lt. ....(P) K. Holme
              (S.A.T.C.O.)
Commander (E)   D.J. Hoare
              (Executive Officer)
       (P)(A/E) P.C. Gibson
              (Training Commander)
Lt.-Com. (E) ..(P) R.C. Pearson
              F.A.J. Pilcher
              (A.E.D.)
              P.J. Nops
              T.M. Myles
              (A.E.D.)
              M. Roberson
              (A.E.D.)
Lt. (E) .... D.W.G. Robotham
              D.J. Turner
              (A.E.D.)
              G.W. Holroyd
              (A.E.D.)
              S.K. Sharrock
Lt. (L) .... G.T.V. Harris
Instr. Com. ...... W.D. Jenkin, MBE,AMIEE
Instr. Lt.-Com. .. D.L. Jones, MSC
Instr. Lt. .... D.E. Stevenson, MA
              (Emgcy)
              D.E. Harbour
              J.D. Christie, MA
              G.L. Tomlinson, BSC
              J.R. Hardy
              N.A. Baynes, BSC
              C. Orpe, BSC
Chaplain .....Rev. J.K. Boulton Jones,
              BA, BD, LLD(hon)
Chaplain,
(C. of S) Rev. C.R.M. Macleod
Commander (S) .... E.J. Shelbourne
Lt.-Com. (S) ..... J.R. Tournay
Tempy.,   )   W.C. Shepherd, MB, chB
Surg. Lt.,   )   (act)
R.N.V.E.   )   J.H. Wallington, MB,
                  BS, (act)
Lt. (S) .... F.G. Hogben
Tempy. Lt. (S),   A.M. Morris
R.N.V.R.

April 1953

Captain (E) ...... R.F. Storrs
              (In Command)
Secretary,
Lt.-Com.(S) ...... A.E. Parsons
Lt.-Com.   (P) J.M. Bruen, DSO, DSC
              (Lt.-Com. (Air))
Lt. ....(P) K. Holme
              (S.A.T.C.O.)
Commander (E) .... A.G. Oliver, OBE
              (Executive Officer)
       (P)(A/E) P.C. Gibson
              (Training Commander)

Lt.-Com. (E) ....(P) R.C. Pearson
              F.A.J. Pilcher
              (A.E.D.)
              P.J. Nops
              T.M. Myles
              (A.E.D.)
              M. Roberson
              (A.E.D.)
Lt. (E) .... D.W.G. Robotham
              D.J. Turner
              (A.E.D.)
              J. Goodchild
              (A.E.D.)
       (A/E) D.G. Little
       (P) P.J. Bing
              N.F.J. Howe
Lt.-Com. (L) ...... G.T.V. Harris
Lt. (L) .... C.L. Palmer
Instr. Commander ... W.D. Jenkins, MBE,
              AMIEE
Instr. Lt.-Com. .... D.L. Jones, BSC
Instr. Lt. .... D.E. Stevenson, MA
              J.D. Christie, MA
              J.R. Hardy
              N.A. Baynes, BSC
              C. Orpe, BSC
              D. Henderson, BSC
Chaplain ....Rev. J.K. Boulton Jones, BA,
              BD, LLD(hon)
Chaplain (U.B.) Rev. C. Hughes
Commander (S) ...... E.J. Shelbourn
Surg. Lt.-Com. (D).. A. Simpson, LDS
Lt.-Com. (S) .... J.R. Tournay
Tempy. Surg.Lt.,)   W.C. Shepherd, MB, chB
R.N.V.R.   )   J.H. Wallington, MB, BS
Lt. (S) .... F.G. Hogben

October 1953

Captain (E) .... R.F. Storrs
              (In Command)
Secretary,
Lt.-Com. (S) .... A.E. Parsons
Lt.-Com.   (P) E.W. Lockwood
              (Lt.-Com.(Air))
Commander (E) ...... A.G. Oliver, OBE
              (Executive Officer)
       (P)(A/E) P.C. Gibson
              (Training Commander)
Lt.-Com. (E) ....(P) R.C. Pearson
              F.A.J. Pilcher
              (A.E.D.)
              P.J. Nops
              M. Roberson
              J.R.P. Landerson
              (A.E.D.)
       (A/E) D.G. Little
Lt. (E) .... D.W.G. Robotham
              D.J. Turner
              (A.E.D.)
              J. Goodchild
              (A.E.D.)
       (P) P.J. Bing

104

```
                          N.F.J. Howe (ret)
                          D.J. Ogg
Lt.-Com. (L) .....  G.T.V. Harris
Instr. Com.         W.D. Jenkin, MBE,
                          AMIEE
Instr. Lt.-Com.     D.L. Jones, BSc
Instr. Lt. .......  J.D. Christie, MA
                          J.R. Hardy
                          N.A. Baynes, BSC
                          C. Orpe, BSC
                          D. Henderson, BSC
                          A.H. Jones, BA
                          J.H.C. Horton, BSC
                          J. Merritt, BSC
                          A.A. Hollis, BSC
Chaplain......Rev. R.W. Richardson, MA
Chaplain (U.B)Rev. C. Hughes
Commander (S) ....  E.J. Shelbourn
                          A.S. Smith
Surg.Lt.-Com. (D)   A. Simpson, LDS
Surg. Lt. ........  J. Smith, MB, chB
Tempy. Surg. Lt.,)  W.C. Shepherd, MB, chB
R.N.V.R.          )  J.H. Wallington, MB, BS
Lt. (S) ..........  F.G. Hogben
```

July 1954

```
Captain (E) ......  R.R. Shorto, DSC
                          (In Command)
Secretary,
Lt.-Com. (S) ....   A.E. Parsons
Lt.-Com.        (P) W. Dobson, OBE
                          (Lt.-Com. (Air))
              (P/T) H.A. Rice
Lt. .............  P.H. Fowler
Commander (E) ....  A.G. Oliver, OBE
                          (Executive Officer)
          (P) (A/E) P.C. Gibson
                          (Training Commander)
                          D.L. Alexander
Lt.-Com (E)(P)(A/E)M.J.W. Norman
                          J.R.P. Landsdown
                          (A.E.D.)
              (A/E) D.G. Little
              (A/E) C.W. Edgar
Lt. (E) .......(P) P.J. Bing
                          N.F.J. Howe (ret)
              (A/E) R.H. Leeson
Instr. Com. ......  W.D. Jenkin, MBE
Instr. Lt.-Com. ..  J. Merritt, BSC
                          J.H.C. Horton, BSC
Instr. Lt. .......  W. Wood, BSC
                          N.A. Baynes, BSC
                          C. Orpe, BSC
                          D. Henderson, BSC
                          A.A. Hollis, BSC
                          W.E. Harborow, BSC
Chaplain......Rev. R.W. Richardson, MA
Chaplain (U.B)Rev. C. Hughes
```

```
Commander. (S).....  R.A.H. Vaughan-
                          Cox
Lt.-Com. (S) ......  A.S. Smith
Surg. Lt. ........  J. Smith, MB chB
                          D.E. Mackay, MB,chB
Lt. (S) ..........  E.G. Hogben
```

July 1955

```
Captain (E) .......  R.R. Shorto, DSC
                          (In Command)
Secretary,
Lt. (S). ..........  D.I. Carter
Lt.-Com. .......(P)  W. Dobson, OBE
                          (Lt.-Com. (Air)9
              (P/T)  W.G. England
                          P.H. Fowler
Commander (E) .....  R.A.H. Bartley
                          (Executive Officer)
          (P)(A/E)  J.E. Dyer-Smith
                          (Training Commander
              (A/E) C.W. Edgar
Lt.-Com.(E)(P)(A/E) M.J.W. Norman
                          J.R.P. Landsdown
                          P.A. Turner
              (A/E) R.H. Leeson
Lt. (E)       (A/E) M.E. Scadding
Instr. Com. ......  V. Lamb
Instr.Lt.-Com. ....  J. Merritt
Instr. Lt. ........  W. Wood
                          E. Blackman
                          D. Henderson
                          R.E. Ashworth
                          E. Blackman
                          W.E. Harborrow
                          F.W. Gilbert
                          D. Gibson
Chaplain ......Rev. R.W. Richardson
Chaplain (U.B.)Rev. W.M. Lamont
Commander (S) .....  R.A.H. Vaughan-
                          Cox
Lt.-Com. (S) ......  A.J. Withers
Surg. Lt. ........  J. Smith
Tempy. Surg.Lt.,)   I.S. McRobbie
R.N.V.R.          )
```

October 1956

```
Captain  (E) ......  W.L.G. Porter
                          (In Command)
Secretary,
Lt. (S) ..........  M.E. Coleman
Lt.-Com.        (P) W. Dobson, OBE
                          (Lt.-Com.(Air)
              (P/T)W.G. England
                          A.G. Mitchell
Commander (E) .....  R.A.H. Bartley
                          (Executive Officer)
          (P)(A/E)  J.E. Dyer-Smith
                          (Training Commander
Lt.-Com. (E) ..(A/E) L.F. Coulshaw
              (A/E) D.G. Rowles
                          P.D.V. Weaving
```

```
Lt. (E) ......(A/E) M.E. Scadding        Chaplain        Rev. E. Williams
                    J.F. Waterhouse      Surg. Com. (D)      R.R.B. Gjertsen
               (A/E) G.A. Prince
                     I.G.T. Ewies        January 1961
               (A/E) R. Baker
Instr. Commander ... V. Lamb             CONDOR (T.R.S.B.421249)
Instr. Lt.-Com. .... F.H. Crossman
                     F.W. Gilbert        (R.N.A.S. Arbroath, Angus)
                     J.D. Christie
Instr. Lt. ......... D.R. Hub            Captain    E      P.H.C. Illingworth
                     R. Johnstone                          (In Command)
                     I.S. Young
                     J.S. Lewis          JANUARY 1961
                     D. Kidd
                     J.G. Gulliver       Commander  X      T.S. Sampson
Chaplain .......Rev. J.R. Malkinson                        (Executive Officer)
Chaplain(U.B.) Rev. W.M. Lamont                     S      A.J. Boyd
Commander (S) ...... H.E.B. Jenkinson               E      M.Roberson
Surg. Lt.-    }                          Lt.-Com.   X      N.C.W. Tetley
Com (D),      }      R.R.B. Gjertsen                       (1st. Lt.)
Lt.-Com.   (S)... A..J. Withers          Lt.        S      N.G. Dolan
Surg. Lt. ......... K.J. MacLean                           (Captain's Secretary)
                                         Instr. Com        D.G. Turnbull
July 1957                                Surg. Com.        R.T. John
                                         Surg. Com. (D)    B.F. Rogers
Captain    E      W.L.G. Porter          Chaplain   Rev.   L.L.R. Griffiths
                  (In Command)
Secretary,                               July 1962
Lt.        S      M.E. Coleman
Commander  S      H.E.B. Jenkinson       CONDOR (T.R.S.B.421249)
           S      G. Clarke              (R.N.A.S. Arbroath, Angus)
           E(AE)  H.J.S. Banks
           E(P)   L.C. Darling           Captain    EngM   K.R. Hickson, AFC
           (AE)                                     (P)    (In Command)
Chaplain .......Rev. J.R. Malkinson      Commander  X      T.S. Sampson
                Rev. E. Williams                          (Executive Cfficer)
Surg. Com. (D)    R.R.B.Gjertsen                    S      A.B. Hilliar
                                                          (Supply Officer)
January 1958                                        EngM   D.W. Cramond
                                         Lt.-Com.   X      P.G. W. Morris
Captain    E      W.L.G. Porter                            (1st. Lt.)
                  (In Command)           Lt.        S      M.P. Marcell
Secretary,                                                 (Captain's Secretary)
Lt.        S      M.E. Coleman           Instr. Com.       D.G. Turnbull
Commander  S      H.E.B. Jenkinson       Surg. Lt.-Com.    J.F. Ryan
           E(AE)  H.J.S. Banks           Surg. Lt.-Com.(D) F.R.B. Mathias
           E(P)   L.C. Darling           Chaplain   Rev.   V.H. Jones
           (AE)                          First Officer     V.F. Mottershaw
Chaplain      Rev.E. Williams                             (In Charge W.R.N.S.)
Surg. Com.    (D) R.R.B. Gjertsen

January 1958                             April 1963

Captain    E      W.L.G. Porter          CONDOR
                  (In Command)
Secretary,                               (R.N.A.S. Arbroath, Angus)
Lt.        S      M.E. Coleman
Commander  S      H.E.B. Jenkinson       Captain    EngM   K.R. Hichson, AFC
           E(AE)  H.J.S. Banks                            (In Command)
           E(P)   L.C. Darling           Commander EngM    D.W. Cramond
           (AE)                                     S      E.A. Berrey, MBE
                                         Lt.-Com.   X(P)   S.C. Farquhar
                                                          (1st. Lt.)
                                         Lt.        S      P.M. Marcell
                                                          (Captain's Secretary)
```

Instr. Com.   D.G. Turnbull
Surg. Lt.-Com.   J.F. Ryan
Surg. Lt.-Com. (D)   F.R.B. Mathias
Chaplain   Rev. V.H. Jones
First Officer   V.F. Mottershaw
                           (In Charge W.R.N.S.)

July 1964

CONDOR

(R.N.A.S. Arbroath, Angus)

Captain   EngM   R.H. Webber
                           (In Command)
Commander   EngM   D.W. Cramond
                           (Training Commander)
                EngL   R.G. Lewis-Jones
                (O)   (Executive Officer)
                S   E.A. Berrey, MBE
Lt.-Com.   X(P)   S.C. Farquhar
                           (1st. Lt.)
Lt.   S   P.M. Marcell
                           (Captain's Secretary)
Instr. Com.   A.E. Willsteed, OBE
Surg. Com.   J.F. Ryan
Surg. Lt.-Com. (D)   R.S. Haigh
                           (S.D.S.)
First Officer   V.F. Mottershaw
                           (In Charge W.R.N.S.)

April 1965

CONDOR

(R.N. Air Station and R.N. Air Engineering School, Arbroath, Angus)

Captain   EngM   R.H. Webber
                (P)   (In Command)
Secretary, Lt. S   N.J. Wilkinson
Commander   EngM   G.L. Coates
                           (Training Commander)
                EngL   R.G. Lewis-Jones
                (O)   (Executive Officer)
                S   M.W. Morris
Lt.-Com.   X(P)   S.C. Farquhar
                           (1st. Lt.)
Instr. Com.   A.E. Willsteed, OBE
Surg. Com.   E.H.P. Warburton
Surg. Lt.-Com.(D)   R.S. Haigh
                           (S.D.S.)
Chaplain   Rev. A.B. O'Ferrall
First Officer   J.M. Witney
                           (In Charge W.R.N.S.)

April 1963

CONDOR

(R.N.A.S. & R.N.A.E. School. Arbroath)

Captain   E(P)   H.W. Sylvester
                           (In Command)
Secretary, Lt. S   N.J. Wilkinson
Commander   E   G.L. Coates
                           (Training Officer)
                S   M.W. Morris
                S   J.A. Hassard-Short
                           (Executive Officer)
Lt.-Com.   X(P)   J.R.N. Gardner
                           (1st. Lt.)
Instr. Com.   A.E. Willsteed, OBE
Surg. Com.   E.H.P. Warburton
Surg. Com.   (D)   R.S. Haigh
                           (.S.D.S.)
Chaplain   Rev. A.B. O'Ferrall
Chaplain   Rev. D.G. Prosser
First Officer   J.M. Witney
                           (In Charge W.R.N.S.)

April 1967

CONDOR

(R.N.A.S. & R.N.A.E. School. Arbroath.)

Captain   E(P)   H.W. Sylvester
                           (In Command)
Secretary, Lt. S   N.J. Wilkinson
Commander   S   J.A. Hassard-Short
                           (Executive Officer)
                E   D.L.J. Corner
                S   J.A. Watt
Lt.-Com.   X(P)   J.R.N. Gardner
                           (1st. Lt.)
Instr. Lt.   B. Hay
Chaplain   Rev. N.M. Denlegh-
                           Maxwell
Chaplain   Rev. A.W.D. Ritson
Surg. Lt.-Com. (D)   G.C. Taylor
                           (S.D.S.)
First Officer   O.V. Thomas
                           (In Charge W.R.N.S.)

October 1968

CONDOR

(R.N.A.S. & R.N.A.E. School. Arbroath.)

Captain   E   J.W. Mott, MVO
                           (In Command)

```
Secretary, Lt.  S    J.J. Brecknell
Commander       E    P.J. Bing
                S    J.A. Watt
                X(O) F. Bromilow
Lt.-Com.        X(P) S.C. Farquhar
                     (1st. Lt.)
Instr. Com.          O.J. Roberts
                     (S. Instr. O)
Surg. Com.      (D)  G.C. Taylor
                     (S.D.S.)
Chaplain        Rev. J.A.G. Oliver
First Officer,       O.V. Thomas
W.R.N.S.             (In Charge W.R.N.S.)
```

July 1969

CONDOR

(R.N.A.S. & R.N.A.E. School. Arbroath)

```
Captain         E    J.W. Mott, MVO
                     (In Command)
Secretary, Lt.  S    J.J. Brecknell
Commander       E    P.J. Bing
                S    J.A. Watt
                X    D.H.D. Merron
                     (Executive Officer)
Lt.-Com.        X(P) S.C.Farquhar
                     (1st. Lt.)
Instr. Com.          P. Carr
                     (S. Instr. O.)
Surg. Com.      (D)  G.C. Taylor
                     (S.D.S.)
Chaplain        Rev. J.A.G. Oliver
First Officer,       O.V. Thomas
W.R.N.S.             (In Charge  W.R.N.S.)
```

April 1970

CONDOR

(R.N.A.S. & R.N.A.E. School. Arbroath.)

```
Captain         E    T.F.G. Hardy
                     (In Command)
Secretary, Lt.  S    J.J. Brecknell
Commander       E    P.J. Bing
                S    J.A. Watt
                X    D.H.D. Merron
                     (Executive Officer)
Lt.-Com.        X(P) S.C. Farquhar
                     (1st. Lt.)
Instr. Commander     P.Carr
                     (S. Instr. O.)
Chaplain        Rev. J.A.G. Oliver
Second Officer,      R.M. Maskell
W.R.N.S.             (In Charge W.R.N.S.)
```

Chapter 3

Wrens

I make no apologies for placing WRENS before most others as, apart from contractors and administrators, it was they that were the vanguard, the pioneers, who made the station into a habitable ship whilst building took place all around them. Sea boots being almost the rig of the day ...

H.M.S. CONDOR 1940 - 41.

"Join the Wrens and Free a Man For the Fleet", that's what the recruiting poster said, so my sister Nancy, and myself, took up the challenge, and were posted to H.M.S. Condor , Arbroath , Scotland, in June 1940.

We shared a railway compartment with two Dutch sailors, who entertained us singing "I've got sixpence", a popular song of the day, and intrigued to hear we were on our way to become "lady sailors", as they said. We were met at Arbroath station, and were taken in an R.N. van and arrived at the gates of H.M.S. Condor. We were not impressed looking at this large sprawling area, which seemed deserted, no proper roads, once inside we passed along identical rows of brick buildings , with windows, end to end. We stopped by one of them, and inside joined approximately a dozen other volunteers. This was the "Wrennery", and we were in Queen Anne dormitory, two long rows of beds either side, covered with anchor patterned bedspreads, small lockers separated the beds.

We were told this was Fleet Air Arm base, which puzzled us, but learned later, what an important part of the Royal Navy it was. The next morning we were issued with a duffel coat , sea boots and stockings and slithered down to the Officers' quarters. In the kitchen area were tea chests containing crockery and kitchen utensils, for two weeks we washed and stacked the contents, were homesick and on three weeks probation , if we lasted that long. A pep talk from Captain Abel Smith assured us how essential this task was in the formation of this new Fleet Air Arm station.

The first troops to arrive and billeted opposite our Quarters were Polish, followed by Black Watch, this was only temporary. Much later a six foot wall was built around the Wrennery, the sailors said it was to keep the Wrens in, we said otherwise.

We signed on the dotted line one week later, and were issued with our uniforms , and learned to march across the country lanes, with many a blistered heel, as the shoes were very uncomfortable. We were often mistaken for Girl Guides , but our distinctive H.M.S. tallybands proved otherwise, and all this for King and Country. We were also taught fire drill.

We were transferred to the main galley, serving the meals to the ever increasing squadrons from the Fleet Air Arm, so very different from the day we arrived wondering "What sort of Navy was this, where are the sailors?". We soon learned they were in their "boiler suits".

More Wrens arrived, some joined us and we learned to cook in large quantities, under the watchful eyes of the Chief Cooks, we gradually took over the duties of the men, swabbed the decks etc., and everything had to be "ship shape for Officers' rounds". We opened up endless tins of food, especially evaporated milk, every tin had to be flattened for easy storage and collection.

We were not allowed to speak to our counterparts , going to and from duty, nor allowed "ashore" after late turn duty, as it was a 3 a.m. call the following morning. We now had a dance hall on the camp, with an R.A.F. band, and enjoyed our trips "ashore" to the cinemas, and the well frequented Webster dance hall, and were allowed one late pass per week. If our partners on the night were waiting for "pay day", it was "see you inside", or a trip to the Y.M.C.A. The camp concert was very successful, and the Wrens were often asked out to tea on Sundays by the local residents, and the popular walking area was along by the cliffs, and the sea shore.

The menus in the galley were planned for the maximum of vitamins. Friday was the most popular, fish and chips, so there were endless queues. One afternoon the Red watch, sometimes we were known as the "Mad" watch, were very busy making salmon fishcakes, and all had a part to play in the completion. I was at the end of the line, and decided to make them look a little different, so dented each one in the centre. Shortly afterwards in rolled 'Lofty', a Chief cook, took one look , and yelled "Wren Winn, what do you reckon you're on - doughnuts?". Had he not heard the well known saying "All work and no play etc.,", obviously not!

A group of us Wrens had walked from Arbroath to the camp one evening, singing as we approached the gates of the camp. A voice boomed out "Stop, who goes there?". a chorus answered "Wrens", the stern reply was " Step forward and be recognised", we did so , obediently and quietly. We realised afterwards this was a serious matter, and essential for security reasons, and remembered the posters , "Walls have ears", and "No talking in crowds".

We were sent to the shelters very often. Sometimes firebombs, on one occasion a seaplane dropped a bomb that penetrated through several of the men's quarters, causing mainly structural damage. It was defused and taken away to be disposed of at sea, by the local fishermen.

But the most memorable was one early evening a message came over the tannoy saying, "This is your Captain speaking, enemy aircraft approaching, take cover". We grabbed our duffel coats, gas mask and tin helmet, and scrambled to our nearby shelter. Having just got seated, out of the darkness came loud shouting," Wrens, you are to make your way down to the main galley, on the double", which we did without asking , why? We heard rumours that a bomb had been dropped, and later our shipmates who had been ashore, joined us, and we slept on the dining room tables that night. It must have been an unusual sight for the "Night flyers", who were on their way to the galley , for their cup of hot ship's cocoa. We served breakfast the next morning to the bleary eyed personnel. It was confirmed the following morning , that a land mine had been dropped, the night before , in the vicinity of the 'Wrens' quarters', and 'Downlands House', which was the Captains' residence , and the guard from there had sounded the alarm. Later we realised how lucky we had been, when we saw the photograph, as they used to say under those circumstance, "Our name was not on it", as it did not detonate. The disposal team defused and removed it, and we were allowed back to our quarters , after lunch, to catch up on some 'Shut eye'.

King George VI visited the camp on a morale boosting mission , and planted a tree , in March 1941, and wonder, if it was as resilient , as we had been.

Business went on as usual , several more squadrons arrived , for extra training , and eventually were formed into 880 Squadron , and were drafted to the new Fleet Air Arm carrier, H.M.S. Indomitable. We reminisced and thought there goes our dancing partners, but as always wished all our counterparts, "God speed and a safe return", as we remembered , the words on the small card we always carried inside our hats, on it were the words of the Wren's prayer.

In December , the Winn Sisters put in a transfer, to the Newcastle area, to H.M.S. Calliope, that was 1941, but we never had any regrets about our 'Rookie days', only fond memories , where we learned to be tolerant , independent, and the comradeship. I'm sure Lord Nelson would have been proud of us , we certainly were.........

We revisited the now R.M. Condor in 1987, and reminisced in the company of the Royal Marine Wrens, the dance hall was now a gymnasium, the galley the same, and so many memories. The Wrens' wall had been demolished, so we were able to walk once again, past the Wrennery, and the Queen Anne dormitory although with new occupants, we remembered so vividly, after all it had been our home, we retraced our steps, down to the familiar signpost, 'Downlands House', and paused awhile to remember, it was all so very long ago.

H.M.S. Condor 1940 The Winn Sisters

Our final visit to the reunion, in June 1996, so very many changes now at 'Condor', we remembered as it was, but the Galley virtually unchanged, held the most vivid memories , of all the personnel who waited patiently for their meals , and the rum ration, of course, in those early days. We Wrens that were there, and had met frequently over the years, could say with pride," We were the Jenny Wren pioneers at H.M.S. Condor", and is now a part of our history.

Madge Helm.

1940 - REFLECTIONS.

As we look back over many years , the beginning of our mission,
From all walks of life we came, to join a great tradition.
Leaving our homes, what was in store? How long would it last,
We had travelled many a lonely mile, leaving behind the past.
As raw recruits we were kitted out in suits of navy blue,
Learned how to march down country lanes, and parade ground too.
We settled down to learn a trade, some very strange and new,
Sleepless nights, second thoughts, what were we going to do.
Jack the lad taught Jenny Wren, what life was like in the 'Navy'
As according to the song of the day , they had 'All the gravy'
On early duty to the Galley, we sang pop songs all the way,
We signed up for King and Country , for four pence a day.
Awakened by the tannoy, make and mend, fall in, rise and shine,
No matter what the weather , we were assured it always fine.
As the flag was lowered at sunset , we were halted on our way,
Came to attention, and pondered, almost the end of another day.
We looked forward to going 'Off-duty', and always went 'ashore',
The bus became 'The Liberty Boat', the deck, was never the floor.
Back at the camp late evening, "Halt, who goes there?". Came the call,
We advanced, and went our separate ways, towards 'Wrennery' wall.
Kit inspection caused some panic, a 'Chit' to visit the store,
Replacing a missing item , "All present and correct once more",
"Enemy aircraft approaching, take cover", was what our Captain said,
Grabbing tin hat, duffel coat, and gas mask ,we scrambled out of bed,
Stumbling in the darkness, to the shelter , half asleep and yawning,
It's no good 'Turning in' again , we're early duty in the morning.
'Trainees' flying round the camp, crews waiting for their draft,
Now expert in the knowledge, the meaning of forward and Aft',
The squadrons move at intervals, to an unknown destination,
'Careless talk costs lives, walls have ears", a threat to the Nation.
As new recruits were drafted in, we went obediently on our way,
 One way ticket, pausing to remember, our arrival on the first day,
Buildings under construction, fields of mud, weather, cold and damp,
As we were part of the structure, of this busy functional camp.

The search goes on to trace our 'Shipmates', and reminisce we do,
We remember the very close friendships, of the Wrens in navy blue.
It's now a part of History, but the memories will always last,
For the bond is just as strong today, as it was in the past.
We look forward to our reunions, our friendships we will renew,
And drink a toast to the Fleet Air Arm, and the Royal Navy too.

MADGE HELM (Ex - L/Wrenn Winn).

Joy Freeman - Bomb Range Marker at Monifieth. Billetted in Letham Grange, complete with mice, occasionally sleeping in the conservatory.

The Acc. Room H.M.S. Condor 1942

Mrs K. Garry - Joined Condor in 1939 , Captain's Steward - moved to sub-base Dundee, accommodated in Marriat Hall.

Patricia Stanton - nee Traill - Billetted first at the Guynd then Letham Grange - passing Italian P.O.W.'s as she cycled into Condor . Aircraft Chocker in storage section later Cypher Officer in Bristol.

Muriel Wood - Switchboard Operator - accommodated in Letham Grange - moved into Nissan huts on Condor complete with earwigs and D.D.T. powder.

Margaret A.M.Taylor - Quarters P.O. at Letham Grange - 1945 to after V.J. day - gained commission , moved to Dundee '51 to '56 as Wren's Staff Officer , Tay Division R.N.V.R.

Taken at Carnoustie after trip to firing range at Moniefieth

Outside Photography Section 1940

Peggy Blackburn - nee Erwin -accommodated in Letham Grange 1945-1946 - walks to Colliston Inn.

Wendy Hogarth - nee Jones - sent to Condor with 737 Squadron 1944 billeted at Letham Grange - Petty Officer Radio Mechanic - daily inspections and maintenance of A.S.V.X. - Sunday divisions at Condor - at the weekends joined liberty flats for runs ashore - smokies in the Waverley Temperance Hotel, near the railway station - First encounters with working Christmases and eye opening Hogmanays.

Betty Gibson served on 'Condor' June 1943 to December 1944 as P.O. Wren Radio Mechanic on 751 Squadron , installing and maintaining radar equipment. The squadrons main function being training of observers in the operation of radar. Basic aircraft were Ansons and Swordfish. There were also a Walrus and a Wellington which were fitted with several sets and used as a small flying classroom. The Wellington suffered severe vibration.

Off duty day would cycle to harbour before crack of dawn and go out with the fishermen collecting lobsters and crabs from their pots. The Harbour fish bar, where we were able to enjoy a delicious plateful of fish and chips for 9d.

Letham Grange was a mansion requisitioned for W.R.N.S. quarters where there was no electricity and a little generator couldn't always cope so candlelight was usual. Walking up the drive in the dark , storm, and snow. Transport to and from the station was only allowed to the road end.

Took part in dramatic society production as 'Miranda Blue' in 'Quiet Wedding'. The producer was Hedley Goodall (professional B.B.C. experience) who was serving as photographic officer. Deciding the play to the presentation took only two hectic weeks in case of drafts disrupting rehearsals.

Wren L. Hume - I joined 'Condor' at the age of 18 in September 1940 and had to wait for one month for a uniform. The supply of Wren uniforms was , at that time, slowly building up. By the time they started calling girls up in 1941 the supply had greatly improved.

I was only 5ft and weighed 7st 1lb and was employed as Battery Charger (I had no idea what that was) and soon found myself working alongside the men working on the aircraft. I was later recommended for the first class of Wren Air Mechanic (L) in 1943.

We had very stormy weather in March 1941 when the King (George VI) officially opened the camp, in fact, the night before, the roof of one on the hangars was blown off.

We were prepared for the King's visit but despite that, the officer in charge forgot to bring the Wrens to attention and we were standing at ease as he inspected us, after which he planted the tree.

Another amusing incident during that wild month , I was sent to 754's hangar for a saw which was required for a job. Flying had been cancelled , and, as I returned to the main workshops, I had to cross the end of the runway, saw under arm. Suddenly a gust of wind caught the saw and being of light weight , I was blown down the runway. The only way I could regain my feet was to

Wren March Past - 1946

drop the saw. You can imagine the amusement this caused when I told of my predicament.

We also had heavy falls of snow that winter and the camp was riddled with ditches for various reasons (since the camp was still actually being built around us) and these ditches were sometimes completely obliterated and twice I fell into those traps, gumboots filled with snow, water and mud (I've no doubt others were also victims).

In those early days there were fears of invasion and we had various instructions of procedure should this happen. Wrens were informed they had to remove the buttons on their uniforms and disperse into the countryside.

HOW LUCKY WE WERE !

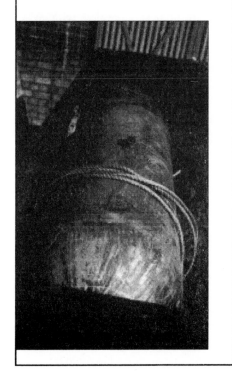

This Landmine landed between the Captains house and the Wrennery. We were all evacuated "on the double" down to the main galley where we stayed overnight. The mine was dismantled the following day and taken away.

One Sunday afternoon, without warning, a lone raider sneaked in and the first we knew was our quarters were being machine gunned. Those at their meals ducked below tables , etc., of course. Next day everyone was discussing what they were doing at that time and the funniest episode was, as the 'plane passed over, the men from one mess ran for the shelter but, half way there, the plane had turned back. The lads turned round and ran back to the mess. But, the first one in shut the door and held it shut, the others were left banging on the door on the outside. (Not all are born to be heroes). The 'plane was shot down.

The night the land mine was dropped, I was on duty and had to do fire watching, (it came down quietly , just a sort of swishing sound through the trees). Because it was near the Wrens' quarters we could not return to bed and we were bedded down on the tables in the main galley, two to a table. A most uncomfortable night , but grateful it was no worse.

We always had a show at Christmas - 'Condordrome' - it was usually organised by a seaman called 'Nally'? It was surprising the talents that were found on the camp. 'Gracie Fields' also did a show on 'Condor'. Ralph Richardson , I believe was parachute officer for a short period, and potato crisp people (Smith's) had a son who trained as observer. (We were well supplied with crisps during that period).

Wrens grew in number and many were moved out to 'The

Guynd', 'Woodville', and 'Letham Grange', but eventually , with the arrival of Wren Air Mechanics who were involved in night flying, it was necessary that they remained on the main camp and we moved into half of one of the men's blocks. The passages and ablutions had to be boarded half way. Of course , the lads would tell tales of knocking out the knots in the wood and tell tales of what they saw.

Most of the men accepted the Wren Air Mechanics but a few were a little resentful, especially when we began getting rated up to P.O., but on the whole I found little trouble.

We had an outbreak of meningitis in 1941 and all leave was cancelled, a Wren died , a cook in the main galley, and one sailor was affected, he recovered. We were fortunate they were the only two cases, but precautions had to be taken. Wrens suffered an outbreak of lice which led to periodic hair inspections, or , as the lads referred to them 'Hair Raids' . The girls who were affected were most embarrassed , but these things could be expected.

There were many other things, the 3d picture shows in the gym, dances, the day a squadron of Grumman Martlets arrived with American pilots, our own aircraft which we had a great respect for, V.E. day, V.J. day, which brought the sorrow of a Barracuda crash with the death of the pilot and two Wrens.

Joy Freeman - Bomb Range Marker at Monifieth. Billetted in Letham Grange, complete with mice, occasionally sleeping in the conservatory.

Mrs K. Garry - Joined Condor in 1939, Capyain's Stweard - moved to sub-base Dundee, accommodated in Marriat Hall.

Patricia Stanton - nee Traill - Billetted first at the Guynd then Letham Grange - passing Italian P.O.W.'s as she cycled into Condor. Aircraft Chocker in storage section later Cypher Officer in Bristol.

Muriel Wood - Switchboard Operator - accommodated in Letham Grange - moved into Nissan huts on Condor complete with earwigs and D.D.T. powder.

Margaret A.M. Taylor - Quarters P.O. at Letham Grange - 1945 to after V.J. day - gained commission, moved to Dundee '51 to 56' as Wren's Staff Officer, Tay Division R.N.V.R.

Peggy Blackburn - nee Erwin - accommodated in Letham Grange 1945 - 1946 - walks to Colliston Inn.

Wendy Hogarth - nee Jones - sent to Condor with 737 Squadron 1944 - billetted at Letham Grange - Petty Officer Radio Mechanic - daily inspections and maintenance of A.S.V.X. - Sunday divisions at Condor - at the weekends joined liberty flats for runs ashore - smokies in the Waverley Temerance Hotel, near the railway station - First encounters with working Christmases and eye opening Hogmanays.

Officers outside Wrens Mess 1950

On roof of Letham Grange 1944

Wrens I. Burdon, M. Strangeman & M. Gray

Letham Grange, Colliston. Used as WRNS Quarters - 1944

Officers outside Wrens Mess 1950

Wrens outside Officers Mess 1950

Wren Officers Mess 1950
³/o Cynthia Colomros, ³/o Mary Hall, ³/o "Bobby" Cumming, ³/o Pamela Sharpe, Sister Dorothy Bong.
Sister "Nicky" Nicholson, ²/o "Kate" Carney, ¹/o Phyllis Cooper, ²/o Irene Austen, ³/o Iris Taylor.

The Gynd, used as WRNS quarters - 1944

³/o Pamela Sharpe & ²/o Irene Austen - 1950

Radio Mecs 1944

The Winn Sisters (Return) "Condor 1987"
Nancy, left, and Madge, with their hands on that famous sign. With
other Wrens who were at Condor later.

Radio Mecs 1944

Betty Gibson served on 'Condor' June 1943 to December 1944 as P.O. Wren Radio Mechanic on 751 Squadron, installing and maintaining radar equipment. The squadrons main function being training of observers in the operation of radar. Basic aircraft were Ansons and Swordfish. There were also a Walrus and a Wellington which were fitted with several sets and used as a small flying classroom. The Wellington suffered severe vibration.

Off duty day would cycle to harbour before crack of dawn and go out with fishermen collecting lobsters and crab from their pots. The Harbour fish bar, where we were able to enjoy a delicious plateful of fish and chips for 9d.

Letham Grange was a mansion requisitioned for W.R.N.S. quarters where there was no electricity and a little generator couldn't always cope so candlelight was usual. Walking up the drive in the dark, storm, and snow. Transport to and from the railway station was only allowed to the road end.

Took part in dramatic society production as 'Miranda Blue' in 'Quite Wedding'. The Producer was Hedley Goodall (professional B.B.C. experience) who was serving as photographic Officer. Deciding the play to presentation took only two hectic weeks in case of drafts disrupting rehearsals.

Extract from 'The Arbroath Guide' Saturday March 17th. 1951.

CONDOR PRESENTS.

'Enclosed Premises' by Paul Johnson, which was the station entry in the Royal Naval Drama Festival, was faultless performance, reliably handled throughout by a cast who could have credibly graced a professional stage.

Dual honours were claimed by Mary Hall, as the respectable, shrewish, 'Esta Moon', and Charles Pratt her long suffering husband. Mother-in-law was given brilliant expression by Kate Carnby. Irene Austen and Mervyn Collins were first class supporting players.

Charles Pratt was also responsible for production. The sets, which were perfect in detail , were built by P.J. Moore. The stage managers were Dennis Franks and Cynthia Colombos.
(President Birmingham WRNS Association - Vice President Association of WRNS).

Mrs Muriel Currie MBE (nee Strangeman) - CONDOR 1942-43 -joined with Joan Donaldson - put in Guardroom with M.A.A. George Dear and a couple of three badgers with rather ripe language. became writer to Commander Woods whose daughter also served on the station.

Always hungry due to bracing winds (nothing new) - billetted at the Guynd , ferrying back and forth. Dances at the Seaforth, badminton, swimming, cycling. Wren Irene Bundin worked in control tower. Wren Muriel Gray , workplace not known (see photograph of Redcastle).

Jo Veale was a signals Wren whose duties consisted sending and receiving signals in the teleprinter room, in M.S.O. typing signals for distribution and control tower listening out or passing information to pilots. They also did night watches in the P.C.B. , checked the confidential books daily and raised/lowered the ensign at RARA - the R.D.F. equipment on the airfield was also set as a daily duty.

June 1943

W.R.N.S.

First Officer ....J.V. Wallace-Smith
                 (In Charge W.R.N.S.)
Second Officer ...B.E. Moore

December 1943

W.R.N.S.

Act. Chief   ) J.V. Wallace-Smith
Officer   )(In Charge W.R.N.S.)
Second Officer ...H.E.S. Gower
Act. Second   )
Officer   ) M.C. Foster-Barham

Februrary 1944

W.R.N.S.

Act. Chief   ) J.V. Wallace-Smith
Officer   )(In Charge W.R.N.S.)
Second Officer ...H.E.S. Gower
Act. Second   )
Officer   ) M.C. Foster-Barham

June 1944

W.R.N.S.

Act. Chief   )
Officer   ) N.J. Mitchelhill
Second Officer....H.E.S. Gower
                  B. O'Kelly
                  S.E. Barrington-Ward

October 1944

W.R.N.S.

Act. Chief   )
Officer   ) N. J. Mitchelhill
First Officer ....G.M. Robinson
                 (i/c W.R.N.S.,R.N.A.S.)
Second Officer ...H.E.S. Gower
                  B. O'Kelly
                  S.E. Barrington-Ward

January 1945

W.R.N.S.

Act. Chief   )
Officer   ) N.J. Mitchelhill
Second Officer ...H.E.S. Gower
                  B. O'Kelly
                  S.E. Barrington-Ward

April 1945

W.R.N.S.

Chief Officer .....N.J. Mitchelhill
Second Officer ....H.E.S. Gower
                   B.O'Kelly
                   S.E. Barrington-Ward

July 1945

W.R.N.S.

Chief Officer .....N.J. Mitchelhill
Second Officer ....S.E. Barrington-Ward
                   M.C. Wright
                   D.J. Williams

October 1945

W.R.N.S.

Chief Officer .....N.J. Mitchelhill
                   M.I. Talbot
    (On staff of Cdre. Flying Training)
Second Officer ....J.D. Williams
                   P.M.S. Creagh
                   A.K. Bartlett
                   O.F. Pollok-Morris

July 1946

W.R.N.S.

Chief Officer .... A.I. Watt
                  (On staff of R.A.R.A.)
Second Officer ....I.M. Kilminster
                   M.J. Hill
                   V.G. Hill
                   B.C. Hopkins
                   L.G. Hewit

July 1947

W.R.N.S.

First Officer .....P.P.S. Crocker
Second Officer ....V.G. Hill
                   F.R.M. Garrett

January 1948

W.R.N.S.

Chief Officer .....E.L.E. Hoyer-Millar
First Officer .....P.P.S. Crocker

April 1948

W.R.N.S.

Chief Officer ....S.H. Broster
First Officer ....P.P.S. Crocker

July 1948

W.R.N.S.

First Officer ....P.P.S. Crocker
Second Officer ...F.P.M. Garrett
                 I. Brewis

October 1948

W.R.N.S.

First Officer ....P.P.S. Croker
Second Officer ...F.P.M. Garrett
                 L. Brewis

April 1949

W.R.N.S.

Second Officer ...I. Brewis
                 J.F. Beer

October 1949

W.R.N.S.

First Officer ....P. Cooper
Second Officer ...I.M. Austen

July 1950

W.R.N.S.

Second Officer ...E.E.L. Carney
                 J.L. Turnbull

October 1951

W.R.N.S.

First Officer ....J.E. Sutton
Second Officer ...E.E.L.Carney

April 1952

W.R.N.S.

First Officer ....J.E. Sutton

October 1952

W.R.N.S.

First Officer ....J.E. Sutton
Second Officer ...A.M. Richards

April 1953

W.R.N.S.

First Officer ....E.L.M. Hill
Second Officer ...A.M. Richards

October 1953

W.R.N.S.

First Officer ....E.L.M. Hill
Second Officer ...A.M. Richards

July 1954

W.R.N.S.

First Officer ....E.L.M. Hill
Second Officer ...M.N. France

July 1955

W.R.N.S.

First Officer ....E.L.M. Hill
Second Officer S.M. Underwood

October 1956

W.R.N.S.

First Officer ....M.I. Talbot

July 1957

W.R.N.S.

Chief Officer ....M.M. Kettlewell

January 1958

W.R.N.S.

Chief Officer .... M.M. Kettlewell

Blackburn Roc

Corsair

Bristol Blenheim

Fairey Seal

Chance Vought Chesapeake

D.H. Dominie

Chapter 4

Squadrons

"TROUBLE IN H.M.S. CONDOR."

825 Squadron (Lt. Cdr. Eugene Esmond) found itself in H.M.S. Daedalus (Lee on the Solent) after disembarking from H.M.S. Furious after an unsuccessful search for Hipper. The Squadron was ordered to go to H.M.S. Condor (Arbroath). We were to be fitted with a A.S.V. Mark 2 N , the first F.A.A. Sqdn. to be fitted with radar. We went to Arbroath in easy stages, on the 9th September Sub. Lt. Jackson, myself and Leading Airman Pinlott took off from Lee to Blackpool (took 2 hours 55 minutes) ,10th September Blackpool to Prestwick (1 hour 55 minutes), same day Prestwick to Evanton (1 hour 55 minutes). Note , we were unable to fly direct to Arbroath because of very low cloud, poor visibility and snow. On 11 th December , 1940 we were able to go to Arbroath via the Caledonian Canal, the cloud covered either side, snow lay on the ground - quite spectacular to fly through what looked like a tunnel , arriving 1 hour 50 minutes later at Arbroath.

The airfield was very much in the embryo stage with many hazards like unfilled ditches , frozen water , snow everywhere , unmade paths , general chaos of an airfield in the making. The procedure of fitting and testing the new A.S.V. went on in the early part of the new year (1941). The equipment was collected from stores with an armed guard and an officer , security was so strict that even my log book referring to A.S,V. was deleted by the senior observer, Lt. Cdr. Sanderson and 'SE' put instead.

One particularly cold and unpleasant day one of the Swordfish had problems with its air speed indicator (A.S.I.). Tim Cardew (Lt.R.N.) 'Dapper' Berrill, Angus Fraser, Sub. Lts. (A) R.N., and myself were told to calibrate the A.S.I. This involved attaching to the Pilot Head a Manometer, I was raising the column of mercury to simulate the air speed in knots. Tim Cardew was in the pilot's cockpit and one of the others in the rear cockpit. I must emphasise that the temperature in the hangar was below zero and it was snowing outside, things were not going well and we asked for assistance from the P.O. Instrument Technician. The aluminium tubes were disconnected at the wing root, one tube comes from the actuating gear at the bottom of the Oleo-leg for the activating gear of the M-type dinghy which normally sits in a cavity on the port upper main plane inboard. The other tube goes to the Pilot Head ; once more attempting to assimilate the air speed there was a terrible noise, the sound of tearing canvas and things breaking out and to our utter horror the M-type dinghy stood up above the Swordfish main plane ejecting itself from its stowage and rising like a genie and surrounded by white vapour as the CO_2 bottle inflated it! Tim Cardew decided this was no place for him and abandoned the cockpit post haste, leaping to the deck and running out of the hangar, followed by the rest of us! All four of us were severely reprimanded and consequently various 'trades' were involved in putting matters right!

All four of us repaired to the Seaforth Hotel in Arbroath where we were joined by Tim's wife who was Sir Henry Wood's daughter where we had a splendid meal and recovered from the shock. I earned the nickname Trouble by complaining of something to the waitress who said in broad Scottish "Och away, your name should be Trouble" and to this day I'm still known by it, even by my 93 year old Aunt!

Later the Squadron left for Furious, then some of the crews were despatched to 810 Sqdn. Ark Royal and finally some of the crews were despatched to Malta to join 830 Sqdn. where the A.S.V. made its mark.

Mr. William Darcy Damiens (84) - R.A.F. A/F Fitter manufacturing and fitting radar aerials - served from 1935 to 1945 - July '40 - October '41 778 squadron.

3 R.A.F. 2 R.N. 2 civilian - Capt. Abel Smith, Lt Cdr. Tillarde, Lt.Cdr. Ward-Thompson, Lt. Furlong.

a.m. 16/09/53. Sea Fury Mk.XI from Condor , last seen 1015. Serial no. VW590, 811 Squadron, call sign 108J. A wide search was carried out, involving H.M.S. Eagle, Gourdon lifeboat, H.M.S. Battleaxe, Arbroath lifeboat and Broughty Ferry lifeboat, nothing found.
A shooting party of Americans led by a local man from Edzell arrived at Glen Esk for a grouse shoot a approx. 1240, they noticed smoke and flames on the slopes of Wirren, they found a crater 15 feet deep and 12 feet across, the heat was too intense to carry out a rescue but the pilot obviously died on impact. (S/Lt. F.D. Beardsall).
This was the second loss by this Squadron,. the first crash on 07/09/53 in a field at Wormiston, Crail, the pilot was killed (Lt. J.C. Ladd). Aircraft serial no. VW718.

Call sign for both aircraft 108 ??.

FLIGHTS OF THE CONDOR

Squadron	Dates	Aircraft	Task	Commanding Officer
703 A Flight	22.2.54 6.54	Firefly		Lt. Cdr. P.D. Lowndes RN
731 East Haven	5.12.43	Swordfish, Fulmar, Sea Hurricane. Seafire		Lt Cdr(A) K. Stilliard RNVR
735 Detachment	28.8.44 15.4.45	Anson, Barracuda, Hellcat		Lt Cdr(A) J.H. Mayne RNVR
737	8.44	Anson		Lt Cdr(A) L.P. Dunne RNVR Lt Cdr(A) E.J. Staveley RNVR Lt Cdr F.V. Jones RNVR
740	4.5.43 5.8.43	Walrus, Swordfish, Kingfisher	Observer training	Lt Cdr D.H. Angel RN
741	1.3.43 19.3.45	Swordfish	Observer training	Lt Cdr(A) O.H. Cantrill RNVR Lt Cdr(A) R.M.C.A. Stratton RNVR
751	19.8.40 13.8.44	Walrus	Observer training	Lt Cdr(A) J.H. Sender RN Lt Cdr(A) F. Leach RNVR
753	23.8.40 1.11.45	Shark, Seal, Swordfish, Albacore, Reliant, Barracuda	Observer training	Capt A.C. Newson RM Lt Cdr(A) L.A. Cubitt RN Lt Cdr(A) A.C. Mills RNVR Lt Cdr(A) F.R. Steggall RNVR Lt Cdr(A) R.E. Stewart RNVR Lt Cdr(A) A.J. Phillips RN
754	7.9.40 27.3.46	Proctor, Lysander, Albacore, Reliant, Swordfish	Observer training	Lt Cdr E.J.E. Burt RN Lt Cdr(A) H.E.S. Pritchett RNVR Lt Cdr(A) A.P.E. Payen RNVR Lt Cdr(A) D.A. Horton RNVR Lt Cdr(A) W.E. Dunn RNVR
758 East Haven detachment	14.10.40 1.2.41 .43 .44	Skua, Proctor	T.A.G training. (Torpedo air gunner)	Lt Cdr(A) F. Leach RNVR
763	15.10.40 2.41		T.S.R. Plans to reform cancelled	

751 Squadron - Radio Mecs, Fitters & Riggers - June 1944

751 Squadron Emblem

751 Squadron & others posed on an Anson

751 Squadron - Radio Mecs, Fitters & Riggers - 1944

December 1940

825 Squadron

S/Lt (A) RNVR	*S/Lt (A) RNVR*	*S/Lt (A) RNVR*	*S/Lt (A) RNVR*
A.J. Griffith	*R. Hodgetts*	*Peter Meadway*	*"Dapper" Berrill*

	Lt RN	*S/Lt (A) RN*	
	Tim Cardew	*Angus Fraser*	

767 East Haven	8.7.40 5.5.43 15.7.40	Swordfish, Albacore, Barracuda, Firefly, Corsair, Seafire	Deck Landing training	Lt Cdr P.L. Mortimer RN Lt Cdr J.A.L.Drummond RN Lt Cdr D.N. Russell RN Lt Cdr A.G. Leathem RN Lt R.L. Williamson DSC RN Lt R.S. Baker-Faulkner RN Lt C.H.C. O'Rorke RN Lt Cdr W.J. Mainprice RN Lt Cdr(A) T.T. Miller RN Lt Cdr(A) J.L. Fisher RNVR Lt Cdr(A) B.W. Vigrass RNVR Lt Cdr(A) D.R. Park RNZNVR Lt Cdr(A) S.G. Cooke RNVR Lt(A) D.C. Hill MBE RNZNVR Lt Cdr(A) F.A.S. Wanton DSC* RN Lt. J.C.S. Wright RN
768	13.1.41 1.3.43	Swordfish, Fulmars, Martlet, Sea Hurricane, Hooked Spitfire	Deck Landing Trials	Lt Cdr V.C. Grenfell RN Lt Cdr(A) F.D.G. Jennings RN Lt N.G. Hallett RN Lt J.C.M. Harman RN Lt(A) P.J. Jackson RN Lt Cdr(A) D.M. Brand RNVR
769 East Haven	29.11.41 7.11.43 29.10.45	Albacore, Swordfish, Tiger Moth, Fulmar, Sea Gladiator, Sea Hurricane, Barracuda		Lt W.H. Crawford RN Lt Cdr W.H. Nowell RN Lt Cdr(A) S.P. Luke RN Lt Cdr P.N. Medd RN Lt Cdr(A) D. Brookes DSC RNVR Lt Cdr G.C. Edwards RCNVR Lt Cdr(A) G. Bennett DSC RNVR
770 Detachment	3.9.45 14.9.45	Mosquito		Lt Cdr(A) J.M.L. Wilson RNZNVR
771 Detachment	13.10.48 3.9.51	Mosquito		Lt Cdr C.R. Bateman RN Lt Cdr(A) R.W.M. Walsh RN Lt Cdr J.G. Baldwin DSC RN Lt Cdr J.A. Welply RN Lt Cdr M.W. Rudorf DSC RN
772 Detachment Detachment	16.10.45 10.1.46 7.46 26.6.47 13.10.48	Martrinets, Wildcats, Mosquito Mosquito Seafire	Fleet Requirement Unit	Lt Cdr P. Snow RN Lt F.G.B. Sheffield DSC RN Lt Cdr C.H. Filmer RN LT(A) W.C. Larkins RN

778	6.7.40 5.3.43	Swordfish, Walrus, Skua, Roc, Albacore, Fulmar, Martlet, Sea Hurricane, Seafire, Chesapeake, Kingfisher, Barracuda	Service Trials Unit	Lt Cdr J.P.G. Bryant RN Lt Cdr A.J. Tillard RN Lt Cdr H.P.Bramwell DSO DSC RN
	15.8.44 9.8.45	Avenger Corsair, Firebrand, Firefly		Lt Cdr P.B. Schonfield RN Lt Cdr E.M. Britten RN
783	9.1.41 15.5.47	Swordfish, Albacore Walrus, DH86, Wellington, Anson, Firefly, Barracuda, Avenger	ASV Radar Training	Lt Cdr(A) J.M. Waddell RNVR Lt Cdr(A)J.M.Keene-Miller RNVR Lt Cdr(A) D.M. Brown RNVR Lt Cdr(A) R.P. Mason RNVR Lt Cdr(A) T.B. Horsley RNVR Lt(A) W.L.M. Daubney RNVR Lt(A) E.H.G. Child RNVR Lt Cdr(A) A.M. Tuke RN
787 'Y' Flight	12.6.44 6.8.44	Seafire, Avenger, Blenhiem, Dominie, Swordfish	Fighter Affiliation	Lt Cdr(A) R.E. Bibhy DSO RNVR
791	15.10.40 10.12.44	Roc, Skua, Swordfish, Defiant, Albacore, Sea Gladiator, Sea Hurricane	Target Towing	Lt Cdr(A) L. Gilbert RNVR Lt Cdr(A) K.G. Brotchie RNVR Lt J.C.M. Harman RN Lt Cdr(A) C.A. Crichton RNVR Lt Cdr(A) A.P.T.Pierssene RNVR
800 'Y' Flight	2.5.41 12.5.41 5.8.41 11.8.41	Fulmar Sea Hurricane	(Bismark)	Lt Cdr J.A.D. Wroughton DSC RN
801 Transit	7.11.41 30.4.48 21.5.48	Sea Hurricane Sea Hornet	(Tirpitz)	Lt Cdr(A) R.A. Brabner MP RNVR Lt Cdr(A) D.H. Richards RN
802	7.5.45 21.6.45 2.2.53 29.4.53	Seafire Sea Fury		Lt Cdr R.C. Hargreaves DSC RN Lt Cdr D.M. Steer RN
803	15.6.45 23.9.45	Seafire		Lt Cdr(A) L.D.Wilkinson DSC RNVR
807	15.6.51 14.7.51	Sea Fury		Lt Cdr A.J. Thomson DSC RN
809	18.6.50 5.7.50	Sea Hornet		Major J.O. Annour RM

810	8.10.40 29.10.40	Swordfish	(Bismark)	Lt Cdr M. Johnstone DSC RN
	29.5.51	Firefly		Lt Cdr G.R. Coy RN
	25.7.51			Lt Cdr D.E. Johnson RN
811	1.11.41	Swordfish		Lt Cdr W.J. Lucas RN
	16.3.42			Lt Cdr H.S. Hayes DSC RN
	17.8.53			
	19.8.53	Sea Fury		Lt Cdr L.G. Morris RN
813	26.4.48	Firebrand		Lt Cdr(A) C.R.J. Coxon RN
	21.5.48			
	14.5.51			
	6.5.51	Firebrand		Lt Cdr L.W.A. Barrington RN
814 Transit	8.8.44	Barracuda		Lt Cdr J.S.L. Crabbe RN
815 Detachment	14.5.48 4.10.48	Barracuda		Lt Cdr K.S. Patterson DSC RN
	14.5.51 28.5.51	Barracuda		Lt Cdr C.R.J. Coxon RN
818	12.7.41 28.7.41	Swordfish		Lt Cdr T.P.Goode RN
819 Detachment	21.7.67 23.6.67 20.7.68 21.7.68	Wessex		Lt Cdr P.H.G. Rogers RN
	14.7.80 24.5.81	Sea King		Lt Cdr A. Finnes RN
	28.5.81 7.12.81 11.12.81 12.12.83			Lt Cdr P.F. Southon RN
	13.12.83 26.1.87			Lt Cdr M.J. Priestley RN
	29.1.87 21.4.87			Lt Cdr J.J. Carter RN
	24.4.87			Lt Cdr C.J. Denny RN
820	10.1.44 1.2.44	Barracuda		Lt Cdr(A) W.R. Nowell RN
Detachment	15.5.67 26.5.67	Wessex		Lt Cdr A. Casdagli RN
Detachment	12.7.76 23.7.76	Sea King		Lt Cdr C.A. Robertson RN
821	10.11.41 18.9.51	Swordfish		Lt C.W.B. Smith RN
	8.11.51	Firefly		Lt Cdr B.H. Notley RN
824 'A'Flight	6.12.81 9.12.81	Sea King		Lt Cdr I.S. McKenzie MBE RN

825 Detachment	11.12.40 19.12.40	Swordfish	(Bismark)	Lt Cdr(A) E. Esmonde DSO RN
826 East Haven Detachment	15.8.45 11.10.45 4.7.66 11.7.66 13.10.66 5.11.66	Barracuda Wessex		Lt Cdr E.S. Carver RN Lt Cdr R.A. Duxbury RN
841 Transit	26.2.44	Barracuda		Lt Cdr(A) R.J. Fisher RNZNVR
845 Detachment	29.11.73 4.12.73 29.11.74 5.12.74 24.7.78 28.7.78 6.11.78 10.11.78 10.79 19.10.81 22.10.81 14.5.84 31.5.84 7.5.85 17.5.85 6.5.86 22.5.86 7.7.86 10.7.86 29.10.86 7.11.86 27.4.87 1.5.87 11.10.87 23.10.87 5.12.89 8.12.89 5.7.89 13.7.89 4.6.90 7.6.90	Wasp Wessex Sea King		Lt Cdr G.S. Clarke RN Lt Cdr Ray Bridges RN Lt Cdr A.C.Gratton-Cooper RN Lt Cdr T.J. Stanning RN Lt Cdr C.J. de Mowbray RN Lt Cdr D.G.Widgery RN Capt P.S. Belding AFC RM Lt Cdr P.S. Belding AFC RN Cdr Ledingham RN

846 Detachment	9.5.69 22.5.69	Wessex	Lt Cdr D.J. Lickfold MBE RN
	29.4.79 3.5.79 19.11.79 23.11.79		Lt Cdr R.P.Seymour AFC RN
	19.10.81 23.10.81	Sea King	Lt Cdr T.J. Yarker RN
	1.3.82 5.3.82		Lt Cdr S.C. Thornewill DSC RN
	5.12.82 10.12.82 11.7.83 15.7.83		Lt Cdr N McMillan RN
	4.9.85 12.9.85 18.10.85 25.10.85 4.11.85 15.11.85 1.12.85 6.12.85		Lt Cdr S.P.K. Rooke RN
880	15.1.41 29.6.41	Martlet Sea Gladiator Sea Hurricane	Lt Cdr F.E.C. Judd RN
883	18.9.45 7.11.45	Sea Fury	Lt Cdr(A) T..A. King-Joyce RN
885 Transit	21.8.42	Sea Hurricane	Lt Cdr(A) R.H.P.Carver DSC RN
898	4.7.51 24.7.51	Sea Fury	Lt Cdr T.L.M. Brander DSC RN
1771	10.3.45 12.3.45	Firefly	Lt Cdr(A) W.J.R.MacWhirter DSC RN

STATION FLIGHT

Tiger Moth II	Proctor II	Reliant	Dominie
Expediter C2	Sea Otter	Anson I	Swordfish II
Martinet TTI	Firefly Ti, T2, FR5		Harvard 2B, T3
Sea Fury T20	Sea Prince T1, C1, C2		Sea Devon

STORAGE SECTION

Dominies   Harvards 2a, 2b, & 3

Name	Regiment	Rank	Regiment Number
WILKINSON	R.N.V.R	S/k (a) Lt (A)	Notes. 1949 See S/L (Sp)
A	HMS Condor, Abbotsinch Sea Lt	"	Sp = Steam Driver Seniority date = 16/10/48

Medal	Roll	No	Remarks
Victory	39/45 Star		1) Royal Life Saving Society Medal in B2. June 1935
BWM	Africa Star		2) Aquatics May 1944 Free Style Relay 1st S/k (A) A. Wilkinson
1914 Star	War Medal		3) Athletics July 1944 Inter Part Relay 1st kt Wilkinson
14/15 Star	Defence Medal		4) Rugby 7-a-side. Winners Lt (A) A Wilkinson RNVR. 737 Squadron.
Theatre of War			
Date of entry			

"Barra" crashes

Sir,
It was with great interest that members of the Bournemouth Branch of the Fleet Air Arm Association read the excellent article by Derek Collier Webb on the prototype Fairey Barracudas in your June issue. Members include old "Barra drivers", so it inspired some lively discussion.

I was at RNAS Arbroath in 1944 when 753 Sqn received theirs. With 741 Sqn's "Stringbags" they must have flown hundreds of sorties, training observers and telegraphist air gunners.

I can recall only two major incidents. I watched with horror when a Barra, making a good landing approach, suddenly fell from the sky when a wing tore off! It crashed just outside the perimeter. I was first on the scene, but the crew were killed instantly and the engine had bored several feet into the ground. It was subse-quently deduced that a wing retaining pin (manufactured from an incorrect material specification) had sheared. Indeed, a fellow member at Bournemouth recalls a Technical Instruction on his squadron at that time for test-ing the pins with a hammer and punch.

Another incident occurred on night flying, when an air-craft, already in the circuit, got in trouble over Arbroath. The aircraft crashed on a piece of waste ground, but the pilot baled out. This was a matter of intense surprise to 753 Sqn pilots who watched it come down, as it was never consid-ered that a pilot had much chance at that altitude.
TED PHILLIPS (ex AMII)
Wimborne
Dorset

Aeroplane Monthly, August 1996

THE PLANE CRASH AT ARBROATH.

Sir,—In connection with the crash of a naval aircraft in Arbroath on Friday night last, fortunately without loss of life, I wish to mention two points. Firstly, the account in your paper did not mention the very early arrival and efficient work put in by the crash tender from this station. Secondly, on arrival of one of my officers the remark was made to him by a civilian, when it was still thought three bodies were burning in the wreckage that "that will teach them to low fly."

There may be instances of unauthorised low flying in the county of Angus by aircraft from this station, in which case I trust wit-nesses will report the fact, together with, if possible, the type and number of the air-craft involved, when the necessary discip-linary action will be taken, but in this case the cause of the accident was a failure of the equipment, necessitating the immediate abandonment of the aircraft, which the pilot did with considerable skill.

It would appear necessary to remind cer-tain residents in Arbroath that there is still a war to be won in the Pacific, and that the least they can do is to put up with a certain amount of inconvenience with a good grace while our young aircrews are learning to fit themselves for the hazardous work they must soon undertake.

I shall be glad if you will publish this letter.—I am, yours faithfully
R. Sherbrooke, capt., Royal Navy.
R.N. Air Station, Arbroath.
June 25, 1945.

THE officers and men of H.M.S. Condor yesterday received the Freedom of Arbroath. It was the burgh's way of marking the 21st anni-versary of the naval air station.

Civic dignitaries from neigh-bouring burghs and representa-tives of local organisations were present with the public at the ceremony in Webster Hall.

Town Clerk Mr W. D. Smith read the Town Council minute conferring the Freedom on the station. Then the Burgess Register was signed by Provost D. A. Gardner, the Town Clerk and Condor's C.O., Captain P. H. C. Illingworth. Captain Illingworth received the framed burgess ticket from the Provost. Outside, the Provost inspected a guard of honour, and publicly

proclaimed the Freedom to the officers and ratings.

The scroll was presented to the youngest apprentice, P.O. Apprentice H. A. Haines, who marched with it at the head of the guard (see picture above).

Preceded by the Royal Marine band and the Condor instru-mental band, the guard fixed bayonets, and the parade marched past Provost Gardner

751 Squadron - Pilots June 1944

Station Flight - Condor 4th September 1950 (Author 4th from right)

753 Squadron

768 Squadron 1941

754 Squadron 1944

Main Galley Staff 1941

December 1940

751 SQUADRON

Lt.Cdr. (A).......(P) J.H. Sender
                      (In Command)
Lt. ....(P) B.P.H. Brooks
Tempy.Lt. (A)....((P) H.E.S. Pritchett
R.N.V.R.   ((P) J.C. Moore

753 SQUADRON

Captain, R.M. ....(P) A.C. Newson
                      (In Command)
Tempy.Lt. (A)   ((P) G.A. Alderson
R.N.V.R.   ((P) J.C. Crammond

754 SQUADRON

Lt.Com. .... (P) E.J.E. Burt(ret)
                      (In Command)
Tempy.Lt (A)   )(P) K.B. Brotchie
R.N.V.R.   )(P) Cameron
)(P) P.G. Aldrich-Blake
                  (P) D.E. Swann

758 SQUADRON

Tempy.Lt.   )(P) F. Leach (act)
Com. (A)   )   In Command)
R.N.V.R.   (
Tempy.Lt. (A)   )(P) A.C. Mills
R.N.V.R.   )

767 SQUADRON

Lt.Com. ....(P) J.A.L. Drummond(ret)
                      (In Command)
                 (O) S.T.C. Harrison
                 (O) (IR) F.D. Howie
                 (P) A.F. Hall
                 (O) E.H.C. Chapman
                 (P) W.G.C. Stokes
Lt. ....(P) P.G. Sugden
                 (P) D.W. Waters
                 (O) Hon. W.A.C. Kepple
                 J.H.R. Medlicott-Vereker
                      (Acting Observer)
Lt. (A) ....(P) C.B. Ealand
                 (P) P.B.H. Butler
                 (And for Instructional Duties)
Tempy.Lt. (A)   (P) W.F.C. Garthwaite
R.N.V.R.   ((P) C.G. Pountney
Lt. (E) ....(P) J.L. Sedgewick
Captain, R.M. ....(P) A.R. Burch DSC

778 SQUADRON

Lt.Com. ....(P) J.G.P. Bryant
                 (In Command)
                (P) A.J. Tillard(ret)
                (O) A.F.P. Frenfell(ret)
                (O) A. Yeoman
                (O) W.Thompson
Lt. ....(P) W.J. Lucas
                (P) R.H. Furlong

791 SQUADRON

Tempy.Lt.-   )
Com. (A),   )(P) L. Gilbert
R.N.V.R.   )
        For Miscellanious Duties
Tempy.   )
Lt. (A),   ) W.G. Robson
R.N.V.R.   )

December 1941

751 SQUADRON

Tempy. Lt.-)
Com. (A),   )(P) F. Leach (act)
R.N.V.R.   )
Tempy.   )
Lt. (A),   )(P) H. Jones
R.N.V.R.   )

753 SQUADRON

Tempy. Lt.-)
Com. (A),   )(P) A.C. Mills (act)
R.N.V.R.   )   (In Command)
Tempy.   )(P) J.G. Crammond
Lt. (A)   )(P) I.D.F. Proctor
R.N.V.R.   )(P) W.A. McElroy
             (P) A.F. Hetherington
             (P) F.C. de la C. de
                 Labilliere

754 SQUADRON

```
Tempy. Lt.-   )
Com. (A),     )(P) H.E.S. Pritchett(act)
R.N.V.R.      )    (In Command)
Tempy.        )(P) K.B. Brotchie
Lt. (A),      )(P) A.G. Cameron
R.N.V.R.      )(P) H.M. Pollock
              (P) A.N. Bardolf
              (P) H. Barrett
              (P) T.B. Horsley
              (P) N.J. Corries
              (P) D.E.W. Hutchinson
              (P) C.A. Crichton
              (P) F.H. Horn
              (P) H. Jones
Lt. (E) .....(P) P. Goddard
              (P) F.G. Hood
```

767 SQUADRON

```
Lt. .........(P) A.G. Leatham
              (O) J.R. Lang
              (P) R.S. Baker-Falkner
              (P) D.F. Godfrey-Faussett,
                  DSC
              (P) W.H. Crawford
              (P) A.S. Whitworth,DSC
              (P) A.T. Darley
          (And for Instructional Duties)
Lt. (A) .....(P) K.S. Pattison
              (P) J.W.G. Wellham,DSC
              (P) H.I.A. Swayne
              (P) M.G.W. Clifford
```

768 SQUADRON

```
Lt. .........(P) J.C.M. Harman
              (In Command)
Sub.Lt. (A)..(P) P.B. Jackson
```

778 SQUADRON

```
Lt. Com. ....(P) H.P. Bramwell
              (In Command)
Lt. .........(P) J.M. Bruen
              (O) E.S. Carver
Lt. (A) .....(P) G. Smith
                  E.W. Sykes
Tempy.        )(P) W.B. Caldwell
Lt. (A),      )    J.H.P. Bryner
R.N.V.R.      )
```

783 SQUADRON

```
Tempy. Lt.-   )(P) J.M. Keene-Miller
Com. (A)      )    (act)
R.N.V.R.      )
Tempy.        )(P) D. Holdsworth
Lt. (A),      )(P) J.P. Inderwick
R.N.V.R.      )
```

791 SQUADRON

```
Tempy. Lt.-   )
Com. (A),     )(P) L. Gilbert(act)
R.N.V.R.      )
Lt. .........)(P) H.G. Thom
R.A.N.V.R.    )
```

811 SQUADRON

```
Lt.Com. .....(P) W.J. Lucus
              (In Command)
Lt. .........(O) W.S. Hayes,DSC
Lt. (A) .....(P) M.F.S.P. Willcocks
              (P) A.S. McTurk
```

818 SQUADRON

```
Lt. .........(O) T.W.B. Shaw,DSC
              (P) N.T. O'Neil
                  T.A. Stewart
                  (Acting Observer)
Lt. (A)......(P) A.S.Campbell
Tempy.        )
Lt. (A),      )(P) H.E. Shilbach
R.N.V.R.      )
```

June 1942

751 SQUADRON

```
Tempy. Lt.-   )
Com. (A),     )(P) F. Leach(act)
R.N.V.R.      )
Lt..(P).........S.M. Howard
Lt., R.N.V.R.(P) B.C. Lyons(act)
Tempy.,       )
Lt. (A)       )(P) H. Jones
R.N.V.R.      )(P) T.J. Arthur
```

753 SQUADRON

```
Tempy. Lt.,   )(P) A.C. Mills(act)
Com. (A),     )    (In Command)
R.N.V.R.      )
Tempy.        )(P) E.H. Garland
Lt. (A),      )(P) O.H. Cantrill
R.N.V.R.      )(P) C.H. Dupere
              (P) R.T.F.Pragnell
              (P) H. Robinson
              (P) R.A. Edmonds
```

754 SQUADRON

```
Tempy. Lt.-   )
Com. (A),     )(P) D.A. Horton(act)
R.N.V.R.      )    (In Command)
Tempy. Lt.    )(P) C.R. Holman
R.N.R.        )
```

Tempy.Lt.   )(P) A.G. Cameron
(A),   )(P) H.M. Pollock
R.N.V.R.   )(P) T.B. Horsley
               (P) F.G. Hood
               (P) D.E.W.Hutchinson
               (P) C.A. Crichton
               (P) E.H. Horn
               (P) H. Jones
Lt. (E) ......(P) B. Goddard

767 SQUADRON

Lt. ....(P) A.G. Leatham
             (P) R.S. Baker-Falkner
             (P) C.H.C. O'Rorke
Lt. (A) ......(P) M.G.W. Clifford

768 SQUADRON

Lt. (A) ......(P) P.B. Jackson
             (In Command)
Tempy. Sub-   )
Lt. (A),   )(P) A.E.R. Wilkinson
R.N.V.R.   )

769 SQUADRON

Lt. ....(P) W.H. Crawford
             (In Command)
Lt. (A) ......(P) J.W.G. Wollham,DSC
             (P) S.G. Cooper
             (P) W.R. Nowell

778 SQUADRON

Lt.-Com. .....(P) H.P. Bramwell
             (In Command)
Lt. ....(0) E.S. Carver
Lt. (A) ......(P) G. Smith
             (P) E.W. Sykes
Tempy. Lt.,   )
(A),   )   J.H.P. Brymer
R.N.V.R.   )(P) G.K. Pridham

783 SQUADRON

Tempy. Lt.-   )(P) J.M. Keene-Miller
Com. (A),   )   (act)
R.N.V.R.   )
Tempy. Lt.,   )(P) D. Holdsworth
(A),   )(P) D.M. Brown
R.N.V.R.   )

791 SQUADRON

Tempy.   )
Lt. (A),   )(P) K.B. Brotchie
R.N.V.R.   )   (in Command)

Tempy.Sub-   )(P) A.D. Richardson
Lt. (A)   )(P) M. Lees
R.N.V.R.   )(P) R.H. Flintoff
              (P) K.L.W. Gilbert
              (P) M. Wargent

811 SQUADRON

Lt. ....(0) H.S. Hayes,DSC
             (In Command)
Lt. (A) ........H.G. Mays
             (Acting Observer)
Tempy.   )
Lt. (A),   )(P) P. Bentley
R.N.V.R.   )

December 1942

751 SQUADRON

Lt.-Com.,   )
R.N.R.   )(P) T.E. Sargent
Lt. ......)
R.N.V.R.   )(P) D.F.H. Dunn
Tempy. Lt.,   )(P) C.R. Holman
R.N.R.   )
Tempy.Lt.-   )
Com.(A),   )(P) F. Leach (act)
R.N.V.R.   )
Tempy.Lt.   )(P) P. Jones
(A),   )(P) C. Hammonds
R.N.V.R.   )(P) G. Windsor

753 SQUADRON

Tempy.Lt.-   )
Com. (A),   )(P) F.R. Steggall (act)
R.N.V.R.   )   (In Command)
Tempy.Lt.,   )(P) O.H. Cantrill
(A),   )(P) C.H. Dupere
R.N.V.R.   )(P) R.T.F. Pragnell
              (P) J.E. Randell
              (P) J.L. Wordsworth
              (P) H.O. Haughton
              (P) R.G. Averill

754 SQUADRON

Tempy.Lt.-   )(P) D.A. HORTON (act)
Com, (A),   )   (In Command)
R.N.V.R.   )
Tempy.,   )(P) H.M. Pollock
Lt., (A),   )(P) T.B. Horsley
R.N.V.R.   )(P) F.G. Hood
              (P) D.E.W. Hutchinson
              (P) C.A. Crichton
              (P) E.H. Horn
              (P) G. Lunt
Lt., (E)....(P) B. Goddard

767 SQUADRON

Lt. ....(P) C.H.C. O'Rorke
        (P) W.J. Mainprice
Lt. (A) .....(P) T.T. Miller

768 SQUADRON

Lt. (A) .....(P) D.J.W. Williams
        (P) A.E.R. Wilkinson

769 SQUADRON

Lt. ....(P) W.H. Crawford
        (In Command)
Lt. (A) .....(P) S.G. Cooper
        (P) W.R. Nowell

778 SQUADRON

Lt.Com. ......(P) H.P. Bramwell
        (In Command)
Lt. ....(O) E.S. Carver
Lt. (A) .....(P) H.M. Ellis,DSC,DFC
        (P) E.W. Sykes
Tempy.Lt.,(A))
R.N.V.R.   } J.H.P. Brymer

783 SQUADRON

Tempy. Lt.-)
Com. (A), }(P) D.M. Brown (act)
R.N.V.R.   ) (In Command)
Tempy. Lt.(A))(P) D. Holdsworth
R.N.V.R.   )(P) K.D. Parkhouse

791 SQUADRON

Lt. ....(P) J.C.M. Harman
        (In Command)
Tempy.Lt.,(A))(P) P.D. Eastham
R.N.V.R.   )

June 1943

740 SQUADRON

Lt.-Com. .....(P) D.H. Angel (act)
        (In Command)
Tempy. Lt.,)
R.N.R.   }(P) H.A.P. Bullivant (act)
Tempy. Lt.,)
R.N.V.R.   }(P) L.F. Plant

741 SQUADRON

Tempy. Lt.-)(P) O.H. Cantrill (act)
Com. (A),   ) (In Command)
R.N.V.R.   )
Sub-Lt. (A)...(P) M.C. Nicholson
        (P) D. Grant

751 SQUADRON

Lt.Com.,)
R.N.R. }(P) T.E. Sargent
Tempy. Lt.,)(P) H. Jones
(A),   ) (In Command)
R.N.V.R.)(P) G. Windsor

753 SQUADRON

Tempy.Lt.,)(P) F.R. Steggall (act)
Com. (A), } (In Command)
R.N.V.R.)
Tempy.Lt.,)(P) C.H. Dupere
(A),   )(P) J.L. Wordsworth
R.N.V.R.)(P) H.O. Haughton
        (P) R.G. Averill
        (P) W.E. Reynolds
        (P) G.R. Dence
        (P) J.D.R.G. Thomson
        (P) H.S. McKane

754 SQUADRON

Tempy.Lt.-)(P) D.A. Horton (act)
Com. (A),) (In Command)
R.N.V.R.)
Tempy. Lt.)(P) H.M. Pollock
(A),   )(P) T.B. Horsley
R.N.V.R.)(P) F.G. Hood
        (P) D.E.W. Hutchinson
        (P) E.H. Horn
        (P) J.L. Long
        (P) D.S. Appleyard
        (P) F.L. Haigh
Lt. (E)......(P) B. Goddard

767 SQUADRON

Lt.Com. ......(P) W.J. Mainprice (act)
        (In Command)
Lt. (A) .....(P) T.T. Miller
        (P) S.P. Luke
Tempy.,)(P) L.C. Watson,DSC
Lt. (A), }(P) J.L. Fisher
R.N.V.R.)

768 SQUADRON

Lt. (A).......(P) A.E.R. Wilkinson
Sub-Lt. (A)...(P) M.A. Lacayo

769 SQUADRON

Tempy.,)(P) D.L.R. Hutchinson
Lt. (A), }(P) R.D. Kingdon
R.N.V.R.)

740 Squadron 1944

753 Squadron 1944

754 Squadron

791 Squadron 1941

783 SQUADRON

Tempy. Lt.-
Com. (A),   )(P) R.P. Mason
R.N.V.R.   )   (In Command)
Lt.,   )(P) P.P. Pardoe-Mathews
R.N.R.   )
Tempy.,   )(P) D. Holdsworth
Lt. (A),   )(P) J.T. Howard
R.N.V.R.   )(P) J.A. Currie
             (P) A.N. Bardolph

791 SQUADRON

Tempy. Lt.-
Com. (A),   )(P) C.A. Crighton (act)
R.N.V.R.   )
Tempy.,   )
Lt. (A),   )(P) P.D. Eastham
R.N.V.R.   )

December 1943

740 SQUADRON

Lt. (A) ....(P) D.J. Cole
Tempy.   )(P) C.T.D. Hosegood
Lt. (A),   )(P) W.A.R. O'Connor
R.N.V.R.   )(P) S.C. Huxham
             (P) R.A.J. Lea

741 SQUADRON

Tempy. Lt.,)(P) O.H. Cantrill (act)
Com. (A),   )   (In Command)
R.N.V.R.   )
Tempy. ,   )
Lt. (A)   )(P) J.A. Higginson
R.N.V.R.   )

751 SQUADRON

Lt.-Com........(P) D.H. Angel (act)
               (In Command)
Lt.-Com.,   )
R.N.R.   )(P) T.E. Sargent
Lt. (A) ....(P) E.A. Humphreys
Tempy.,   )
Lt. (A),   )(P) W.R. Blatchley
R.N.V.R.   )
Tempy.   )
Lt. (A),   )(P) S.W. Richards
R.N.Z.N.V.R.)

753 SQUADRON

Tempy. Lt.·)(P) F.R. Steggall (act)
Com. (A),   )   (In Command)
R.N.V.R.   )

Tempy.,   )(P) C.H. Dupere
Lt. (A),   )(P) J.L. Wordsworth
R.N.V.R.   )(P) H.O. Haughton
             (P) J.J. Parker
             (P) W.E. Reynolds
             (P) G.R. Dence
             (P) J.D.R.G. Thomson
             (P) H.S. McKane
             (P) J.C. Fratter

754 SQUADRON

Tempy. Lt.-)(P) W.E. Davis (act)
Com. (A),   )   (In Command)
R.N.V.R.   )
Tempy. Lt.,)(P) F.G. Hood
(A),   )(P) D.E.W. Hutchinson
R.N.V.R.   )(P) E.H. Horn
             (P) D.S. Appleyard
             (P) A. Guthrie
             (P) W.A. Walls
Lt. (E).......(P) B. Goddard

767 SQUADRON

Tempy.,   )(P) L.C. Watson,DSC
Lt. (A),   )(P) J.L. Fisher
R.N.V.R.   )(P) D.L.R. Hutchinson

768 SQUADRON

Lt. (A).......(P) A.E.R. Wilkinson
Sub.Lt. (A)...(P) M.A. Lacayo

769 SQUADRON

Lt.-Com.(A).......S.P. Luke (act)
                 (In Command)
Tempy.   )(P) D.L.R. Hutchinson
Lt. (A),   )(P) J.T. Pratt
R.N.V.R.   )(P) R.T. Kingdon

783 SQUADRON

Tempy. Lt.-)(P) R.P. Mason (act)
Com. (A),   )   (In Command)
R.N.V.R.   )
Tempy. ,   )(P) J.T. Howard
Lt. (A),   )(P) J.P. Isserverdens
R.N.V.R.   )

791 SQUADRON

Tempy. Lt.-)
Com. (A),   )(P) C.A. Crighton (act)
R.N.V.R.   )
Tempy. ,   )
Lt. (A),   )(P) P.D. Eastham
R.N.V.R.   )

For (0) Duties and Course.

```
Lt. .........(0) A.S. Marshall
            (0) E.J. Treloar
            (0) C.H. Jeffery
Lt. (A) .....(0) A.D. Corkhill
            (0) G.S. Dormand
            (0) J.H.D. Tapscott
            (0) D.C. Fields
Tempy.      )(0) B. White,DSC
Lt. (A),    )(0) R.C. Neil
R.N.V.R.    )(0) S.S. Laurie
            (0) R.A.R. Wilson
            (0) J.A. Barnes
            (0) O.J. Griffith
            (0) F.W. Turner
            (0) B.E. Shaw
            (0) J.H. Lewis
```

February 1944

740 SQUADRON

```
Lt. (A)......(P) D.J. Cole
Tempy.,     )(P) C.T.D. Hosegood
Lt. (A),    )
R.N.V.R.    )(P) S.C. Huxham
```

741 SQUADRON

```
Tempy. Lt.- )
Com. (A),   )(P) O.H. Cantrill (act)
R.N.V.R.    )   (In Command)
Tempy.,     )
Lt. (A),    )(P) G.W. Sweeting
R.N.V.R.    )
Tempy.,     )
Lt. (A),    )(P) J.M. Chapman
R.N.Z.N.V.R.)
```

751 SQUADRON

```
Lt.Com. .....(P) D.H. Angel (act)
            (In Command)
Lt.Com.,    )
R.N.R.      )(P) T.E. Sargent
Lt. (A)......(P) E.A. Humphreys
Tempy,      )(P) W.R. Blatchley
Lt. (A),    )(P) J.U. Reid
R.N.V.R.    )(P) J.P. Issaverdens
Tempy.      )
Lt. (A),    )(P) S.W. Richards
R.N.Z.N.V.R.)
```

753 SQUADRON

```
Tempy. Lt.- )(P) F.R. Steggall (act)
Com. (A),   )   (In Command)
R.N.V.R.    )
```

```
Tempy.,     )(P) C.H. Dupere
Lt. (A),    )(P) J.L. Wordsworth
R.N.V.R.    )(P) H.O. Haughton
            (P) J.J. Parker
            (P) W.E. Reynolds
            (P) G.R. Dence
            (P) J.D.R.G. Thomson
            (P) H.S. McKane
            (P) H. Montgomery
```

754 SQUADRON

```
Tempy. Lt.- )(P) W.E. Davies (act)
Com. (A),   )   (In Command)
R.N.V.R.    )
Tempy.,     )(P) F.G. Hood
Lt. (A),    )(P) D.E.W. Hutchinson
R.N.V.R.    )(P) E.H. Horn
            (P) D.S. Appleyard
            (P) A. Guthrie
            (P) W.A. Walls
            (P) H.M. Fenelon
```

769 SQUADRON

```
Lt.-Com.(A).......S.P. Luke (act)
                (In Command)
Tempy. Sub.- )   J.M.C. Paton
Lt. (A),     )   (Acting Observer)
R.N.V.R.     )   N.F. Tolleton
```

783 SQUADRON

```
Tempy. Lt.- )(P) R.P. Mason
Com. (A),   )   (In Command)
R.N.V.R.    )
Tempy.      )
Lt. (A),    )(P) J.T. Howard
R.N.V.R.    )
```

791 SQUADRON

```
Tempy. Lt.- )
Com. (A),   )(P) C.A. Crighton (act)
R.N.V.R.    )
Tempy.,     )
Lt. (A),    )(P) P.D. Eastham
R.N.V.R.    )
Tempy.,     )
Lt. (A),    )(P) I.E. Sweeney
R.N.Z.N.V.R.)
```

For (0) Duties and Course.

```
Lt. ...........(0) A.S. Marshall
            (0) E.J. Treloar
            (0) C.H. Jeffery
Lt. (A)........(0) A.D. Corkhill
            (0) G.S. Dormand
            (0) J.H.G. Tapscott
```

Tempy.   )(O) B. White,DSC
Lt., (A),   )(O) R.C. Neil
R.N.V.R.   )(O) S.S. Laurie
           (O) R.A.R. Wilson
           (O) J.A. Barnes
           (O) A.J. Griffith
           (O) F.W. Turner
           (O) B.E. Shaw
           (O) L. Wilkings,DSC
           (O) D.H. Stokes

June 1944

740 SQUADRON

Tempy.   )
Lt., (A),   )(P) N.R. Walker
R.N.V.R.   )
Tempy. Sub-   )
Lt. (A),   )(P) G.H. Parker
R.N.Z.N.V.R.)

741 SQUADRON

Tempy. Lt.-   )
Com. (A),   )(P) R. McA. Stratton (act)
R.N.V.R.   )   (In Command)
Tempy.,   )
Lt. (A),   )(P) J.M. Chaplin
R.N.Z.N.V.R.)

751 SQUADRON

Lt.-Com.,   )(P) T.E. Sargent, RD
R.N.R.   )   (In Command)
Tempy.   )(P) W.R. Blatchley
Lt. (A),   )(P) L.F. Thame
R.N.V.R.   )(P) S.A. Green
           (P) J.C. Kennedy
           (P) E.N. Shearly
Tempy,   )(P) S.W. Richards
Lt. (A),   )(P) R.W.M. Williams
R.N.Z.N.V.R.)

753 SQUADRON

Tempy. Lt.-   ) R.E. Stewart (act)
Com. (A),   ) (In Command)
R.N.V.R.   )(P) J.J. Parker (act)
Tempy.,   )(P) C.H. Dupere
Lt. (A),   )(P) J.L. Wordsworth
R.N.V.R.   )(P) H.O. Haughton
           (P) J.D.R.G. Thomson
           (P) H.S. McKane
           (P) D.S. Appleyard
           (P) D.E.W. Hutchinson
           (P) R. Shirley-Smith

754 SQUADRON

Tempy. Act.,   )(P) J.G.V. Burns
Sub-Lt.(A),   )(P) D.C. Pritchard
R.N.V.R.   )(P) K.H.J. Fletcher

783 SQUADRON

Tempy. Lt.-   )
Com. (A),   )(P) R.P. Mason
R.N.V.R.   )   (In Command)
Tempy.,   )(P) T.J. Howard
Lt.(A),   )(P) D.R. Walker
R.N.V.R.   )(P) E.G. Pearce

791 SQUADRON

Tempy. Lt.-   )(P) A.P.T. Piersscne (act
Com. (A),   ) (In Command)
R.N.V.R.   )
Tempy.   )
Lt. (A),   )(P) P.D. Eastham
R.N.V.R.   )
Tempy.   )
Lt. (A),   )(P) I.E. Sweeney
R.N.Z.N.V.R.)

For F.F.D. and Course.

Tempy.   )(P) S.W. Birse,DSC
Lt. (A),   )(P) K.G. Talbot
R.N.V.R.   )

For (O) Duties and Course.

Tempy. Lt.-   )
Com. (A),   )(O) T.D. Haskey,DSC (act)
R.N.V.R.   )
Lt. (A)........(O) D.J. Cook
           (O) T.A. de V. Hunt
Tempy.   )(O) D.J. Price
Lt. (A),   )(O) W.L. Orr
R.N.V.R.   )(O) D.O. Rees
           (O) T.E.R. Moore,DSC
           (O) D.W. Glassborow
           (O) J.M. Robertson,DSC
           (O) W.R. McPherson
           (O) N.P. Piercey
           (O) A. Eckersley

October 1944

737 SQUADRON

Tempy. Lt.-   )(O) L.F. Dunne (act)
Com. (A),   ) (In Command)
R.N.V.R.   )(P) A. Baker
           (P) A. Wilkinson

Stinson Reliant

De Haviland Sea Devon

Sea Fury

De Haviland Tiger Moth

Vickers Wellington

Walrus

Grumman Widcat

```
Tempy. Lt.,          )(P) A.J. Tanner              (P) C.A. Stroud
R.C.N.V.R.           )                             (P) D.R. Carter
Tempy.,              )(O) F.G.V. Hanroth           (O) J.R. Home
Lt. (A),             )     (act)                   (O) R.L.R. Morgan
R.N.V.R.             )(O) W.W.N. Balkwill           (O) D.E. Johnson
                     )     DSC (act)
                      (O) J.T. Teesdale        783 SQUADRON
                      (O) K.A. Austin (act)
                      (O) I.P.M. Macdonald     Tempy. Lt.-)(P) T.B. Horsley (act)
                          (act)                Com. (A),  )    (In Command)
                      (O) K.E.J. Tyell (act)   R.N.V.R.   )(P) A.T.C. Hazledine (act)
                      (O) A.J. Snelgrove (act)            )(P) J.T. Howard (act)
                                               Tempy.,    )(P) D.R. Walker
741 SQUADRON                                   Lt. (A),   )(P) E.G. Pearce
                                               R.N.V.R.   )
Tempy. Lt.-          )(P) R. McA. Stratton (act)
Com.   (A),          )    (In Command)         787 SQUADRON
R.N.V.R.             )
Tempy.,              )(P) R. Williams          Tempy. Lt.,)(P) P.H. Williams (act)
Lt. (A),             )(P) A.G. Coles           R.N.V.R.   )
R.N.V.R.             )                         Tempy.Lt.- )(P) J.D. Buchanan
Tempy.,              )                         Com. (A),  )(P) J.M. Richmond
Lt. (A),             )(P) J.M. Chaplin         R.N.V.R.   )(O) D.J.Keating
R.N.Z.N.V.R.         )
                                               791 SQUADRON
753 SQUADRON
                                               Tempy. Lt.-)(P) A.T.P. Pierssene (act)
Tempy.               )(P) R.E. Steward (act)   Com. (A),  )    (In Command)
Lt.Com. (A),         )    (In Command)         R.N.V.R.   )
R.N.V.R.             ) (P) J.J.Parker (act)    Tempy.,    )
Tempy.,              )(P) J.D.R.G. Thomson     Lt. (A),   )(P) P.D. Eastham
Lt. (A),             )(P) H.S. McKane          R.N.V.R.   )
R.N.V.R.             )(P) D.S. Appleyard       Tempy,     )
                      (P) R. Shirley-Smith     Lt. (A),   )(P) I.E. Sweeney
                      (P) H.A. Epps            R.N.Z.V.N.R)
                      (P) W.A. Allkins
                      (P) A.C. Pitman          For F.F.D. and Course.
Tempy. ,             )(P) S.W. Richards
Lt. (A),             )(P) D. Dorizac           Tempy.,    )(P) S.W. Birse,DSC
R.N.Z.N.V.R.         )                         Lt. (A),   )(P) I.H.M. Gunn
                                               R.N.V.R.   )
754 SQUADRON
                                               For (O) Duties and Course.
Tempy. Act.          )(P) J.G.V. Burnes
Sub-Lt. (A),         )(P) D.C. Pritchard       Lt. Com.....(O) C.L.F. Webb (act)
R.N.V.R.             )(P) K.H.J. Fletcher      Lt. (A).....(O) D.J. Cook
                                                           (O) I.A. de V. Hunt
778 SQUADRON                                               (O) C.H. Pain
                                               Tempy.     )(O) W.L. Orr
Lt.Com..........(O) P.B. Schondfeldt (act)     Lt. (A),   )(O) D.O. Rees
                    (In Command)               R.N.V.R.   )(O) T.F.R. Moore,DSC
Lt. (A).........(P) L.R. Tivy                              (O) W.R. McPherson
                (P) P.G. Lawrence                          (O) N.I. Piercey
                (P) J.R.N. Gardner                         (O) A. Eckersley
Tempy.          )(P) J.F. Urquhart                             K. Chapelow
Lt. (A),        )(P) E.S. Morrell                             (Acting Observer)
R.N.V.R.        )(P) A.C. Powell
                (P) D.P. Adamson
                (P) J.F. Underwood
```

January 1945

737 SQUADRON

Lt.-Com. (A).....(O) G.J. Staveley (act)
                 (In Command)
Tempy. Lt.-   )(P) A. Baker
Com. (A),   )(P) A. Wilkinson
R.N.V.R.   )
Tempy.,   )(O) F.G.V. Hanrott
Lt. (A),   )(O) K.A. Austin (act)
R.N.V.R.   )(O) I.P.M. MacDonald
               (O) K.E.J. Tyrrell (act)
               (O) A.J. Snelgrove
               (P) L.T. Radford
               (O) J.M. Hutton (act)
               (O) D. O'D. Newbery
               (O) M. Powell (act)
Tempy. Sub-   )(P) F.R. Patterson
Lt. (A),   )(P) E. Goss
R.N.V.R.   )   A.C. Langham
                  (Acting Observer)
               (P) R.S.J. Morgan

741 SQUADRON

Tempy. Lt.-   )(P) R. McA. Stratton (act)
Com. (A),   )   (In Command)
R.N.V.R.   )
Tempy.   )(p) R. Williams
Lt. (A),   )(P) A.G. Coles
R.N.V.R.   )(P) S.D. Clayton
Tempy.   )
Lt. (A),   )(P) J.M. Chaplin
R.N.Z.N.V.R.   )

753 SQUADRON

Tempy. Lt-   )(P) R.E. Stewart (act)
Com. (A),   )   (In Command)
R.N.V.R.   )(P) J.J. Parker (act)
Tempy.   )(P) J.D.R.G. Thomson
Lt. (A),   )(P) H.S. McKane
R.N.V.R.   )(P) D.S. Appleyard
               (P) R. Shirley-Smith
               (P) H.A. Epps
               (P) A.C. Pitman
               (P) P.D. Eastham
               (P) E.H.G. Child

778 SQUADRON

Lt.-Com........(O) P.B. Schondfeldt (act)
               (In Command)
Lt. (A)........(P) L.R. Tivy
               (P) J.R.N. Gardner
Tempy.   )(P) J.P. Urquart
Lt. (A),   )(P) E.S. Morrell
R.N.V.R.   )(P) A.C. Powell
               (P) D.P. Adamson

(P) J.F. Underwood
(P) C.A. Stroud
(P) D.R. Carter
(O) J.R. Hone
(O) R.L.R. Morgan
(O) D.F. Johnson
(P) A.B.B. Clark
(O) E.G. Richardson
(P) J. Elliot

783 SQUADRON

Tempy. Lt.-   )(P) T.B. Horsley (act)
Com. (A),   )   (In Command)
R.N.V.R.   )(P) A.T.C. Hazledine (act)
Tempy Lt.,   )(P) J.W. Stewart
R.C.N.V.R.   )(P) L.F. Page
Tempy.   )
Lt. (A),   )(P) L.A.C. Madley
R.N.V.R.   )

For F.F.D. and Course.

Lt. (A).......(P) G.H.P. Hunt
Tempy.,   )
Lt. (A),   )(P) S.W. Birse,DSC
R.N.V.R.   )
Tempy.,   )
Lt. (A),   )   C. Honore
R.N.Z.N.V.R.   )

For (O) Duties and Course.

Lt. Com. (A)   )(O) P.H. Phillips,DSC (act)
R.N.V.R.   )
Lt. (A).......(O) P.D. Lloyd
               (O) R.V. Hinton
               (O) M.S. Cardwell
               (O) C.H. Pain
Tempy. Lt.,   )(O) T.A. Wilson
(A),   )(O) G.M. Evans
R.N.V.R.   )(O) R.O. Bonnett
               (O) K.L. Jones
               (O) H. Taylor
               (O) T.S. Hall
               (O) A.D. Midgley
               (O) S.S. Laurie
Tempy.,   )
Lt. (A),   )(O) D.K. McIntosh
S.A.N.F.(V)   )

April 1945

737 SQUADRON

Tempy. Lt.-   )(O) F.V. Jones (act)
Com.,   )   (In Command)
R.N.V.R.   )
Tempy,   )(O) I.P.M. MacDonald
Lt. (A),   )(O) K.E.J. Tyrrell
R.N.V.R.   )(O) A.J. Snelgrove

154

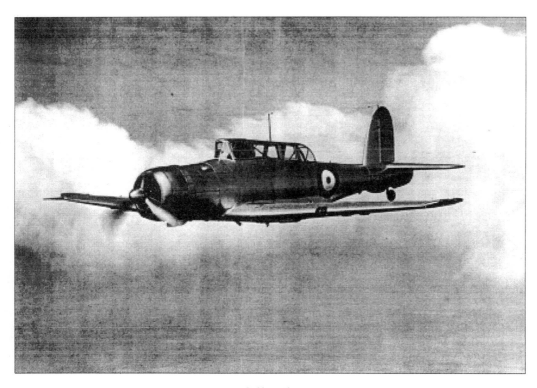

Blackburn Skua

Sea Prince

```
                    (P) L.T. Radford              Tempy.,     )(P) L.A.C. Madley
                    (0) J.M. Hutton (act)         Lt. (A),    )(P) (P) S.W. Mings
                    (0) D.O'D. Newbery            R.N.V.R.    )
                    (0) M. Powell (act)
                    (0) S.C. Yeo                  For F.F.D. and Course.
                    (0) S.C. Abel
                    (0) J.R. Culshaw (act)        Tempy.,     )(P) S.W. Birse, DSC
                    (0) A.S. Le Good              Lt. (A),    )(P) A.R. Astin
                    (0) D. Fairbairn (act)        R.N.V.R.    )(P) J. Robertson
                    (P) A. Wilkinson                          (P) C.E. Price
```

741 SQUADRON

```
Tempy.,          )(P) R. Williams
Lt. (A),         )(P) A.G. Coles
R.N.V.R.         )
Tempy. Sub-      )
Lt. (A),         )(P) L.F. Harper
R.N.V.R.         )
```

753 SQUADRON

```
Tempy. Lt.-      )(P) R.E. Stewart (act)
Com. (A),        )   (In Command)
R.N.V.R.         )(P) J.J. Parker (act)
Tempy.,          )(P) J.D.R.G. Thomson (act)
Lt. (A),         )(P) H.S. McKane
R.N.V.R.         )(P) A.C. Pitman
                 (P) P.D. Eastham
                 (P) E.H.G. Child
                 (0) G.M. Evans
Tempy. Lt. (A)   )(P) J.M. Chaplin
R.N.Z.N.V.R.     )
```

778 SQUADRON

```
Lt. Com........(P) E.M. Britton (act)
                  (In Command
Lt. (A)........(P) L.R. Tivy
               (P) J.R.N. Gardner
Tempy.,        )(P) D.P. Adamson
Lt. (A),       )(P) C.A. Stroud
R.N.V.R.       )(0) R.L.R. Morgan
               (P) A.B.B. Clark
               (0) E.G. Richardson
               (P) J. Elliot
               (P) S.N. Harris
               (P) W.N. Preston
               (0) A. Hutchinson
               (P) J. Swift
Tempy.Lt.(A),  )(P) I.D. Scades
R.N.Z.N.V.R.   )
```

783 SQUADRON

```
Tempy. Lt.-    )(P) T.B. Horsley (act)
Com. (A),      )   (In Command)
R.N.V.R.       )(P) A.I.C. Hazledine (act)
Tempy. Lr.,    )(P) J.W. Stewart
R.C.N.V.R..    )(P) L.F. Page
```

July 1945

737 SQUADRON

```
Lt. (A),       )
R.N.V.R.       )(0) M. Powell (act)
```

741 SQUADRON

```
Tempy.,        )
Lt. (A),       )(P) A.G. Coles
R.N.V.R.       )
Tempy. Sub-    )
Lt. (A),       )(P) L.F. Harper
R.N.V.R.       )
```

753 SQUADRON

```
Tempy. Lt.-    )(P) R.E. Stewart (act)
Com. (A),      )   (In Command)
R.N.V.R.       )(P) J.J. Parker (act)
Lt. (A).......(0) H.E. Rumble
Tempy.,        )(P) J.D.R.G. Thomas
Lt. (A),       )(P) H.S. McKane
R.N.V.R.       )(P) P.D. Eastham
               (P) E.H.G. Child
               (P) A.H. Steel
               (P) A.M. Palmer
```

778 SQUADRON

```
Lt. Com......(P) E.M. Britton (act)
                (In Command)
Tempy.,        )(P) D.P. Adamson
Lt. (A),       )(P) C.P. Stroud
R.N.V.R.       )(P) A.B.B. Clark
               (0) E.G. Richardson
               (P) J. Elliot
               (P) S.N. Harris
               (P) W.N. Preston
               (0) A. Hutchinson
               (P) J. Swift
               (0) D.J. Keating
               (0) K.L. Jones
               (P) D.A. Stevenson
                  (D.L.C.O. Duties)
Tempy.Lt.(A),  )(P) I.D. Scanes
R.N.Z.N.V.R.   )
```

<u>783 SQUADRON</u>

Tempy. Lt.- Com. (A), R.N.V.R.	)	(P) T.B. Horsley (act) (In Command)
Tempy., Lt. (A), R.N.V.R.	)))	(P) L.A.C. Madley (P) S.W. Mings (P) J.S. Wagstaff (P) H.D. Glendinning (P) J.W. Reader

For F.F.D. and Course.

Tempy., Lt. (A), R.N.V.R.	)))	(P) S.W. Birse,DSC (P) A.R. Astin

<u>October 1945</u>

<u>737 SQUADRON</u>

Tempy. Lt.- Com., R.N.V.R.	)))	F.V. Jones (act) (In Command)
Tempy., Lt. (A), R.N.V.R.	))	(O) M. Powell (act)

<u>741 SQUADRON</u>

Tempy. Lt. (A), R.N.V.R.	)	(P) A.G. Coles
Tempy. Sub- Lt. (A), R.N.V.R.	)))	(P) L.F. Harper

<u>753 SQUADRON</u>

Lt.Com. (A)......(P) A.J. Phillips (act)		
		(In Command)
		(P) J.J. Parker (act)
Lt. (A).........(O) H.E. Rumble		
Tempy., Lt. (A), R.N.V.R.	)))	(P) P.D. Eastham (P) E.H.G. Child (P) A.M. Palmer

<u>783 SQUADRON</u>

Tempy. Lt.- Com. (A), R.N.V.R.	)))	(P) T.B. Horsley (act) (In Command)
Tempy. , Lt. (A), R.N.V.R.	)))	(P) L.A.C. Madley (P) S.W. Mings (P) J.S. Wagstaff (P) R.H. Owen (P) A.W. Goadby

For F.F.D. and Course.

Tempy. Lt. (A), R.N.V.R.	))	(P) S.W. Birse,DSC

<u>July 1947</u>

<u>783 SQUADRON</u>

Lt. Com. (A).....(P) A.M. Tuke (act)		
Lt. (A)............B. Lee		
		G. Jones
		D.O. Rees
Tempy. Lt. (A), R.N.V.R.	))	(P) W.E. Byrne

<u>January 1948</u>

<u>772 SQUADRON</u>

Lt. (A).........(P) D.M. Rouse	
	(P) W.C. Larkins
	(P) M.D. Stanley
	(P) N.L. Sharrock
	(O) N. Clark
	(O) J.R. Mably

<u>April 1948</u>

<u>772 SQUADRON</u>

Lt. (A)..........(P) D.M. Rouse	
	(P) W.C. Larkin
	(P) M.D. Stanley
	(P) N.L. Sharrock
	(P) H.J.E. Wombwell
	(O) N. Clark
	(O) J.R. Mably

<u>July 1948</u>

Lt.-Com..........(P) C.H. Filmer	
	(In Command)
Lt. (A)..........(P) D.M. Rouse	
	(P) W.C. Larkins
	(P) M.D. Stanley
	(P) N.L. Sharrock
	(O) N. Clark
	(O) J.R. Mably
	(O) J.T.R. Dutton

<u>October 1948</u>

<u>772 SQUADRON</u>

Lt. (A)..........(P) W.C. Larkins	
	(In Command)
	(P) M.D. Stanley
	(O) N. Clark
	(O) J.R. Mably
	(O) J.T.R. Dutton

Chapter 5

Apprentices

This is a very clear portrayal of apprentice life. A change of names and dates and it could be any apprentice...............

1940 - REFLECTIONS - HMS CONDOR - RNAS ARBROATH.

I was one of the 180 young lads of 15/16 years of age who joined the Fleet Air Arm on the 11th August 1945 at the RN Stockheath Camp (site 2) at Bedhampton, near Havant in Hampshire, named HMS DAEDALUS 3. We joined as Naval Aircraft Artificer Apprentices and formed JERVIS DIVISION, undertaking initial training there of drill, lectures and sport etc., whilst kitting up in ' fore and aft rig' and marking same. We were taken on trips to see HMS VICTORY, Fleetlands Aircraft Repair Yard, and a short flight in a Lancaster Bomber from RAF Thorney Island. In charge of us was a fearsome elderly Chief GI 'Killer' Kent, assisted by another Chief GI named Dyer. Four days after joining VJ DAY was declared (which made us wonder if we were really the ultimate deterrent and not the atom bomb!) and at the end of that month we were split in two groups with one half going west to HMS FISGARD at Torpoint in Cornwall, and the others (myself included) northwards on the overnight train via London and Edinburgh, to Rosyth. Here we joined HMS CALEDONIA the RN Artificer Training Establishment (RNATE) and commenced our schooling and technical training for the next ten months, as 'temporary lodgers'; and being Fleet Air Arm (Airy Fairies) we were looked upon as 'untouchables' by the ERA/EA and OA (Fish-head) Apprentices whose establishment it was! My prime memory of this place was learning to swim by being made to jump off the top diving-board at the swimming pool and left to flounder, after the seemingly endless drop through air and water! (PTIs with long wooden rods were at hand to hook out those attempting to drown!)

On June 29th next year (1946) we moved further north, again by rail ,to Arbroath where at HMS CONDOR we were reunited with our other half, officially joining on the 30th. (It was whilst marching at the Drum Head Service for the 1996 CONDOR REUNION that I realised that it was exactly fifty years ago to the day that we had joined RNAS ARBROATH.) As CONDOR was then just starting up as a training establishment (previously FAA Apprentice training having been carried out at Newcastle - under - Lyme). I recall that for the first few days we had to set up work benches in the factory and school furnishings etc., Although this station had ceased being a front-line flying establishment, there was still a certain amount of air activity, with a Station Flight and Reserve Squadrons , plus gliding. We were to remain here for the next three years, completing our four years apprenticeship. The majority were, like myself, 'engines and airframes' trade, although at one stage (quickly abandoned after a short while) we were being taught 'electrical and ordnance' also, but some of our division were exclusive to those latter two trades.

As we were arriving at HMS CONDOR the senior Division HOOD were about to pass out on completion of training, which then left Raleigh as the seniors (H Class), followed by EFFINGHAM, KEPPEL, COCHRANE and then our JERVIS Division, with six-monthly intervals between each, and then DRAKE came next. From now on however, with the war over, the entry numbers were reduced from the usual 180 or so who previously went through the system. (these same names were revived for later intakes, so another JERVIS Division came along a few years later.) To complicate matters, at CONDOR they

Section of a Meteor before assembly to fuselage

Front - Attacker Fuselage.
(This A/C used in the film "The Sound Barrier")
Sea Vampire.
2 Sea Fires.
Sea Otter Fuselage & Otter fuselage in centrre.

An Instructor Officer explains the behaviour of an aerofoil

Tailplane now assembled to Meteor - early 1950's

Chief Craxton supervising Meteor Tailplane assembly

Apprentices study an Attacker airframe

devised a scheme which, if I remember rightly didn't last long either, of taking classes out of each entry to create separate Divisions which would contain apprentices of mixed ages, and these were designated as BLAKE, COLLINGWOOD, EXMOUTH and HAWKE Divisions (I was in COLLINGWOOD, but our loyalties always remained with your own entry connections!)

It was a constant round of Parade drill, school studies, technical training in the large factory (sheet-metal work, fitting and turning, welding, fabric repairing, engine operation, etc.) with plenty of sport added. There was also religious instructions under the watchful eyes of 'The Rover Gover' (Chaplain Thomas E. Gover) who roamed the camp in a black cloak, and in his spare time ran a 'Rover Scout' group. His assistant was the Reverend Gilbert Wall's Webster who was as tall and thin as the other was short and 'rotund', rather like a ' Laurel and Hardy ' combination! (For RC's it was Father B. Cunningham , and for 'Wee Frees' the Rev. F. Street). Of the other characters of that time, I recall that our Commander (Cdr. (E) J.E. Esmonde OBE, DSC) was the brother of a wartime FAA pilot Lt. Cdr. Eugene Esmonde RN. of 825 Squadron who won the VC posthumously for attacking the German SCHARNHORST and GNEISENAU; and the much feared Coxswain (CPO Bradbury) was referred to as 'The Swine', and who according to the apprentices was formerly a warder at Glasgow's Barlinnie Jail, particularly by the defaulters who nightly had to double round the parade ground wearing a steel helmet and carrying a rifle! Of the WRENS I remember one called 'Timber' (Woods?) who was a regular comedienne of the Joyce Grenfell type, and took part in concerts and plays. On the instrumental side was CPO Joe Riley (teaching propellers and the internal combustion engine), CPO 'Viscosity' Clark (hydraulics), and the civilian metal-work teacher Hughie Hodges who, whilst warning a class to be careful when operating the sheet metal guillotine, accidentally cut off some of his own fingers! He was a keen footballer, and ran a local team. I also recall a civvie messman called 'Dave', who was very good to us lads in the dining hall. One of my colleagues recalled German POW's being employed to clear the snow from roads in the camp that first winter of '46/ '47, and I do know that there were a lot of them in the Arbroath area, working on farms etc., some of whom stayed on after the war and married local girls.

Because of the shortage of accommodation, our division were later that year made to move our bedding out to East Haven Camp, the former RNAS HMS PEEWIT (at one time CONDOR 2), about three miles south of Arbroath, between the roadway and railway line to Dundee. If you are lucky you got a bus ride to CONDOR morning and night, otherwise it was the back of a three ton lorry more often than not! This camp was run by a CPO Davidson, who later, I believe, married into the Swankie fishing family and took residence in Arbroath. It was during the severe winter of 1946/7 that we became snowed in at East Haven for a few days, giving some concern to our 'Masters' at CONDOR, since there was little store of provisions at this camp, and eventually the roadway was cleared part way to us, enabling lorries to transport bread and other victuals to a pick-up point which we managed to rendezvous on foot, and carry the goods back with the aid of some improvised sledges.

I don't recall anyone of us being in the least concerned at our predicament; rather it was all quite fun, and we had escaped lessons and drill, which was a respite! One rather tall tale I recall is that the smokers were shaving the fluff off the blankets to roll into their 'tickler papers' in lieu of tobacco ... but I cannot vouch for that! Apart from all the travelling I didn't mind being at this satellite camp, despite the very basic Nissen hutted accommodation as compared to the relative comfort of the CONDOR dormitories; in fact it was a more relaxed routine there, particularly at weekends , and was easier to get to when going ashore to Dundee as there was then a station nearby, or a bus stopped at the end of the road about 500 yards away. There is little trace of this camp now ; just the odd building used by farmers as barns or storage huts. I imagine that we were only there about six months, because a new entry of apprentices came twice a year so we would no longer be the junior division (Sprogs) and thus moved back into CONDOR which at that time was a real show-piece, with the grounds kept immaculate and white-painted chains marking off the pathways , which regrettably bears no resemblance today! (My diary for 1949 mentions that I returned to sleeping at East Haven from the 9th January to 19th February).

Due to the labour shortage so soon after the war we were hired out to the local farmers during the summer to assist in 'Tattie-howking' (potato picking) which was definitely unpopular backbreaking work. The Navy took the bulk of the payment , but I received three shillings 'back-pay' for it on 17th February 1949, yet cannot recall how many days or hours I worked! There was one incident when a class rebelled because the tractor driver was coming round too fast, so they pelted him with ' tatties ' and then stopped work! They were immediately returned to the camp and had sore back-sides afterwards by a caning! There was also an annual pageant during the summer re-enacted at the Abbey, with a parade through the town, when a few of the lads volunteered to act as medieval soldiers or horsemen.

Whilst some will recall the town by the many pubs they frequented (names I recall are the 'Vaults' - 'Tutties Neuk' - 'Panmure' - 'Shakespeare' - and 'Thistle' plus the Marine Ballroom (now standing derelict), there was also a canteen for the Navy (which I helped prepare for opening) in Hill Street if I remember correctly, on the opposite side to the post office. However, my prime memories were of the excellent fish supper cafes (particularly Joe Dora's), and the smokies, haggis and mealie puddings etc.; plus the harbour activities and the cliff walks. There were then three cinemas in town, the Palace, Playhouse, and Olympia, and a frequent bus service to the camp from Kirk Square. Most of all, I remember those long overnight train journeys down south on leave, rushing to get on the special steam driven train first to grab the corner seats, and the subsequent hours spent in the smoke filled haze (no windows open of course!). periodically relieved when the train stopped at a station where, barely before the train halted, a mass of 'tiffies' leaped out onto the platform to rush at the tea trolleys positioned at intervals! I took note that we left Arbroath in one instance at 1745, to arrive Kings Cross at 0615 next morning, and on the return left at 1845 to arrive back in Arbroath at 0600. (Intercity trains are certainly better these days!). Sunday Divisions were regular on the parade ground, followed by compulsory church service in the gymnasium, (RC's and Non-Conformists having been fallen out beforehand), and at other times short services or prayers on the daily parades. Then we were allowed ashore after lunch; but as I had relations living out in the countryside at Carmyllie, many Sundays I walked the three miles out there for my lunch and tea. Saturday mornings were also, of course, working days then, so free time was only the weekend afternoons .... if you were not on 'extra factory' or some similar default on Saturdays!

Coach trips were sometimes organised to the Caird Hall in Dundee for concerts, and I went on at least two of these, seeing the great Italian tenor Gigli on one occasion, and the piano players Jose Iturbi and his sister Amparo on another. High tea was always booked at the Keillers Restuarant nearby beforehand. I believe these were organised by the EVT section, but recall on one occasion at least that 'Rover Gover' was i/c of the run. This reminds me that the EVT room, at the western end of the long Nissen hut at the top end of the Senior Rates rows of huts (near the sickbay where the road leads to the Wardroom), was a favourite place for me to look in, to read 'Ditty Box' and other expensive magazines that I could ill-afford to buy! When I returned in 1955 I believe that this had become the 'Buffers Store'.

I joined the camp's Choral Society which held rehearsals over the road in 'Woodville House', occupied by the Wrens (in addition to huts behind 'the wailing wall' in the main camp). On one occasion a coach outing was organised by this group to Glen Clova, which I thoroughly enjoyed. The only other occupation I can recall here was as church organist, alternating with a CPO Adams. From my 1949 diary, I also note that I went fire-fighting somewhere near Brechin on April 11th; sweets came off the ration on April 24th; I went on a gunnery course at Barry Ranges 15-18 June; our Divisional dance was held on Sunday June 26th and the 'Passing Out Parade' in a hangar, due to wet weather routine, on Tuesday 28th. We were to miss the 'Open Day' (Air Day) scheduled for July 20th.

On the 29th of June, all those successful on the course set off on draft to various ships or shore bases to complete a minimum 14 years service (including two years as boys), and in my case it was to RNAS Stretton, near Warrington (HMS BLACKCAP), rising at 0430 for a 0645 departure and arrival at 'BLACK-CAP' at 1700. On the 6th July those who joined me on this draft saw the Captain to be rated Aircraft Artificer 5th class, and proudly sewed a hook on our sleeves! This was not to be my last contact with Arbroath however, for I was destined to return to CONDOR on the 8th June 1956, this time on the staff! The CONDOR Apprentices had their own military band, and an excellent dance band, most of whom (including the singer Roy Nutley) belonged to my Division (JERVIS), In the 'Brass Section' were 'Taff' Jones, (now living in OZ), Dickie Lawes (Arbroath), 'Lofty' Arnold (Lancs), and Joe Harrild (deceased); 'Reeds Section' Tony Cooke (Woking), Jock Aird (Dorchester) and Bob Gravestock. On Drums 'Fishy' Lowe (Gloucester), Double Bass was 'Virgo' Vernon-Jones, and the leader on piano was 'Plonk' Underhill. Gravestock and 'Suds' Sutherland (on guitar) were not of our division.

Apprentices also had their own vocabulary which I believe we inherited from the ' Fish-head Tiffies' of CALEDONIA and FISGARD, as per some examples:-

'Goss ' (uniform cap).
'Buck' ((Camp cinema).
'Gobbi' (Civilian cleaner). and
'Lobs' (watch/look out) !!!

The bright boys amongst us were given promotion in the final 18 months of training as F-G and H Classes, and a 'Leading App.' had an inverted chevron on the lower end of one sleeve; the 'Petty Officer

App.' one inverted chevron that included a star, and the 'CPO App.' a chevron plus star on both sleeves, and they were known as 'Hook Boys', or in the case of the latter it was 'Chief Hook'. There were four 'Chief Hooks' in our Division, and this rank was only given in the senior term (H Class), as a Division came and left every six months. Ours were Gerry 'Snip' Cotton, Joe Barrett, Derek Silas Algar and M. W. 'Ben' Tillett, with the first named being the senior one.

At CALEDONIA (as at FISGARD also I am told) the ' Fish-head Hook Boys ' operated like the prefects of public schools and had the younger lads 'fagging for them'. I remember being caught by one and given some menial task to do but did nothing about it , and on being rounded up later I received a 'tanning on the backside' in the 'Hooks Room' (amongst their gathering). This practice did not operate at CONDOR I am glad to say, to the best of my knowledge, so we did not walk in fear of the 'Hook Boys' there! Several years ago there was a film THE GRUDGE FIGHT on TV written by an ex-Tiffy John Hale who served at HMS FISGARD as an apprentice, which depicted the bullying tactics of the 'Hook Boys' of H Class there, but I am certain nothing of that sort happened at CONDOR during my three years at least, nor during my later two years on the staff.

No self-respecting apprentice wore his uniform cap straight from stores in our days; there was the ritual of cutting an inch or so from the 'grommet', then soaking the cap in hot water, and tying it up in a large cloth to bend it into shape and then left to dry out, so that it resembled more the cap of the German SS! I recall once on Divisions hearing the Captain say to the Commander, as he inspected us, "What do they do with these caps ..... boil them?". Some were also to 'gussets' sewn into uniform trouser leg bottoms to give a wider flare, but were often caught and reprimanded for it!

We missed out on the war medal by a few days (the previous entry 'COCHRANE DIVISION' who joined in January 1945 did get it), but we did qualify for 'War Gratuity' and received seven pounds one shilling on the 31st October 1946! At the fortnightly payment we picked up 11 shillings , but part payment was held back for leave periods. We were not therefore 'big spenders', and I recall the horror of once having to borrow a shilling to get a haircut.

By the time that I returned to CONDOR on the 8th June 1956 , I was now promoted to AA2 rank and thus accommodated in the CPO's Mess, with a cabin in the new two-storey block up near the sickbay, and I was attached to the 'Training Aids' section in the factory which was producing models and other practical aids for classrooms. I was also on the duty roster for supervising the apprentices at meal times, which entailed sleeping in a cabin of 'A' block (opposite the parade ground) to do night rounds and "wakey-wakey" morning calls. Thus I had come full circle! I recall that by this time the establishment was not solely for apprentices but also Air Mechanicians and other branches.

I joined the CADS (amateur dramatic society) and performed in three plays there; 'ON MONDAY Next' (Dec 1956), 'Simon AND LAURA ' (Mar '57), both comedies, and the Agatha Christie thriller "The HOLLOW" (Dec '57), by which time my next draft had already come through, and I left on January 17th following to join HMS EAGLE at Devonport.

My only other claim to fame here was sharing the Herbert Lott Trust Fund Award for 1957 with Chief Cook Jackson; he for the construction of field kitchens, and I for organising a group of 'faked casualties' for an Admiralty film on the after-effects of an enemy attack. I recall visiting several butchers in the area to get hold of large bones, and added to this were plaster-cast broken limbs etc., all swilled down with gallons of red ochre to make up a scene of total devastation in an old derelict building on the airfield. I also joined the 'casualties' (of whom the only one I can recall by name was an electrical rating 'Sandy' Hindmarsh) and was told afterwards that quite a few of the matelots sent in to 'rescue' us were unprepared for what they met , and became a little 'off-colour'! That last remark reminds me that I was a patient in the sickbay for four weeks with a severe case of Glandular Fever, and being looked after by Nursing Sister Pat Gould, who later went on to be the senior nurse at Haslar Hospital.

COMMANDING OFFICERS.
During my first stay at CONDOR, the Captain was B.H. Cronk DSC. and the Commander J.W. Esmonde OBE.DSC. (replaced by Cdr. M. Cursham on 23rd April 1947). On my second draft there it was Captain W.L.G.Porter and Cdr. R.A.H. Bartley RN.

JERVIS DIVISION PERSONALITIES.
Apart from the Dance Band aforementioned, we had some outstanding sportsmen: e.g. Sam Gilbert and 'Buzz' Hartfree (swimmers), Riley Curtis (shooting and basketball), Peter Ware and Brian Smith (hockey), Brian Chubb and Gary Smith (rugby), Dan Ferris, Alan Marsden, John Platts and Doug Asbury (football). Anyone overlooked - I beg forgiveness.
At least five of our number gained commissions, although none made it to senior positions. These were Tony Drake, Tony Hayward, 'Lofty' Elner, Alec Tizard and 'Doc' Hopkins.
We have held reunions at Portsmouth every five years since leaving the F.A.A., and five of us were in attendance at the '96 CONDOR Reunion.

Tony Perrett.

Apprentices on Parade 1946

Raleigh Division March Past 1946

Raleigh Division 1946

Division 1970

Vice Admiral Power Inspection - summer 1946

Divisions 1957

Captain Tanner, Lt/Cdr Michael Keen(e) 1960/61

Instructional Staff

Workshops Service.
C.A.A. P. Slater.
A.A. T. Baker.
A.A. G. A. Low.
A.A. D. A. Skeens.
A.A. E. V. Rollason.
A.A. H. Wilkshire.
A.A. B. C. Carrington.
E.R.A. C. Malkin.
E.R.A. J. Mitchell.
E.R.A. H. Tait.
E.R.A. H. Thomson.
A/Mech. D. Benjamin.
A/Mech. R. Bonney.
A/Mech. L. C. Bennett.
A/Mech. S. Davidson.
A/Mech. D. Mackay.
A/Mech. R. Starkie.
A/Mech. G. T. C. Gee.
A/Mech. E. R. Jennings.
A/Mech. J. A. Glyde.

Workshops—Civilian.
Mr. F. E. Allum.
Mr. J. Burns.
Mr. F. Florence.
Mr. W. Guild.
Mr. H. Hodgens.
Mr. W. Hood.
Mr. R. Jones.
Mr. J. Mackay.
Mr. R. Mackay.
Mr. R. Miller.
Mr. J. Morrison.
Mr. J. Roark.
Mr. W. Smith.
Mr. A. Stewart.
Mr. C. Yule.

'A' Section.
C.A.A. D. McLeod.
A.A. G. Wilkins.
A.A. A. Kirkman.
A.A. C. Bourne.
A.A. A. Fuller.
A.A. D. Westlake.
A.A. S. R. Hands.
A.A. P. Sparks.
A/Mech. S. D. Hardwick.
A/Mech. J. Youngs.
A/Mech. J. Glyde.

'O' Section.
C.A.A.(O) J. V. Harley.
C.A.A.(O) M. Ayling.
A.A.(O) N. F. Curnow.
A.A.(O) M. Wheeler.
A.A.(O) T. Radley.
A/Mech. C. E. Gray.

'E' Section.
C.A.A. S. Dolman.
C.A.A. W. Brown.
A.A. D. Freeman.
A.A. R. Crate.
A.A. T. E. Evans.
A.A. R. F. Skipworth.
A.A. D. Rollo.
A.A. F. A. Bryant.
A.A. D. G. Humphrey.
A/Mech. A. Heald.
A/Mech. S. J. O'Neill.

Flight Servicing.
C.A.A. J. T. Milne.
A.A. M. E. Bliss.
A.A. F. Mundy.
A.A. D. J. Read.
A.A. V. N. Cavill.
A/Mech. W. R. Munro.
A/Mech. G. Bezzant.

Examinations.
C.A.A. F. E. Jones.
A.A. A. Gutteridge.
A.A. J. Firth.

Training Aids.
A.A. D. Loving.
A.A. W. B. Stevenson.
A.A. T. C. McArthur.
A.A. A. J. Perrett.
A.A. L. E. Laver.
A.A. N. J. Bush.
A.A. A. W. Groves.
A/Mech. L. M. Woods.
A/Mech. W. E. Whalley.
A/Mech. E. Wimberley.

Training Maintenance.
A.A. L. G. Addy.
A.A. A. J. Martin.
A/Mech. J. McDiarmid.
C.A.E.(A) L. T. Brant.
P.O.A.F. R. R. Roose.
A/P.O.A.F. B. Jolliffe.

Parade Training.
C.P.O. G.I. J. E. O. Bartlett.
P.O. G.I. W. C. Brooks.
P.O. G.A.I R. O'Neill, D.S.M.*
P.O. A.F. D. Eldridge.

Physical Training.
C.P.O. P.T.I. P. J. Parkes.
P.O. P.T.I. J. Carnochan.
P.O. P.T.I. T. V. Smith.
Ldg. Sn. P.T.I. K. Martin.

S.A.M.C.O.
C.A.A. K. Clayton.
C.A.A. C. A. McCluskie.
C.A.A.(O) K. G. Sims.
A.A. A. P. Russell.
A.A. G. Adamson.
A.A. C. French.
A.A. F. R. S. Cumbleton.
A.A. J. Kitcatt.
A.A. P. Vella.
A.A. D. J. Richardson.
A.A. W. J. McKeon.
A.A. J. E. W. Hutchinson.
A.A. H. S. Tiffins.
A.A. P. G. Gray.
A.A. R. Hicks.
A.A. D. Walker.
A.A. D. G. W. Whyte.
A.A. J. A. Swift.
A.A.(O) J. W. Robertson.
E.A. D. E. Eames.
E.A. D. J. Burns.
A/Mech. K. Wardle.
A/Mech. K. B. Ashton.
A/Mech. P. J. T. Warren.
A/Mech. J. C. Williams.
A/Mech. J. B. Pollard.

H.M.S. "Condor"

Captain W. L. G. Porter—Commanding Officer.
Lieutenant M. E. Coleman—Captain's Secretary.

Commander R. A. H. Bartley—Executive Officer.
Commander J. E. Dyer-Smith—Commander (Training).
Commander G. Clarke—Supply Officer.
Instructor Commander J. C. Gascoigne, O.B.E., B.Sc., A.R.C.S., D.I.C.—Senior Instructor Officer.
Surgeon Commander P. S. Edgecombe, B.A., M.R.C.S., L.R.C.P., D.I.H.—Medical Officer.
Surgeon Lieutenant Commander (D) R. R. B. Gjertson, L.D.S.—Dental Officer.
Reverend J. R. W. Malkinson, M.A.—Chaplain.
First Officer J. S. Rae—Officer-in-Charge, W.R.N.S.

Executive Department.
Lieut. Cdr. J. E. Stevenson.
Lieut. Cdr. A. G. Mitchell.
Sub. Lieut. D. R. Bayley.
Sub. Lieut. J. Watson.

Air Department.
Lieut. Cdr. I. D. Roberts.

Communications Department.
Lieut. D. J. Donovan.

Training and Engineering Department.
Lieut. Cdr. D. W. Cramond.
Lieut. Cdr. D. C. Rowles.
Lieut. Cdr. L. F. Coulshaw.
Lieut. Cdr. J. F. Waterhouse.
Lieutenant K. E. A. Shattock.
Lieutenant R. Baker.
Lieutenant G. A. Prince.
Lieutenant D. G. Edwards.
Lieutenant L. P. Thomas.
Lieutenant D. S. J. Wightman.
Lieutenant J. Salter.
Sub. Lieut. C. Moore.
Sub. Lieut. F. Buckley.
Sub. Lieut. J. Colbeck.
Sub. Lieut. W. B. Putman.
Sub. Lieut. J. L. Freeman.

Instructional Department.
Inst. Lieut. Cdr. F. H. Crossman, B.Sc.
Inst. Lieut. Cdr. J. D. Christie, M.A.
Inst. Lieutenant R. Johnston, B.Sc.(Eng.).
Inst. Lieutenant D. R. Hub, B.Sc.
Inst. Lieutenant J. S. Lewis, B.Sc.
Inst. Lieutenant I. S. Young, B.Sc.
Inst. Lieutenant J. G. Gulliver, B.Sc., M.Sc.
Inst. Lieutenant D. Kidd, B.Sc.
Inst. Lieutenant F. S. Murfin, B.A., Ph.D.

Supply and Secretariat Department.
Lieut. Cdr. Smith.
Sub. Lieut. M. D. Maclean.
Sub. Lieut. J. G. Norfolk, B.E.M., M.H.C.I.
Sub. Lieut. M. C. Cawthorne.

Electrical Department.
Lieutenant J. E. Philpott.

Medical Department.
Surg. Lieut. K. J. Maclean, M.B., Ch.B.

W.R.N.S.
Third Officer Machonochie.

Q.A.R.N.S.
Snr. Nursing Sister P. Gould.

Flag Officer Reserve Aircraft

Staff of the Flag Officer Reserve Aircraft
Rear Admiral J. D. N. Ham, C.B.—Flag Officer Reserve Aircraft.
Lieutenant R. G. C. Smith—Flag Lieutenant.

Commander G. H. Moore—Admiral's Secretary.
Lieutenant Barnes—Assistant Secretary.
Captain E. C. Beard, M.I.Mech.E., A.F.R.Ae.S.—Chief Staff Officer.
Lieutenant D. H. Bates—Secretary to Chief Staff Officer.

Captain J. E. Langdon—Staff Supply Officer.

Commander V. C. Grenfell.
Commander A. E. Hargrave.
Commander H. J. S. Banks.
Commander F. H. Starks.
Lieut. Cdr. J. G. O. Hofman.
Lieut. Cdr. Sheppard.
Lieut. Cdr. R. H. Tremaine.
Lieut. Cdr. C. A. Johnson.
Lieut. Cdr. J. R. Pedder.
Lieut. Cdr. A. Greenhalgh.
Lieut. Cdr. D. A. Yeo.

Lieut. Cdr. H. J. Barnes.
Lieut. Cdr. H. A. Benner.
Squadron Leader G. G. Fowler.
Lieut. Cdr. A. Walker.
Lieut. Cdr. A. C. Kennedy.
Lieutenant J. C. Calderwood.
Sub. Lieut. B. A. Edgell.

W.R.N.S.
Chief Officer E. G. Lucas.
Third Officer W. H. Ness.

Instructional Staff

Workshops—Service.
C.A.A. P. Slater.
Ch.A.M. L. C. Bennet.
A.A. T. Baker.
A.A. G. A. Low.
A.A. E. V. Rollason.
A.A. H. Wilkshire.
A.A. B. C. Carrington.
A.A. S. J. Rayfield.
E.R.A. C. Malkin.
E.R.A. H. Tait.
E.R.A. H. Thomson.
E.R.A. E. Childs.
A/Mech. D. Benjamin.
A/Mech. R. Bonney.
A/Mech. S. Davidson.
A/Mech. D. Mackay.
A/Mech. R. Starkie.
A/Mech. J. A. Glyde.

Workshops—Civilian.
Mr. F. E. Allum.
Mr. J. Burns.
Mr. F. Florence.
Mr. W. Guild.
Mr. H. Hodgens.
Mr. W. Hood.
Mr. R. Jones.
Mr. A. Mackay.
Mr. R. Mackay.
Mr. R. Miller.
Mr. J. Morrison.
Mr. J. Ruark.
Mr. W. Smith.
Mr. A. Stewart.
Mr. C. Yule.

'A' Section.
C.A.A. D. McLeod.
A.A. G. Wilkins.
A.A. A. Kirkman.
A.A. C. Bourne.
A.A. A. Fuller.
A.A. D. Westlake.
A.A. S. R. Hands.
A.A. P. Sparks.
A/Mech. S. D. Hardwick.
A/Mech. J. Youngs.

'O' Section.
C.A.A.(O) E. Percival.
C.A.A.(O) M. Ayling.
A.A.(O) N. F. Curnow.
A.A.(O) M. Wheeler.
A.A. K. R. J. Brisley.
A.A. J. H. C. Caple.
A.A. P. G. Foster.
A/Mech. C. E. Gray.
A/Mech. R. W. Skeet.
C.A.F.(O) M. Catlow.

'E' Section.
C.A.A. W. Brown.
A.A. D. Freeman.
A.A. R. Crate.
A.A. R. F. Skipworth.
A.A. D. Rollo.
A.A. F. A. Bryant.
A.A. D. G. Humphrey.
A.A. D. S. Macey.
A/Mech. S. J. O'Neill.

Flight Servicing.
C.A.A. J. T. Milne.
A.A. M. E. Bliss.
A.A. F. Mundy.
A.A. D. J. Read.
A.A. V. N. Cavill.
A/Mech. W. R. Munro
A/Mech. G. Bezzant.

Examinations.
C.A.A. F. E. Jones.
A.A. A. Gutteridge.
A.A. J. Firth.

Training Aids.
A.A. D. Loving.
A.A. W. B. Stevenson.
A.A. T. C. McArthur.
A.A. A. J. Perrett.
A.A. L. E. Laver.
A.A. N. J. Bush.
A.A. A. W. Groves.
A/Mech. L. M. Woods.
A/Mech. W. E. Whalley.
A/Mech. E. Wimberley.
A/Mech. D. C. Blackman.
A/Mech. E. R. Jennings.
A/Mech. G. T. C. Gee.

Training Maintenance.
A.A. L. G. Addy.
A.A. A. J. Martin.
A/Mech. J. McDiarmid.
C.A.F.(A) L. T. Brant.
P.O.A.F. R. R. Roose.
A/P.O.A.F. B. Jolliffe.

Parade Training.
C.P.O. G.I. J. E. O. Bartlett.
P.O. G.I. W. C. Brooks.
P.O. G.A.I R. O'Neill, D.S.M.[3]
P.O. A.F. D. Eldridge.

Physical Training.
C.P.O. P.T.I. P. J. Parkes.
P.O. P.T.I. J. Carnochan.
P.O. P.T.I. T. V. Smith.
P.O. P.T.I. K. Martin.

S.A.M.C.O.
C.A.A. K. Clayton.
C.A.A.(O) K. G. Sims.
A.A. G. Adamson.
A.A. C. French.
A.A. F. R. S. Cumbleton.
A.A. J. Kitcatt.
A.A. P. Vella.
A.A. D. J. Richardson.
A.A. J. E. W. Hutchinson.
A.A. H. S. Tullins.
A.A. P. G. Gray.
A.A. R. Hicks.
A.A. D. Walker.
A.A. D. G. W. Whyte.
A.A. J. A. Swift.
A.A.(O) J. W. Robertson.
E.A. D. E. Eames.
E.A. D. J. Burns.

S.A.M.C.O. (Continued).

A/Mech. K. Wardle.
A/Mech. K. B. Ashton.
A/Mech. P. J. T. Warren.
A/Mech. J. C. Williams.
A/Mech. J. B. Pollard.
C.A.F. W. G. Robertson.
C.A.F. J. S. Passmore.
C.A.F. J. S. Smith.
Ch.E.A. L. J. Cooper.

Ch.El. G. Haddigan.
Ch.El. L. Knowles.

Divisional Staff.

C.P.O. D. G. Wilson.
C.P.O. W. E. Sweeney.
C.P.O. A. Brown.
C.P.O. M. Watson.
C.P.O. W. J. Cresser.
P.O. W. McGibbon.

Ship's Company Chief Petty Officers and Petty Officers

M.A.A. D. McIntosh.
C.P.O. R. Cowie.
C.A.A. D. Ritchie, B.E.M.
C.E.R.A. G. Ritchie.
St.C.P.O. F. M. Walpole.
St.C.P.O. W. Grieve.
C.P.O. Steward V. Lynch.
C.P.O. Writer D. Howard.
C.P.O. Cook J. Glennon.
C.P.O. Cook H. Jackson.
S.B.C.P.O. F. W. Drew.
C.P.O.(Air) R. Layton.
C.P.O.(Air) K. T. O. Smith.
R.P.O. G. W. Mutch.
R.P.O. J. S. Gove.
R.P.O. W. S. Faulkner.
P.O. J. Watson.
P.O. R. Dickie.

P.O. R. Raines.
P.O. W. Armstrong.
P.O. J. Hayes.
P.O. T. McGuire.
P.O. W. Kirkpatrick.
R.E.L. M. Carrick.
R.E.A.4. W. Simmonds.
P.O.E.L. R. Stephenson.
St.P.O. H. Watson.
St.P.O. F. Pearson.
P.O.C.K. F. Ely.
P.O.W.T.R. T. Piper.
S.B.P.O. B. Thompson.
A.A.4. A. E. Potts.
P.O.A.F. R. Roose.
P.O.A.F. R. Horsley.
P.O.A.F. A. Nicoll.

Chief and P.O. Wrens

Chief Wren D. M. M. Wardle.
Chief Wren B. J. Jones.
P.O. Wren M. Farthing.
P.O. Wren I. C. Willshire.
P.O. Wren N. F. J. Jarvis.

P.O. Wren M. Hirst.
P.O. Wren C. M. Logan.
P.O. Wren A. M. Hartnett.
P.O. Wren F. Baty.

Chapter 6

Entertainments

Reg Whitear & Jill Chambers

The Chorus

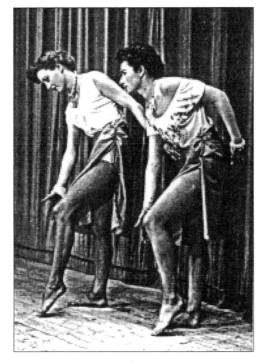
'Deep Purple' Lee Newcombe & Midge Timpson

'Ave Maria' Jean Dobie

By kind Permission of Captain (B) J. H. Illingworth, R.N.

The Condor Amateur

Dramatic Society

PRESENTS

"Blithe Spirit"

(An Improbable Farce)

By NOEL COWARD

Programme : Price 3d

Dundee
Repertory
Theatre

in association with C.E.M.A
Lessee - G. E. GEDDES, Manager
Director of Productions :
A. R. WHATMORE

MONDAY, 18th, to SATURDAY, 30th SEPTEMBER, 1944
Every Evening, 7.15   Matinees—Wednesdays, 2.30; Saturdays, 4.30.
Stalls, 4/· and 3/·. Dress Circle, 3/·. Balcony, 2/· and 1/6.
All Seats Bookable. Telephone 3530.

SHE WANTED A CREAM FRONT DOOR

By A. R. WHATMORE

Next Production—

MONDAY, 2nd OCTOBER, 1944

The Corn is Green

By EMLYN WILLIAMS

H.M.S. CONDOR

Amateur Dramatic Society

Presents

(by kind permission of Capt. R. St. V. SHERBROOKE, V.C., R.N.)

Quiet Wedding

A Comedy in 3 Acts

by

Esther McCracken.

CAST (IN ORDER OF APPEARANCE.)

MIRANDA BUTE,	- -	BETTY GIBSON
FLORENCE BUTE,	- -	MARY KERR
MADAME MIRELLE,	- -	JUNE MUSCANT
BELLA,	- - -	ETHEL JACKSON
MILDRED ROYD (the bride's mother,)		PAMELA PARKER
MARY JARROW,	- -	FELICITY McINTYRE
JANET ROYD (the bride to be,)		PEGGY KINIPPLE
ARTHUR ROYD (the bride's father,)		HEDLEY GOODALL
DALLAS CHAYTON (the bridegroom,)		JOHN FRANCIS
DENIS ROYD (the best man,)	-	GEORGE BAKER
JOHN ROYD,	- -	NORMAN BENWELL
FLOWER LISLE,	- -	ELIZABETH AMBROSE
NICODEMUS,	- -	NICKY
MARCIA BRENT,	- -	PAT BENNETT
JIM BRENT,	- -	GEOFFREY HIDE

The Action of the Play takes place in the Morning Room of the Royd's home in Throppleton and in the Sitting Room of a small flat in Chadston.

ACT 1.   The day before the Wedding—late afternoon.
ACT 2.   Sc. i.   Some hours later.
            Sc. ii.   One hour later.
ACT 3.   The day of the Wedding Morning.

STAGE MANAGER,   -   LEONARD THOMPSON

LIGHTING UNDER THE DIRECTION OF   JOHN CLAY

TAPESTRY AND BACKCLOTH DESIGNED AND PAINTED BY   .   JUNE MUSCANT

SCENERY PAINTED BY   -   -   PETER WOODHAM

THE SCENERY DESIGNED AND BUILT BY GEO. PEARCE

FURNISHINGS kindly supplied by D. T. WILSON & SONS

STAGE STAFF:—MARGARET BEE, CARL DRAPER, BRIDGET DUMAS, FRANK GINN, PEGGY HUTLEY, JUDY KING, THOMAS PARK, BARBARA WILLIAMS, SUSAN WINTLE.

The Play produced by HEDLEY GOODALL.

The C.A.D S. would like to thank all members of the Ship's Company, whose co-operation and help have made this Production possible.

'Rudolph' with Midge Timpson

Midge Timpson

C.A.D.S. 1956 'Cast of 'On Monday Next'

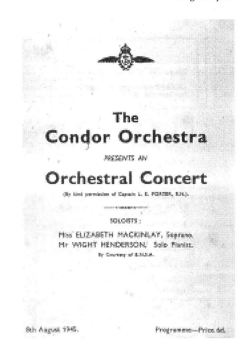

The
Condor Orchestra

PRESENTS AN

Orchestral Concert

(By kind permission of Captain L. E. PORTER, R.N.)

SOLOISTS :

Miss ELIZABETH MACKINLAY, Soprano.
Mr WIGHT HENDERSON, Solo Pianist.
By Courtesy of S.M.S.A.

8th August 1945.   Programme—Price 6d.

Megacycle Mix-up

Nick Webb, Goerge Cowie & Nobby

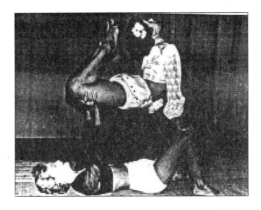

Lee & Midge

C.A.D.S. 1957 'Simon & Laura'

The Cast of 'Oot of the Navy Blue'

Ladies of Chorus - 'Desert Song' 1950

The Cast

A Corruption of a Ditty Sung on a Radio

1

We'll get used to it, We've got to get used to it
The food is pretty bad, We're getting used to it,
In the dining room they say, we get lashed up every day
But as to eat our lunch, we sit, we all know what to do with it
It's Wonderful, It's Marvellous
With Bridies always hot and full of meat
We'll get used to it, We'll get used to it,
Maybe soon we'll get a meal that we can eat.

2

We'll get used to it, We'll get used to it
The factory's such a bind - We're getting used to it
Though our test job wasn't hard, and old Uncle Fred's a card
He smiles, he grins, and winks and nods
Then tells us we have dipped our jobs
It's Wonderful, It's Marvellous,
With breaking backs we stand and file away
We'll get used it, We'll get used to it
At this speed we'll still be here when we are grey.

3

We'll get used to it, We've got to get used to it,
With exams on every week, We're getting used to it
With NAMEB so they say, it gets harder every day
But we've no need to sit and swat, we gave the NAMEB Chief our tot
It's Wonderful, It's Marvellous
We're only working 20 hours a day,
We'll get used to it, We'll get used to it
And there's rumours of an extra rise in pay.

4

We'll get used to it, We've got to get used to it
On Skippers every day, We're getting used to it
Men get rated every day, but before they get away
As quick as you can turn and look
The Skippers whipped away your hook
It's Wonderful, It's Marvellous
The Slops on badges do a roaring trade,
We'll get used to it, We'll get used to it
We've even heard of one who made the grade.

5

We'll get used to it, We've got to get used to it
The pantomime is on, we're getting used to it,
Our producer's quite a type, when our speech is rather ripe,
He turns and gives us such a look
Then marks it down in his black book,
It's Wonderful, It's Marvellous
On I.T.V. this show would be a WOW
We'll get used to it, We'll get used to it
But La Lollas on instead the lucky .... girl!

6

We'll get used to it, We've got to get used to it
The Sun is awfully hot, We're getting used to it
Up in Angus, so they say, there is sunshine every day
But every morning in the murk, we find we have to swim to work.
It's wonderful, It's Marvellous
The water levels rising to our knees,
We'll get used to it, We've got to get used to it.
Now they're treating all the Wrens for ducks disease ....

For the benefit of Patrons going home after the Show the nearest Tube Station is Hyde Park, London.

❖❖❖❖❖

Patrons are earnestly requested not to tread on the cigarette ends as this makes it difficult for the Cast to smoke them after you have left.

❖❖❖❖❖

Any complaints—
please contact P.C. Bloggs, c/o St. Ives Constabulary, Cornwall.

Note :—All complaints must be made in person.

❖❖❖❖❖

Found in High Street :—3 Fur-lined Studded Socks. Anyone with 3 feet please contact the Manager.

❖❖❖❖❖

Please keep this programme—it will come handy later to wrap your ice cream in.

❖❖❖❖❖❖

Continued on Page 10 of the Boomerang Throwers Assistants Bumper Fun Book of 1964.

In case of fire — tear off.

Presenting

OUT OF THE (NAVY) BLUE

A Variety Show

IN AID OF THE POLIO FUND

Webster Memorial Hall,
Arbroath,

At 8 p.m.

Friday, 2nd December 1955.

Programme 3d.

Overture :—Ring out the Bells.

Bell Bottom Blues :—Midge Timpson and Chorus.

Room for the Night :—Keith Tatt, Mick Webb,
Johnny Brown, Jill Chambers.

Ave Maria :—Jean Dobie.

Megacycle Mixup :—Mick Webb, Reg Whitear,
Nobby Clarke, George Cowie,
Ken Poole.

Blue Mood :—Lynn McKye.

Blues in the Night :—Lee Newcombe, Midge Timpson
Mick Webb, Reg Whitear.

Tit for Tat :—   Reg Whitear, Irene Brymner,
Nobby Clarke, Jill Chambers.

Interval.

Deep Purple :—Midge Timpson, Lee Newcombe.

Females on the Beach :--Jill Chambers, Nobby Clarke
George Cowie.

Sailor Boy :—   Midge Timpson, Lee Newcombe,
Jill Chambers, Irene Brymner,
and Chorus.

I believe :—Jean Dobie.

Fate of the Fisherman's Daughter :—Nobby Clarke,
Lee Newcombe, Reg Whitear, Mick Webb.

Rudolph :—   .... Midge Timpson, Reg Whitear,
George Cowie.

Just one of those things :—Chorus.

Finale :—Full Cast.

Chorus :—   Teresa Cox, Daphne Bigsey, Thelma Wicks,
Ruby Hunter, Marjorie Hindley, Kathy Harper.

Orchestrations by Dave Mann.

Choreography by Janet Johnson.

Master of Ceremonies : - Don Treeby.

Produced and Directed by Mick Webb.
Assisted by Reg Whitear.

Stage Managed by .... Ken Poole.

Lighting Effects by ....George Masson.

Make-up by .... John Cotton.

DON'T STAND ON YOUR HEAD TO READ THIS.   YOU MAY OBSTRUCT SOMEONE'S VIEW WITH YOUR FEET.

ARBROATH AMATEUR OPERATIC SOCIETY
PRESENTS

THE
DESERT SONG

By arrangement with SAMUEL FRENCH LTD.
Book and Lyrics by OTTO HARBACH, OSCAR HAMMERSTEIN and FRANK MANDEL
The Music by Sigmund Romberg

THE DESERT SONG

Characters in Order of Appearance

SID EL KAR,	Mr JOHN GORBLE
MINDAR,	Mr R. SOMERVILLE
HASSI,	Mr R. B. BROWN
HADJI,	Mr M. D. W. KINNEAR
MERI,	Miss GRACE W. ALLAN
PIERRE BIRABEAU,	Mr JACK LAMB
BENJAMIN KIDD,	Mr J. A. WELCH
AZURI,	Miss ELSPETH G. EDGAR
Captain PAUL FONTAINE,	Mr IAN SPALDING
Lieutenant LA VERGNE,	Mr A. M. L. RAE
Sergeant DE BOUSSAC,	Mr C. G. McDONALD
SUSAN,	Miss F. H. RITCHIE
EDITH,	Miss J. W. BUICK
MARGOT BONVALET,	Miss G. S. FLEMING
General BIRABEAU,	Mr A. W. BROWN
CLEMENTINA,	Miss S. DUTCH
ALI BEN ALI,	Mr G. S. MORRIS
SHEILA,	

Arabs, Riffs, Soldiers, Spanish Girls, Sabbira Wives, Riffian Dancers, etc.

LADIES OF THE CHORUS:—

Misses A. Ranchart, B. Scott, K. Cobban, J. Duncan, J. Mitchell, E. McFarlane, V. McLean, E. Robertson, B. Smith, E. Suttie, A. Spink, M. Talbot, M. Winton, D. Millar, E. Melville, Arklen, J. Bisa, J. Ballan, Mrs A. Hogg, Mrs A. Hekennice, Misses R. Melvin, E. Malcolm, M. Reas, M. Scott, I. Suttie.

GENTLEMEN OF THE CHORUS:—

Messrs D. H. Espbin, P. S. Kydd, G. Kinloan, G. Smith, R. B. Forbes, G. N. Excel, D. R. Harriet, J. Osborough, M. Wallace, J. V. Roel.

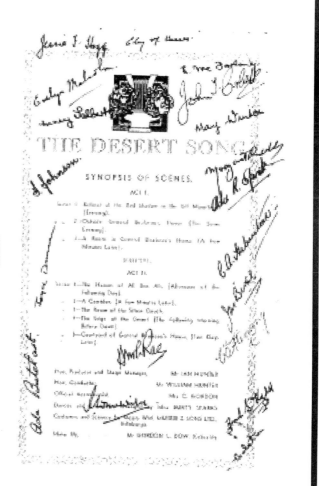

THE DESERT SONG

SYNOPSIS OF SCENES.

ACT I.

ORCHESTRA

FIRST VIOLINS—Mr. F. ROUTLEDGE BELL (Leader) Mr. ANDREW
MORRISON, Mr. GEORGE C. BAIRD; Mr. SIDNEY SCOTT.

SECOND VIOLINS—Miss A. S. REID; Mrs. MINA HAMILTON;
Mr. D. HOWESON.

VIOLA—Mr. JACK DUTCHART.	CLARINET—Mr. D. F. CLAYTON.
CELLO—Mr. F. PHILIPS.	OBOE—Miss NANCY GORDON.
BASS—Mr. D. WILKIE.	TRUMPET—Mr. J. WILLIAMSON.
FLUTE—Mr. GORDON DAVIDSON,	Mr. VICTOR LEWIS.
Mr. A. S. URQUHART.	TYMPS—Mr. C. S. MAXWELL.

POPETTE DESAIRS (Voice or Guitar will be heard in Second
between Acts I and II)

Arbroath Amateur Operatic Society desires to thank Mr W. L.
Reid, who designed the scene, and Arbroath Art Society who designed
it. The Society also wishes to thank all friends who have assisted in
distributing and displaying Bills, Selling Programmes, Stewarding in the
Hall, attending to Advance Booking and in any way assisting the
Society and Lastly the Honorary Members and General Public for their
support

PREVIOUS PRODUCTIONS

THE DESERT SONG

The scene is laid in French Morocco. High in the hills, a band of Riffs desperate are consolidating a series of raid against the weak French. Their trusted leader, Pierre Birabeau, formerly an officer in the French escape police, that area has shown is his lot with the Riffs, and is helping them to avenge the wrongs which he felt as a despairing France. Unaware of his true identity, the Riffs have set only as the Red Shadow, some daring to profess that deed respects with which he surrounds himself.

Birabeau becomes complicated when Zenoir, father, General Birabeau, is appointed to the command of the French troops charged with the duty of exterminating the Red Shadow and his band. The General, the dissonant of the Red Shadow's behaviour, need to admonition of his comrade, is concerned with the inactivity of Pierre, the lieutenant, greatly realising is only assisted by Pierre for the purpose of despise, when not engaged in his exploits as watch leader.

The only in the plot is Margot Bonvalet, the fiancee of a great socially sly and by Pierre. Knowing Pierre only in his abstract true role, Margot contrasts him to his disillusion with the Red Shadow She, indifferent to Pierre, she imagines herself in love with Captain Paul Fontaine. General Birabeau approves of this match for Paul and his association with Azuri a native dancing girl.

Meanwhile the Red Shadow, to prevent her marriage with Paul carries off Margot to the Palace of his friend, Ali Ben Ali, where eventually she submits to the wooing of her desert lover. All this is alarming to the Riffs, who fear reprisals at the hands of the French The situation comes to a head when Azuri, prompted by jealousy and knowing the Red Shadow's secret, brings the General to the Palace. Pierre and we are face to face but only the father knows this. Challenged to a duel, the Red Shadow rather than fight his own father, flings coward-like and is turned adrift into the desert in disgrace.

Returning home with Margot, the General learns the real truth from Azuri, and is overcome with grief on discovering that his lost son has met his death. Great, however, the relations sadden return with the news that the Red Shadow has been killed, and his in no other than Pierre himself. Thus the romance of Margot and Pierre ends in fullest.

In the Play Azuri, who is personated by Jeannine Kehr, Pierre's a Paris revue girl marriage, and Sports, his secretary, was Neil H Kerr and Hassi, two of the Red Shadow's lieutenants, and a one, being a Spanish lady, are lively contributors to the French scene.

CONDOR DROME

(By kind permission of Captain R. B. ... ARMSTRONG, V.C., D.S.O., R.N.)

"HAPPY DAYS,"
OR BARM f NIGHTS.

A SUNNY SUMMER MUSICAL COMEDY, without Plan or Plot, in 4 Acts. Produced by DIANA KING and BEN NALLY.

THE STORY.

Count Lewis Clanham is a Ruritanian nobleman ... in exiling, on the Deed, Pedestrian Shop and ...

THE CAST.

Count Lewis Clanham	Ken Lewis	Dinah	Diana King
Baggage, the Butler	Frankie Guss	Alice	Hilda Kershaw
Chef	Terry Kaufman	Bertha	Margaret Wilkinson
Valet	Robert Wilson	Violette	Audrey Bowman
Chauffeur	Bill Stevens	Georgette	Audrey Carr
Secretary	Len Stevens	Sally	Peggy Elliott
Boots	George Tweddell	Hazel	Hazel Clarence
Gardener	Joseph Bradshaw	Rose	Alice Holden
Kitchen Boy	Joe Thompson	Elizabeth	Jean Warren
Housekeeper	Marie Kennedy	Dorothy	Jenny Duckworth
Patience Nicol	Doll Williams		
Mr Grindle	Frankie Guss		
Joe Grindle	Ben Nally		
Welsh	George Tweddell		
Miss Prendthe	Diana King		
Mine Host	Terry Kaufman		

Script by Ben Nally. Dances and Ensembles arranged by Diana King.

ACT I.

SCENE 1. BELOW STAIRS (The Kitchen in the Count's London Mansion)

"Romancin' in the Kitchen with Dinah"	The Company
"The Visitor and the Porter and the Upstairs Hall"	Diana King
"Chorus"	Frankie Guss
"Can't Help Singing"	Jenny Duckworth
"It's a Hap-Hap-Happy Day"	The Company

SCENE 2. TICKETS PLEASE | Frankie Guss and The Company

ACT II.

SCENE 1. ABOARD THE STEAM YACHT "DIANA"

"In the Middle of Nowhere"	Diana King and Jack Evans
"Up Above, Down Below"	Frankie Guss, Ben Nally, George Tweddell, Terry King
"Paradise for Two"	Marie Kennedy and Ken Lewis
"Appearance that Passes"	Boots, Peggy, Rose, Alice and Hilda
"Musical Medley"	Margaret Wilkinson
"Sailor Dance"	Frankie Guss
"Foxley, the Fisherman"	Ken Lewis and The Company

INTERVAL.

ACT III.

SCENE 1. MR GRINDLE'S SALOON in the Wild and Woolly West.

"Ragtime"	The Company
"The Garden for Miss Grindle"	Frankie Guss, Ben Nally, George Tweddell, Terry King
"Cowboy Songs"	Margaret O'Gorman, Doll Williams, Joe Tweddell

SCENE 2. BARNEY VINTAGE

"Nightingale"	Patrick Tweddell
"Songs of Yesterday"	Jenny Duckworth
"My Dreams are Getting Better"	Diana King, Henry Warren, Bill Stevens

SCENE 3. BACK TO MR GRINDLE'S

"You're Mine"	Ken Lewis
"Don't Fence Me In"	Audrey, Hilda, Jenny, Peggy, Bertha and Alice

SCENE 4. INTERLUDE

"The Mystery Man"	Joe and George Tweddell and Doll Williams

ACT IV.

SCENE 1. RURITANIA'S BEER GARDEN.

"Chit Chat (Tittack-Tweedle) Polka	Diana King, Hilda, Audrey, Peggy, Bertha, Betty, Jenny, Jean and Audrey
"I'm in Love with Vienna"	Marie Kennedy
"Drinking Song"	The Company
"It's a Hap-Hap-Happy Day"	The Company

Express

Blackburn Firebrand Mk V

Fairey Albacore

Heading: These five Glosters Gladiators of No33 Squadron, photographed in 1939

Fairey Fulmar

Grumman Martlet

Chapter 7

Rear Admiral Reserve Aircraft

H.M.S. CONDOR - 1954 to 1956.

With the passage of time my memories of CONDOR are obviously somewhat clouded; I never kept a diary, I can't find my Service record and my time there was really unremarkable. These are a few disjointed that that I do (I think!) remember.

I arrived in October 1954 as a young(ish) Lieutenant , aged 24, to take up an appointment as Secretary to the Chief Staff Officer to the Rear Admiral Reserve Aircraft (RARA). Having just returned from a year spent for the most part in the tropics I remember particularly feeling the cold and piling every blanket, and even my overcoat, on my bed in a rather bare cabin in one of the outbuildings. The Captain, I think , was Captain Storrs (an Air Engineer?) but my boss was Captain Charles Bernard Pratt and the Admiral was Rear Admiral John Dudley Nelson Ham. My short title, Sec/CSO, caused occasional mirth as it sounded like a seductive brand of petrol (sexy ESSO). I still remember the first paper with which I had to deal: It was headed " Requirement for a plunge centreless grinding attachment" and to this day I still do not know what it was ,what it did, why it was centreless or to what it was attached. Charles Pratt was a splendid man to work for. Three particular things standout in my memory:

1.   Being asked to get him a pair of pyjamas from slops and on asking his measurements being told " 44,44,44".

2.   Being buzzed for as he arrived in his office one morning and on going in being sworn at for two minutes solidly and then told "Thank you Derek, I feel better now, you can go".

3.   Being invited to Christmas lunch by Captain and Mrs Pratt (I think it was 1954 but may have been 1955) and following a superb lunch with a glass of vintage port, Taylor's 1908, which was absolutely magnificent.

Charles Pratt was relieved by Eric Beard, a very different personality and a very nice man to work for, of whom I have only pleasant memories and nothing noteworthy. I can remember the names of very few officers on the staff; Sammy Hargrave (who I think was a Naval gold champion), Stephen Banks, Vic "Hooky" Walker the Admiral's pilot, John Hoffman a ferry pilot, but, to my shame, I cannot remember the name of the Admiral's Secretary. I recall the change of title from Rear Admiral Reserve Aircraft to Flag Officer Reserve Aircraft (as a result of AFO 1/56?). There was a comment by some that this meant going from being a RARA AVIS (or rare thing) to be a member of the FORAMINIFERA (a marine animal with a perforated shell).

Of work, I really remember little else. It was a continuous round of "paper-pushing" on subjects of which I had little knowledge and frankly very little interest.

Social life was, I suppose, fairly typical for those days. I took part in most of the amateur dramatics on the station; I remember "Simon and Laura" and " On Monday Next". The usual Saturday night was down to the Lunan Bay Hotel which was far enough off the beaten track not to worry too much about closing time. Or into Arbroath for four quick pints of Bass (at 1/3d a pint, I remember) before going on the town - or to Dundee. And then discovering the Balmoral Hotel at Friockheim which had the most comfortable

R.A.R.A. Staff 1954 - 55

R.A.R.A. Staff

R.A.R.A. Staff

R.A.R.A. Office Staff 1950

R.A.R.A. Staff 1950

Lt. (E) Bailey, Lt. (S) Walters, Lt. (E) Handford, Lt.(E) Johnson, Lt. (S) Collins, 3/0 Austin, Mr Mills, ??, 3/0 Shape
Lt. (E) Jones, Lt. (E) Dodge-Wilcock, Lt. Cdr (E) ?, Lt. Cdr (E) ?, Lt. Cdr (E) Peters, Lt. Cdr Bruin, Lt. Cdr (E) Roberts
Lt. Cdr (E) Milham, Mr Camerson, Lt. Cdr O'Sullivan, Lt. (E) Wilson,
Lt. Cdr (S) Elliot, Surg. Cdr. Grant, ?, Cdr. Pratt, Capt. (E) ?, R. Admiral (E) Jameson, Cdr. (E) Johnstone,
Cdr. (S) Tomkins, Cdr. (E) Lawson, Cdr. (L) Bolwell, Lt. Cdr. Cubitt.π

194

front bar in the business and which was was open for "travellers" on Sundays - and travelling the few miles from CONDOR was ample. I got very friendly with the Strachan family who ran it, and particularly with Freda , the second of the three daughters of the house. We became what I suppose would nowadays be called an "item". She came to dances in the mess; I went to Balls at St. Andrews University where she was studying and we had regular seats at the Dundee Rep.. It was then a fortnightly rep. and we had two seats in the fourth row back and saw some quite superb productions. The only disappointment was seeing the ballet (Rambert I think) from the same seats where it loses the magic as you can hear the "thump" of feet on the stage and see the sweat dropping off the dancers" faces, Freda and I had many good times together and we would run the bar at the Balmoral often on a Sunday night.

I had a big old Austin 16 and I remember driving round the airfield at night with someone (I forget who now) in the back shooting hares out the window. Hares didn't seem to mind cars driving up close; really rather unsporting. I remember driving many hundreds of miles round the countryside working out a route for a motor car treasure hunt. John Calderwood, Jerry Prince and I certainly organised one, and I think two. I recall that the Admiral got lost on one and we were not popular!

I recall "Jumbo" Cramond and "Hooky" Walker, each six feet plus and fifteen stone plus taking off in a Tiger Moth and needing the whole length of the runway to get airborne. I also recall the story (although it may have been apocryphal) of a Royal VIP (Princess Marina?) arriving at the airfield by plane en route elsewhere and a reporter (from the Scottish Daily Mail?) trying to get in to cover the event and being refused admission and the next day the paper produced some snide and untrue comment like" The visit caught the station so much on the hop that Captain Storrs had to rush out and get an immediate haircut". Such was the bitchiness of the press.

Overall I have nothing but pleasant , if clouded, memories of my time at CONDOR. Arbroath smokies. Finnan Haddies. "Dooker" (?) certificates for swimming in the Arbroath swimming pool on New Year's Eve (but not me!). Pleasant, hospitable people. Good beer and a warm welcome at the Balmoral. I have never been back since ; perhaps one day.....

One of the functions of R.A.R.A. was the location and serviceability of all airframes and engines for all types of aircraft. R.A.R.A. later became F.O.R.A. or Flag Officer Reserve Aircraft.

Lt. Cdr. J.C.P. Lansdown RN (retd) 1951-52 AEO to 821 Sqdn. Firefly AS6's - CO Lt. Cdr.(O) B.N. 'Slug' Notley decided to hold night flying, first time in years it had been tried. Runway lighting with paraffin glim lamps, created quite a stir.

Captain was R.F."Farmer" Storrs, a large gentleman from Somerset, hence nickname.

Cdr(X) was R.J.Hoare who set up the assault course and Glen Esk scheme, also outward bound camp at Loch Lee.

July 1947

CONDOR - R.A.R.A.

Rear Admiral (E)...J.L. Bedale, CB
    (In Charge Reserve Aircraft
    and Technical Training)

STAFF

Lt.Com. (A) (P) L.T. Summerfield(act)
Lt. (A) .........L.E. Lucock
    (A.E.D.)
    H.R.S. Pellow
    (A.E.D.)
    T.A. Amos
    (A.E.D.)
    J. Bellingham
    (A.E.D.)
Lt. (E) .........R.P. Grimwood

January 1948

CONDOR - R.A.R.A.

Rear Admiral (E)...J.L. Bedale, KBE
    (In Charge Reserve Aircraft
    and Technical Training)
Secretary,
Lt.-Com. (S) .......J.F.W. Hastings (act)

STAFF

Commander ....M. Cursham
    (Staff Officer Flying)
    H. Duncan
    (Maintenance Commander)
Lt. (C) ....(O) J.D. Jackson
Lt.-Com. (A) ...L.T. Summerfield (act)
Lt. (A) ..........C.T.J. Ware
    F.E. Lucock
    D.A. Conde
    H.R.S. Pellow
    T.A. Amos
    J. Bellingham
    R.A. Whittingham
    (P) F.G. Noble
Captain (E) ....W.B. Axford, OBE (act)
Commander (E) ......W.J. Robb
    (Staff Officer Aircraft)
    E.C. Senjor
Lt.-Com. (E) ....A.L.S.S. Thackara
Lt.-Com. (L) ....H.H. Pain
Lt. (L) ....F.R. Tattersall
Commander (S) ....R.H. Rump
    (Staff Supply Officer)
Lt.-Com. (S) ....J.R. Fenley
Lt. (S) ....M.G. Slattery
    (Secretary to Captain (E))
    G.W.P. Grant

April 1948

CONDOR
(R.N.A.S. Arbroath, Angus)

Rear Admiral (E)   J.L. Bedale, KBE
    (In Charge Reserve Aircraft
    and Technical Training)
Secretary,
Lt.-Com. (S)   J.R. Fenley
Chief of Staff,
Captain (E)   G.E. Ross, CBE
Secretary,
Lt. (S)   M.G. Slattery

STAFF

Commander ....H. Duncan
    (Maintenance Commander)
Lt. (C) (O) J.D. Jackson
Commander (A) (P) G.N.P. Stringer, OBE,
    DFC
    (P) L.A. Cubitt
    (Lt.-Com. (Flying)
Lt.-Com. (A) .......L.T. Summerfield (act)
Lt. (A) .......C.T.J. Ware
    F.E. Lucock
    D.A. Conde
    H.R.S. Pellow
    T.A. Amos
    J. Bellingham
    (P) F.G. Noble
    J.W. Hall
    (A.E.D)
Commander (E).......W.J. Robb
    (Staff Officer Aircraft
    E.A. Morrison
Lt.-Com. (E) .......A.L.S.S. Thackara
Lt. (E) .......A.E. Day
Lt.-Com. (L) .......H.H. Pain
Lt. (L) .......F.R. Tattersall
Commander (S) .......R.A. Braine
    (Staff Supply Officer)
Lt.-Com. (S) .......J.P. Parker
    (ASSO)
Lt. (S) .......G.W.P. Grant
    F.E.J. Warren

July 1948

CONDOR
(R.N.A.S. Arbroath, Angus)

Rear Admiral (E)   Sir John L. Bedale,
    KBE, CB
    (In Charge Reserve Aircraft
    and Technical Training)
Secretary,
Lt. Com. (S)   J.R. Fenley
Chief of Staff...Captain (E)
    G.E. Ross, CBE, AMIMECHE
Secretary,
Lt. (S)   D.B. Jeffery

STAFF

Commander ....H. Duncan
          (Maintenance Commander)
Lt. ......(C)   (0) J.D. Jackson,DSC
                     J.A. Douglas
                 (P.T. & W. Duties)
Commander (A)   (P) G.N.P. Stringer, OBE,
                     DFC
Lt.-Com. (A) ......L.T. Summerfield (act)
Lt.   (A) ...(P) R.E. Dubber
                     C.T.J. Ware
                     (A.E.D)
                     F.R. Lucock
                     D.A. Conde
                     (A.E.D.)
                     H.R.S. Pellow
                     (A.E.D.)
                     J. Bellingham
                     J.W. Hall
                     (A.E.D.)
                     D..W. Wooler
                     (A.E.D.)
                     J.C. Quinlan
                     (A.E.D.)
Tempy. Lt.(A) ......W.R. Bailey (act)
                     (A.O.D.)
Commander (E) ......W.J. Robb
                 (Staff Officer Aircraft)
                     E.A. Morrison
                 (Staff Officer Planning)
Lt.-Com. (E) ......A.L.S.S. Thackara
Lt.-Com. (L) ......H.H. Pain
Lt.   (L) ......F.R. Tattersall
Commander (S) ......R.A. Braine
                 (Staff Supply Officer)
Surg.   )   A.G.G. Troomey
Lt.-Com.   )   (Staff Medical Officer)
Lt.-Com. (S) ......J.P. Parker
                     (ASSO)
Lt.   (S) ......G.W.P. Grant
                     F.E.J. Warren

  Technical Training Staff
Captain   (E) ......G.L. Bailey
Commander (E) ......W.L.G. Porter
Lt.   (A) ......W.F.H. Scott, MBE (act)
Lt.   (E) ......A.E. Day

W.R.E.N.S.

Chief Officer ......S.H. Broster
Second Officer .....I.M. Kilminster
                     E. Abel
                     J. Hatcher

CONDOR
(R.N.A.S. Arbroath, Angus)
Rear Admiral   (E) Sir John L. Bedale,
                     KBE, CB
         (In Charge Reserve Aircraft
          and Technical Training)
Secretary,
Lt.-Com.   (S) J.R. Fenley
Chief of Staff,
Captain ....(E) G.E. Ross, CBE,
                     AMIMECHE
Secretary,
Lt. ....(S) D.B. Jeffery

STAFF

Commander ....H. Duncan
          (Maintenance Commander)
Lt. ....(C) K.M. Teare
                     J.A. Douglas
                 (P.T. & W. Duties)
Commander (A) (P) G.N.P. Stringer,
                     OBE, DFC
Lt.-Com. (A) .....L.T. Summerfield (act
                     E.H. Banfield (act)
                     (A.E.D.)
Lt. (A) ......(P) G.C.J. Knight
                 (P) B.D. Abbott
                     C.T.J. Ware
                     (A.E.D.)
                     D.A. Conde
                     (A.E.D.)
                     H.R.S. Pellow
                     (A.E.D.)
                     J.W. Hall
                     (A.E.D.
                     D.W. Wooler
                     (A.E.D.)
                     J.C. Quinlan
                     (A.E.D.)
                     E.J. Jennings
                     (A.E.D.)
                     A..E. Wilson
                     (A.E.D.)
Tempy. Lt.(A) .....A.R. Bailey (act)
                     (A.O.D.)
Commander (E) ....W.J. Robb, AMIME
                 (Staff Officer Aircraft)
                     E.A. Morrison
                 (Staff Officer Planning)
Lt.-Com (E)......A.L.S.S. Thackara
Lt.-Com. (L) .....H.H. Pain
Lt.   (L) .....F.R. Tattersall
Commander (S) .....R.A. Braine
                 (staff Supply Officer)

Surg.,   ) A.G.G. Toomey
Lt.-Com.   )(Staff Medical-Officer)
Lt.-Com. (S).....J.P. Parker
                (ASSO)
Lt.   (S)....G.W.P. Grant
               F.E.J. Warren

Technical Training Staff
Captain   (E).....G.L. Bailey
Commander (E).....W.L.G. Porter
Lt.   (A).....W.F.H. Scott, MBE (act)
Lt.   (E).....A.E. Day

W.R.N.S.
Chief Officer ....S.H. Broster
First Officer ....J. Daziel-Reid

April 1949

CONDOR
(R.N.A.S. Arbroath, Angus)

Rear Admiral (E)..W.S. Jameson, CBE
            (In Charge Reserve Aircraft)
Secretary   )
Commander (S)) A.L. Tapper
Chief Staff Officer,
Captain   (E) ... G.E. Ross, CBE,
                AMIMECHE
Secretary,
Lt.   (S) ....F.E.J. Warren

        STAFF
Commander .......J.M. Bailey, DSC
            (Maintenance Commander)
            (P) G.N.P. Stringer, OBE, DFC
Lt.-Com. .........J.A. Douglas
            (P.T. & W. Duties)
            (P) ...L.T. Summerfield (act)
Lt.   (C) ...K.M. Teare
            (P) ...G.C.J. Knight
            (P) ...B.D. Abbott
Commander   (E) ...W.J. Robb, AMIME
            (Staff Officer Aircraft)
                E.A. Morrison
            (Staff Officer Planning)
Lt.   (E) ...C.A. Johnson
                C.T.J. Ware
                D.A. Conde
                J.W. Hall
                D.W. Wooller
                I.C. Quinlan
                E.J. Jennings
                A.E. Wilson
                L.R. Symons
                W.J.H. Mills
Tempy.Lt.   (E) ...W.R. Bailey (act)
                (A.O.D.)
Lt.-Com.   (L) ...H.H. Fain

Lt.   (L)...P.A.T. Reeves
Surg. Com. ......F.G.V. Scovell, MRCS,
                L.R.C.P.
Commander (S)...C.E.C. Tomkins, OBE
                (S.S.O.)
Lt.-Com.   (S)...J.P. Parker
                (ASSO)
Lt.   (S)...G.W.P. Grant
                D.B. Jeffery
            (Asst. Secretary)

W.R.N.S.

Chief Officer....S.H. Broster
First Officer....E.M. Carter
Second Officer...I.M. Kilminster
                I.M. Austen

October 1949

CONDOR
(T.R.S.B. 421030)

Rear Amiral (E)..W.S. Jameson, C.B.E.
            (In Charge Reserve Aircraft)
Secretary,
Commander (S)..A.L. Tapper
Chief Staff Officer,
Captain   (E)..P.D. Oliver
Secretary,
Lt.   (S)..F.E.J. Warren

        STAFF
Commander.......J.M. Bayley, DSC
            (Maintenance Commander)
Lt.-Com.   (P) L.A. Cubit
            (Lt.-Com. (Air))
            (P) L.T. Summerfield (act)
Lt.   (C) K.M. Teare
            (P) G.C.J. Knight
            (P) F.D. Adams
                A.P. O'Sullivan
            (P.T. & W. Duties)
Commander   (E) C.B. Pratt
                R.B.H. Johnstone
            (Staff Officer Aircraft)
Lt.-Com.   (E) M.W. Peters
                (A.E.D.)
                J.W. Hall
                (A.E.D.)
                D.W. Wooller
                (A.E.D.)
Lt.   (E) C.A. Johnson
                C.T.J. Ware
                F.D. Willcock
                A.E. Wilson
                B.L. Gagliardi
                L.R. Symons
Tempy. Lt. (E) W.R. Bailey (act)
                (A.O.D.)

198

Lt.-Com.   (L).....H.H. Pain
Lt.   (L) ....P.A.T. Reeves
Surg.Com.   .........W.A.S. Grant, MB,
                       chB
                       (S.M.O.)
Commander   (S) ....C.E.C. Tonkins, OBE
                       (S.S.O.)
Lt.-Com.   (S).....R.M. Levett
                       (ASSO)
Lt.   (S).....G.W.P. Grant
                       D.B. Jeffery
                       (Asst. Secretary)

W.R.N.S.

First Officer ......P. Cooper
Second Officer .....I.M. Kilminster
                    I.M. Austen

July 1951

CONDOR
(T.R.S.B. 421030)
(R.N.A.S. Arbroath, Angus)

Rear Admiral (E)   Sir William S. Jameson,
                       KBE, CB
                    (In Charge Reserve Aircraft)
Secretary,
Lt.-Com.   (S) ...P.C. Elliot
Chief Staff Officer,
Captain   (E) ...P.D. Oliver, ADC
Secretary,
Lt.   (S) ...J.W.T. Walters

            STAFF
Commander   .........B.J. Anderson
                    (Maintenance Commander)
                    (P) ...M. Johnstone, DSC (act)
                       (S.O. (Air))
Lt.-Com.   (P) ...J.M. Bruen, DSO, DSC
                       (Lt.-Com. (Air))
                    (P) ...K. Holme
                       (S.A.T.C.O.)
                       D.F. Trench
                       (P.T. & W. Duties)
Lt.   (P) ...C.G. Hurst
                    (P) ...H.J. Westwood (emgcy)
Commander   (E) ...A.E. Turner
                       M.P. Lawson
                    (Staff Officer Aircraft)
Lt.-Com.   (E) ...J. Milham
                       (A.E.D.)
                       D.P. Ward
                    (P) ...F.P.W. Fison
                       (A.E.D.)
                       C. Rawden
                       (A.E.D.)
                       E.J.B. Jones
                       (A.E.D.)

                       L.R. Symons
                       (A.E.D.)
            (P) ...I. Campbell-Brown
                       (A.E.D.)
                       P.D. Willcock
Lt.   (E) ......A.E. Wilson
                       B.L. Gagliardi
                       A.C.M. Handford
Tempy. Lt. (E)......W.R. Bailey (act)
                       (A.O.D.)
Commander   (L) ......F.T. Searle, OBE (ret)
                       (S.EI.O.)
Lt.   (L) ......F.D.J. Thomas
Surg. Com. .........W.A.S. Grant, MB,chB
                       (S.M.O.)
Commander   (S) ......R.L. Cole
                       (S.S.O.)
Lt.   (S) ......W.E. Pochon
                       J.M.S. Collins

W.R.N.S.

Second Officer ......J.M. Churchwood

October 1951

CONDOR (T.R.S.B. 4210309
(R.N.A.S. Arbroath, Angus)

Rear Admiral (E) Sir William S. Jameson,
                       KBE, CB
                    (In Charge Reserve Aircraft)
Secretary,
Lt.-Com.   (S) ....P.C. Elliot
Chief Staff Officer,
Captain   (E) ....J.P.W. Furze, OBE
Secretary,
Lt.   (S) ....J.W.T. Walters

            STAFF
Commander...........B.J. Anderson
                    (Maintenance Commander)
                    (P) M. Johnstone, DSC, (act)
                       (S.O. (Air))
Lt.-Com.   (P) ....J.M. Bruen, DSO, DSC
                       (Lt.-Com. (Air))
                    (P)   M.P. Price
                    (P)   K. Holme
                       (S.A.T.C.O.)
                       D.F. Trench
                    (P.T. & W. Duties.)
Lt.   (P)   C.G. Hurst(Emgcy)
Commander   (E)   A.E. Turner, MIMECHE
                       M.P. Lawson
                    (Staff Officer Aircraft)
Lt.-Com.   (E) ....J. Milham
                       (A.E.D.)
                       D.P. Ward
                    (P)   F.P.W. Fison
                       (A.E.D.)

C. Rawden
(A.E.D.)
E.J.B. Jones
(A.E.D.)
L.R. Symons
(A.E.D.)
(P)...I. Campbell-Brown
(A.E.D.)
P.D. Willcock

Lt. (E)...A.E. Wilson
B.L. Gagliardi
A.C.M. Handford

Tempy. Lt. (E)...W.R. Bailey (act)
(A.O.D.)

Commander (L)...F.T. Searle, OBE (ret)
(S.EI.O.)

Lt. (L)...E.D.J. Thomas

Commander (S)...R.L. Cole
(S.S.O.)

Surg. Lt.-Com. The Hon. A.G. Gathorne-
Hardy, MB, chB
(S.M.O.)

Lt.-Com. (S)...J.M.S. Collins (act)
Lt. (S)... W.E. Pochon

W.R.N.S.

Second Officer ....J.M. Churchwood

April 1952

CONDOR (T.R.S.B. 421030)
(R.N.A.S. Arbroath, Angus)

Rear Admiral (E) L.E. Rebbeck
(In Charge Reserve Aircraft)
Secretary,
Commander (S) P.C. Elliot
Chief Staff Officer,
Captain (E) J.P.W. Furze, OBE
Secretary Lt.(S) J.M. Powell

STAFF

Commander ........B.J. Anderson
(Maintenance Commander)
(P) M. Johnstone, DSC (act)
(S.O. (Air))
Lt.-Com. (P) M.P. Price
(Ferry Control)
A.E. Burton
Lt., (P) E. Waterhouse
Lt., R.T. Reames
R.N.V.R. (F.I. & W. Duties)
Commander (E) M.P. Lawson
(Staff Engineer Officer)
A.E. Turner, MIMechE,
AFRAes
(S.O. Aircraft Repair)

Lt.-Com. (E) ...J. Milham
(A.E.D.)
D.P. Ward
(P) ...F.P.W. Fison
(A.E.D.)
C.Rawson
(A.E.D.)
E.J.B. Jones
(A.E.D.)
(P) T. Campbell-Brown
(A.E.D.)
J.F. Martin
(A.E.D.)

Lt. (E) B.L. Gagliardi
A.C.M. Handford
J.F. Corfield
(A.O.D.)

Commander (L) F.T. Searle, OBE (ret)
(S.EI.O)

Lt. (L) E.D.J. Thomas
Commander (S) R.L. Cole
(S.S.O.)

Surg. Lt.-Com. The Hon. A.G. Gathorne-
Hardy, MB, chB
(S.M.O.)

Lt. (S) W.E. Pochon
B.D. Wansbury

W.R.N.S.

Second Officer .....J.M. Churchward

October 1952

CONDOR (T.R.S.B. 421030)
(R.N.A.S. Arbroath, Angus)

Rear Admiral (E) ...L.E. Rebbeck
(Rear Admiral (E) Reserve Aircraft)
Secretary,
Lt.-Com. (S) ...G.H. Peters
Chief Staff Officer,
Captain (E) J.P.W. Furze, OBE
Secretary Lt.(S) ...J.M. Powell

STAFF

Commander B.J. Anderson
(Maintenance Commander)
(P) M. Johnstone, DSC,(act)
(S.O. Air)
Lt.-Com. (P) M.P. Price
(Ferry Control)
Lt. (P) E. Waterhouse
Lt., } R.T. Reames
R.N.V.R. } (P.T.D.)
Commander (E) M.P. Lawson
(Staff Engineer Officer)
A.E. Turner, MIMechE,
AFRAes
(S.O. Aircraft Repair)

Sea King

Westland Wasp

Wessex HAS 1

Lt.-Com.   (E) ...J. Milham
               (A.E.D.)
               D.P. Ward
           (P) ...M.M. Gibson
               (A.E.D.)
               E.J.B. Jones
               (A.E.D.)
           (P) ...I. Campbell-Brown
               (A.E.D.)
               J.F. Martin
               (A.E.D.)
          (A/E) .. D.L.J. Corner
          (A/E) ...C.F. Whittaker
Lt.   (E) ...J.F. Corfield
               (A.O.D.)
Commander   (L) ...T.N. Jaggard
               (S.EI.O.)
Lt.   (L) ...E.D.J.Thomas
Surg. Com. .........G.A..S. Anthony, MRCS,
               LRPC (act. int.)
Commander   (S) ...R.L. Cole
               (S.S.O.)
Lt.   (S) ...W.E. Pochon
               B.D. Wansbury

W.R.N.S.

Second Officer ......J.M. Churchward

October 1953

CONDOR (T.R.S.B. 421030)
(R.N.A.S. Arbroath, Angus)

Rear Admiral (E) ...L.E. Rebbeck
     (Rear Admiral (E) Reserve Aircraft)
Secretary,
Commander   (S) ...G.H. Peters
Chief Staff Officer.,
Captain   (E) ...C.B. Pratt
Secretary Lt. (S) ...J.M. Powell

STAFF
Commander   (P) ...V.C. Grenfell, DSO
          (Maintenance Commander)
          (P) ...M. Johnstone, DSC (act)
               (S.O. (Air))
Lt.-Com.   (P) ...G.I.L. Corder
               (Ferry Control)
               H.A. Rice
               (P.T.D.)
Lt.   (P) ...E. Waterhouse
               P.H. Fowler
               (S.A.T.C.O.)
Commander (E)(A/E)...H. Bott
          (Staff Engineer Officer)
           A.E. Turner, MIMechE,
           AFRAes
          (S.O. Aircraft Repair)

Lt.-Com.   (E) (A/E) ...D.W. Wooller
        (P)   M.M. Gibson
               (A.E.D.
        (A/E) ...C.F. Cleary
               J.F. Martin
               (A.E.D.)
        (A/E) ...D.L.J. Corner
        (A/E) ...C.F. Whittaker
Lt.   (E) ........J.F. Corfield
               (A.O.D.)
               J.E. Hommert
               (A.E.D.)
Commander (L) .... T.N. Jaggard, MIN
               (S.ET.O)
Lt.   (L) .........R.W. Nickson
Surg. Commander ........G.A.S. Anthony,
         MRCS, LRCP, (act. int.)
Captain   (S) ....A. Lade, OBE
Lt.-Com.   (S)..........J.C. O'Regan
Lt.   (S) ........B.D. Wansbury

W.R.N.S.

Chief Officer ..........E.M. Drummond
(On Staff of F.O.F.T. and for duty with
F.O.G.T., R.A.R.A. and F.O.S.)

July 1954

CONDOR (T.R.S.B. 421030)
(R.N.A.S. Arbroath, Angus)

Rear Admiral (E) .......L.E. Rebbeck, CB
     (Rear Admiral (E) Reserve Aircraft)
Secretary,
Commander   (S) .......G.H. Peters
Personal Assistant
Lt. (E) (A/E) ..........J.E. Hommert
Chief Staff Officer,
Captain   (E) .... C.B. Pratt
Secretary. Lt. (S) ..... V.D. Jeffreson

STAFF
Commander .... V.C. Grenfell, DSO
         (Maintenance Commander)
        (P) .... E.A. Shaw
           (S.O. (Air))
Lt.-Com.   (P) .... G.I.L. Corder
          (Ferry Control)
Lt.   (P) .... E. Waterhouse
Commander (E) ..(A/E)..H. Bott
         (Staff Engineer Officer)
         (A/E)..A.E. Hargrave
         (S.O. Aircraft Repair)
Lt.-Com. (E) ..(A/E)..D.W. Wooler
        (A/E)..R.B. Horner
        (A/E)..C.F. Cleary
        (A/E)..D.L.J. Corner
        (A/E)..C.F. Whittaker

Lt.   (E) .... A.F.W. Marchall
           (A/E) F.A. Burls -
Commander (L) .... T.N. Jaggard
           (S.EI.0)
Lt.   (L) .... R.W. Nickson
Surg. Commander .. G.A.S. Anthony, MRCS,
           LRCP (act. int.)
Captain   (S) .... A. Lade, OBE
Lt.-Com.   (S) .... J.G. O'Regan
Lt.   (S) .... I.M. Powell

W.R.N.S.

Chief Officer .... E.M. Drummond
(On Staff of F.O.F.T. and for duty
with F.O.G.T., R.A.R.A., AND F.O.S.)

July 1955

CONDOR (T.R.S.B. 421030)
(R.N.A.S. Arbroath, Angus)

Rear Admiral (E).. L.E. Rebbeck, CB
   (Rear Admiral (E) Reserve Aircraft)
Secretary,
Commander   (S).. W.H. Field, DSC
Personal Assistant,
Lt.-Com. (E) (A/E) J.E. Hommert
Chief Staff Officer,
Captain (E) .... C.B. Pratt
Secretary,
Lt.   (S) .... V.D. Jeffreson

STAFF
Commander .... V.G. Grenfell, DSO
        (Maintenance Commander)
        (P) .... E.A. Shaw
           (S.O. (Air))
Lt.-Com. (P) .... G.I.L. Corder
        (Ferry Control)
Lt.   (P) .... E. Waterhouse
Commander (E)(A/E) A.E. Hargrave
        (S.O. Aircraft Repair)
           (A/E) H.J.S. Banks
Lt.-Com. (E)(A/E) D.W. Wooller
           (A/E) R.B. Horner
           (P)(A/E) R.S. Andrew
           (A/E) D.L.J. Corner
           (A/E) B.J.C. Bailey
Lt.   (E) .... A.F.W. Marshall
           (A/E) J.C. Calderwood
Commander (L) .... G.A. Hawkes
           (S.FT.0)
Lt.-Com. (L) .... R.W. Nickson
Instr.Lt. .... R. Johnstone
Surg.Commander ... J. Glass (act)
Captain (S) .... J.E. Langdon
           (S.S.0.)
Surg. Lt.-Com. (D) W.S. Turnbull
Lt.-Com. (S) .... J.G. O'Regan
Lt.   (S) .... A.J. Jury

W.R.N.S.

Chief Officer ..... E.G. Lucas
(On Staff of F.O.F.T. and for duty with
F.O.G.T., R.A.R.A., and F.O.S.)

October 1956

CONDOR (T.R.S.B. 421249)
(R.N.A.S. Arbroath, Angus)

Rear Admiral (E)... J.D.M. Ham, CB
           (Flag Officer Reserve Aircraft)
Secretary,
Commander   (S).... W.H. Field, DSC
Flag Lt. Lt.(E)(A/E) R.G.C. Smith
Chief Staff Officer,
Captain   (E) ... E.G. Beard
Secretary Lt.(S) .. D.H. Bates

STAFF
Commander.........V.C. Grenfell, DSO
           (Maintenance Commander)
Lt.- Com. .... J.G.O. Hofman
Lt.   (P) .. V.A. Walker
Commander (E)(A/E).A.E. Hargrave
           (S.O. Aircraft Repair)
           (A/E).H.J.S. Banks
Lt.-Com. (E)(A/E).C.A. Johnson
           (A/E).R.H. Tremaine
           (A/E).J.C.M. French
           (P)(A/E).J.R. Pedder
           (A/E).A. Greenhalgh
Lt.   (E).... A.C. Kennedy
           (A/E).J.C. Calderwood
Commander (L) .... G.A. Hawkes
           (S.EI.0)
           F.M. Starks
Lt.-Com. (L) .... H.A. Brenner
Captain (S) .... J.E. Langdon
           (S.S.0.)
Surg. Com. .... J. Glass
Lt.-Com. (S) .... D.A. Yeo
           H.J. Barnes

July 1957

Instr. Commander.. J.C. Gascoigne, OBE
           (S.I.0.)
Surg. Commander .. P.S. Edgecombe
           (S.M.0.)

CONDOR (T.R.S.B. 421249)
(R.N.A.S. Arbroath, Angus)

Rear Admiral ......A.J. Tyndale-Biscoe, OBE
           (Flag Officer Reserve Aircraft)
Secretary,
Commander S .   G.H. Moore
Flag Lt.
Lt.   E(AE) R.G.C. Smith
Chief Staff Officer,
Captain   E .. E.G. Beard

                    STAFF

Captain   S ...H.L. Cryer, MVO
                        (S.S.O.)
                  L ...F.H. Starks
                        (S.L.O.)
Commander E(AE) ... J.G.T.D. Atkinson
          X(O) .... A.F. Paterson
          (S.O. Air and Maintenance Commander)
          E(AE) ... E.H. Banfield
Lt.-Com. X(P) ... I.D. Roberts
                  (Lt.-Com.(Air))

January 1958

CONDOR (T.R.S.B. 421249)
(R.N.A.S. Arbroath, Angus)

Rear Admiral ...... A.J. Tyndale-BISCOE, OBE
          (Flag Officer reserve Aircraft)
Secretary,
Commander   S ..... G.H. Moore
Flag Lt.,
Lt.   E(AE) ..R.G.C. Smith

Chief Staff Officer,
Captain   E ... E.G. Beard

                    STAFF

Captain   S ... H.L. Cryer, MVO
             (Captain Admin.)
             L ... F.H. Starks
                    (S.L.O.)
Commander   E(AE) J.G.T.D. Atkinson
             X(O)..A.F. Paterson
          (S.O. Air and Maintenance Commander)
             E(AE) E.H. Banfield
Lt.-Com.   X(P)..I.D. Roberts
             (Lt.-Com.(Air))
Instr.,
Commander ........J.C. Gascoigne, OBE
                    (S.I.O.)
Surg.,
Commander........P.S. Edgecombe
                    (S.M.O.)

Chapter 8

Roll of Honour

They rest here still, forgotten not,
By next of kin in far off lands;
Their farewell smiles and brave hand waves
Their letters home from war,
Then suddenly, no more;
But from this lonely spot on Scotland's eastern shore
They still reach out,
To touch the hearts and souls of those
Who waved them off
So long ago.

Rev. George Fairlie

Casualties of H M S CONDOR, WW 2.
From the Database of The Commonwealth War Graves Commission.

Canada

HALIFAX MEMORIAL - Nova Scotia

DIAMOND, Lieutenant, JOHN EDMUND, H.M.C.S. Condor Royal Canadian Navy Vol. Reserve. 10th July 1942. Age 26. Son of Randolph William and Nellie Emily Diamond, of Trail, British Columbia. Panel 8.

United Kingdom

ANNAN CEMETERY - Dumfriesshire

LAURIE, Sub-Lieutenant (A), ALASTAIR FLETCHER, H.M.S. Condor Royal Naval Volunteer Reserve. 5th June 1942. Age 20. Son of William Gilchrist Fletcher Laurie and Clarissa Mary Laurie. Sec. R. Grave 35.

ARBROATH WESTERN CEMETERY - Angus

AYRE, Lieutenant (A), ANTHONY CHARLES EDWARD, H.M.S. Condor Royal Navy. 8th December 1941. Age 23. Son of Paymaster Captain L. C. E. Ayre, C.B.E., R.N., and Mrs. D. B. A. Ayre, of Wembury, Devon. Compt. D. North Border, Grave 14.

BAKER, Leading Cook, RUFUS ISAAC, P MX49255, H.M.S. Condor Royal Navy. 15th September 1940. Age 26. Son of Thomas George and Lily Elizabeth Baker; husband of Winifred Mary Baker, of Cosham, Portsmouth. Compt. D. North Border, Grave 51.

BRIFFETT, Sub-Lieutenant (A), LEONARD HERBERT, H.M.S. Condor Royal Naval Volunteer Reserve. 10th December 1941. Age 21. Son of Reginald Herbert and Louisa Harriett Briffett. Winner of British Games Junior 100 yards Sprint 1937, and Middlesex Senior 220 yards in 1939. Compt. D. North Border, Grave 13.

BUNCH, Sub-Lieutenant (A), SAMUEL HOSKIN, H.M.S. Condor Royal Navy. 11th June 1941. Age 22. Son of Herbert Ernest and Jane McKenzie Bunch, of Roehampton. London: husband of Sonia Bunch. Compt. D. North Border, Grave 8.

CALWELL, Leading Airman, WILLIAM NOEL, FX85505, H.M.S. Condor Royal Navy. 13th May 1942. Age 23. Son of Dr. Andrew M. Calwell, M.C., M.B., Ch.B., and Ida P. Calwell, of Wilkieston, Midlothian. Compt. D. North Border, Grave 39.

CARPENTER, Sub-Lieutenant (A), SYDNEY JAMES, H.M.S. Condor Royal Naval Volunteer Reserve. 20th October 1941. Age 23. Son of James William and Dorothy Selina Carpenter, of Sandown, Isle of Wight. Compt. D. North Border, Grave 11.

CLARKE, Sub-Lieutenant (A), FRANK DAVID STRICKLAND, H.M.S. Condor Royal Naval Volunteer Reserve. 13th May 1942. Age 25. Son of Frank Clarke, formerly M.P., and of Hilda Mary Clarke, of Hurstpierpoint, Sussex. Compt. D. North Border, Grave 15.

COLLINS, Air Mechanic (E) 1st Class, ARTHUR FREDERICK, FX79072, H.M.S. Condor Royal Navy. 7th August 1941. Son of David and Elizabeth Jane Collins, of Ynyshir, Glamorgan. Compt. D. North Border. Grave 44.

DAVID, Midshipman (A), JOHN ALEXANDER, H.M.S. Condor Royal Naval Volunteer Reserve. 1st May 1941. Age 18. Son of Alexander Noel and Violet Norah David. Compt. D. North Border, Grave 5.

DAVIES, Wren, IVY MARION, 6357, H.M.S. Condor Women's Royal Naval Service, 24th January 1941, Age 44. Daughter of Edward Frederick and Annie Davies, of Finsbury Park, Middlesex. Compt. D. North Border. Grave 47.

DE CUNHA, Leading Airman, THOMAS DAVID, FX95601, H.M.S. "Condor" Royal Navy, 10th August 1943, Age 22. Son of Louis John and Suzy de Cunha, of Jagatdal, 24 Parganas, Bengal, India. Compt. D. North Border. Grave 35.

FURLONG, Lieutenant (A), ROBERT HENRY, H.M.S. "Condor" Royal Navy, 8th July 1941, Age 28. Son of Alfred William and Hilda Florence Furlong; husband of Nancy Furlong, of Newbury, Berkshire. Compt. D. North Border. Grave 10.

GRUBB, Leading Airman, CECIL HERBERT, JX344902, H.M.S. Condor Royal Navy, 10th August 1943, Age 22. Son of Herbert Grubb, and of Margaret Grubb, of Edinburgh. Compt. D. North Border. Grave 37.

HARLEY, Chief Petty Officer, JOHN, P 225427, H.M.S. Condor Royal Navy, 2nd July 1942, Age 54. Son of John and Katherine Harley; husband of Florence Ada Harley, of Copnor, Hampshire. Compt. D. North Border. Grave 42.

HARVEY, Lieutenant (A), JOHN FRANCIS, H.M.S. "Condor" Royal Naval Volunteer Reserve, 11th December 1942. Compt. D. North Border. Grave 17.

JENNINGS, Lieut-Commander (A), FREDERICK GODFREY, H.M.S. Condor Royal Navy, 2nd July 1941, Age 39. Son of Frederick Summers Jennings and Ellen Jennings, of Midhurst, Sussex; husband of Kathleen Elizabeth Jennings. Compt. D. North Border. Grave 9.

JONES, Leading Airman, HAROLD VAUGHAN, FX79222, H.M.S. Condor Royal Navy, 15th December 1940, Age 24. Son of Benjamin and Mabel Jones, of Millhouses, Sheffield. B.Com. Hons. (Lond.). Compt. D. North Border. Grave 49.

MARSH, Petty Officer, SAMUEL ALFRED, 228468, H.M.S. Condor Royal Navy, 20th December 1942, Age 54. Son of Alfred and Emily Marsh; husband of Helen Marsh, of Carnoustie. Compt. D. North Border. Grave 40.

McSHANE, Midshipman (A), JAMES ANTHONY, Midn.(A), R.N.V.R. H.M.S. Condor Royal Naval Volunteer Reserve, 23rd August 1940, Age 1. Son of James and Ellen Annie McShane, c f Ashkirk, Selkirkshire. Compt. D. North Border, Grave 2.

MEYER, Sub-Lieutenant (A), JOHN HAYCROFT, H.M.S. Condor Royal Naval Volunteer Reserve, 23rd October 1940, Age 21. Compt. D. North Border, Grave 6.

PATTERSON, Leading Airman, BRIAN ARTHUR, 2825, H.M.S. Condor Royal New Zealand Navy, 13th May 1942, Age 24. Son of John Samuel Patterson and of Irene Alice Patterson (nee Smart), of Woodville, Hawke's Bay, New Zealand. Compt. D. North Border, Grave 43.

POLLOCK, Lieutenant, HERBERT MERCER, H.M.S. Condor Royal Naval Volunteer Reserve, 10th August 1943, Age 42. Son of James Alexander and Annie Olivia Pollock; husband of Iris Isobel Pollock, of Malone, Co. Antrim, Northern Ireland. Compt. D. North Border, Grave 20.

RAVEY, Sub-Lieutenant (A), WILLIAM, H.M.S. Condor Royal Naval Volunteer Reserve, 17th February 1943, Age 22. Son of David and Annie Mary Ravey, of Ilford, Essex. Compt. D. North Border. Grave 18.

READ, Sub-Lieutenant (A), ROBERT HODGSON, H.M.S.Condor, Royal Naval Volunteer Reserve, 23rd August 1940, Age 21. Son of Robert Hodgson Read and Marie Griffin Read. Compt. D. North Border. Grave 1.

TEAR, Leading Airman, FRANK WILLIAM, FX90669, H.M.S. Condor Royal Navy, 13th May 1942, Age 25. Son of William and Bertha Tear, of Lincoln; husband of Irene Tear (nee Atkinson), of Lincoln. Compt. D. North Border, Grave 41.

THARME, Air Fitter (E), FREDERICK ROBERT, FX88319, H.M.S. Condor Royal Navy, 27th January 1943. Age 19. Son of Robert and Florence Kate Tharme, of Harrogate, Yorkshire. Compt. D. North Border, Grave 38.

THOMPSON, Lieutenant Commander, WARD, H.M.S. Condor Royal Navy, 8th July 1941. Age 31. Compt. D. North Border, Grave 12.

AYR CEMETERY - Ayrshire

ARMSTRONG, Sub-Lieutenant (A), JOHN GEOFFREY, H.M.S. Condor Royal Naval Volunteer Reserve, 2nd December 1944. Age 22. Son of Henry and Katherine May Armstrong, of Denbigh. Sec. R. 1931 Div. Grave 2722A.

BARKING (RIPPLESIDE) CEMETERY - Essex

SINSTADT, Leading Airman, RICHARD ALBERT, FX88469, H.M.S. Condor Royal Navy, 17th February 1943. Age 21. Son of Richard William and Lilian Alice Sinstadt, of Barking. Sec. H. Grave 157.

BELFAST CITY CEMETERY - County Antrim

WADE, Sub-Lieutenant (A), LEONARD PERRY, H.M.S. Condor Royal Naval Volunteer Reserve, 2nd October 1945. Age 23. Son of Flossie L. Wade, of Kelowna, British Columbia, Canada. Glenalina Extn. Sec. B.S. Grave 128.

BLACKLEY (ST. ANDREW) CHURCHYARD - Lancashire

BOARDMAN, Leading Airman, STANLEY, PJX 168146, H.M.S. Condor Royal Navy, 21st May 1943. Age 24. Son of Benjamin and Martha Boardman. Sec. A. Grave 390.

BYLEY (ST. JOHN) CHURCHYARD - Cheshire

REYNOLDS, Petty Officer, GEORGE GEOFFREY, D S M, L FX77304, H.M.S. Condor Royal Navy, 11th February 1946. Age 24. Son of Dennis and Edith Reynolds; husband of Edith Dorothy Reynolds, of Didsbury, Manchester. Sec. E. Grave 1.

CAMBERWELL NEW CEMETERY - London

BEGLEY, Petty Officer(Airman), ROBERT OSMOND, FX114962, H.M.S. Condor Royal Navy, 29th March 1945. Age 30. Son of Henry Thomas Begley and Ethel Begley, husband of Ada Louisa Begley, of East Dulwich. Square 90. Grave 8550.

CHESTER-LE-STREET CEMETERY - Durham

PLACE, Petty Officer, Wre/1, FLORENCE ELIZABETH, 12909, Women's Royal Naval Service, H.M.S. Condor Women's Royal Naval Service, 29th October 1942. Age 38. Daughter of Thomas and Elizabeth Place, of Chester-le-Street. Sec. I. Grave 16.

CHRISTCHURCH CEMETERY - Hampshire

BURDEN, Leading Airman, RICHARD COLIN, FX 77610, H.M.S. Condor Royal Navy, 30th August 1940, Age 20. Son of Reginald Stuart Burden and Dorothy Burden, of Bournemouth. Sec. C. (Uncons. New). Grave 13.

COOKSTOWN NEW CEMETERY - County Antrim

BAYNE, Petty Officer Airman, ALLEN MILLAR CAMERON, FX76845, H.M.S. Condor Royal Navy, 17th February 1943, Age 23. Son of William James Bayne, and of Selina Bayne, of Tinwald, Canterbury, New Zealand. Sec. A. Grave 1116.

COVENTRY (LONDON ROAD) CEMETERY - Warwickshire

HANCOX, Able Seaman, THOMAS, P/223408, H.M.S. Condor Royal Navy, 27th November 1943, Age 56. Son of William Hancox and of Harriet Hancox (nee Slaney), of Coventry; husband of Minnie Hancox (nee Cooley), of Coventry. Square 294. Grave 177.

CRYSTAL PALACE DISTRICT CEMETERY - Kent

CUNY, Leading Airman, GEOFFREY CHARLES GEORGE FX, 89297, H.M.S. Condor Royal Navy, 10th August 1943. Sec. V. 10. Grave 12770.

DEWSBURY CEMETERY - Yorkshire

ANDREWS, Wren, EMILY, 78934, H.M.S. Condor Women's Royal Naval Service, 5th June 1946, Age 19. Daughter of Mr. and Mrs. Arthur Andrews, of Ravensthorpe, Dewsbury. Cons. Sec. A. Grave 436.

DORE (CHRIST CHURCH) CHURCHYARD - Yorkshire

STONE, Wren, DOROTHY JOYCE, 89729, H.M.S. Condor Women's Royal Naval Service, 5th April 1945. West Gate. Grave C.1.

EDINBURGH (SAUGHTON) CEMETERY - Edinburgh

GRAY, Sick Berth Attendant, JOHN, P/MX 94298, H.M.S. Condor Royal Navy, 21st January 1945, Age 31. Son of Walter Scott Gray and Rebecca Donaldson Gray, of Edinburgh; husband of Jane Clark Gray, of Edinburgh. Sec. L. Grave 908.

EDINBURGH (WARRISTON) CREMATORIUM - Edinburgh

HOGG, Sub-Lieutenant (A), GRAHAM ANGUS, D S C and bar, H.M.S. Condor Royal Naval Volunteer Reserve, 18th March 1942, Age 20. Son of William Angus Hogg and of Elsie Harriet Hogg (nee Graham), of Newcastle-on-Tyne. Panel 2.

ENFIELD CREMATORIUM - Middlesex

POCOCK, Lieutenant (A), BERNARD CYRIL, H.M.S. "Condor" Royal Naval Volunteer Reserve, 15th December 1940, Age 29. Son of Henry Edward Percy and Winifred Emily Pocock; husband of Joan Marjorie Pocock, of Winchmore Hill. Panel 3.

GELLYGAER (GWAELODYBRITHDIR) CEMETERY - Glamorganshire

WILLIAMS, Sub-Lieutenant (A), ROBERT ARFON, H.M.S. Condor Royal Naval Volunteer Reserve. 12th November 1942. Age 20. Son of John J. Williams and Kate Williams, of Bargoed. Sec. F. Grave 4289.

GOLBORNE (ST. THOMAS) CHURCHYARD - Lancashire

BROWN, Marine, EDWIN, PO/X 111439. H.M.S. Condor Royal Marines. 11th November 1942. Age 20. Son of Edwin Albert and Jane Brown, of Golborne. Sec. B. Row 4. Grave 3.

GREENWICH ROYAL NAVAL CEMETERY - London

KEMP, Sub-Lieutenant (A), PERCY. H.M.S. Condor Royal Naval Volunteer Reserve. 11th December 1942. Age 19. Son of Bertram Marshall Kemp and Eliza Ellen Kemp, of West Greenwich. Officers' ground. Plot E. Row M. Grave 10.

HASLAR ROYAL NAVAL CEMETERY - Hampshire

BAGG, Petty Officer Telegraphist, GEORGE WILLIAM HENRY, P/JX 128179. H.M.S. Condor Royal Navy. 30th August 1943. Age 35. Son of Henry and Beatrice Bagg; husband of Florence Bertha Bagg, of Chessel, Isle of Wight. E. 64. 9.

HORLEY (ST. BARTHOLOMEW) NEW CHURCHYARD - Surrey

DOWDALL, Able Seaman, THOMAS GEORGE, P/JX224175. H.M.S. Condor Royal Navy. 10th April 1942. Age 21. Son of Thomas George and Lillian Alice Dowdall, of Salfords. Block G. Row N. Grave 1.

IDLE UPPER CHAPEL (CONGREGATIONAL) CEMETERY - Yorkshire

MITCHELL, Sub-Lieutenant (A), LAWRENCE EDMUND. H.M.S. Condor Royal New Zealand Naval Vol Reserve. 10th December 1941. Age 23. Son of Norman and Marion Mitchell, of Remuera, Auckland, New Zealand. Sec. J. Grave 8.

IPSWICH CEMETERY - Suffolk

BAYLEY, Leading Airman, WILLIAM ARTHUR MAXWELL FX. 84984. H.M.S. Condor Royal Navy. 8th December 1941. Age 19. Son of Arthur Maxwell and Marjorie Nella Bayley, of Ipswich. Sec. X.J. Div 2 Grave 199.

KESWICK (ST. JOHN) CHURCHYARD - Westmoreland

DENNISON, Midshipman (A), MAURICE ROBINSON. H.M.S. Condor Royal Naval Volunteer Reserve. 12th July 1942. Son of Robert and Elsie Dennison, of Keswick. Plot B. Grave 132.

LANCING (ST. JAMES THE LESS) CHURCHYARD EXTENSION - Sussex

ADAMS, Wren, PEGGY MAY, 51859. H.M.S. Condor Women's Royal Naval Service. 4th March 1944. Age 20. Daughter of John Henry William and Mabel Alexandra Adams, of Lancing. Plot T. Grave 126.

LEE-ON-SOLENT MEMORIAL. - Hampshire

ANDERSON, Leading Airman, HARRY BEWS, FAA/FX. 85284. H.M.S. Condor Royal Navy. 2nd October 1941. Age 25. Son of Dr. J. Anderson and Mrs. C. Anderson. M.A. Bay 2. Panel 1.

ASHCROFT. Sub-Lieutenant (A), WILFRED JAMES CHARLES, H.M.S. Condor Royal Naval Volunteer Reserve. 14th September 1942. Age 21. Son of Wilfred Ernest and Elizabeth Mary Ashcroft, of Middlesbrough. Bay 3, Panel 7.

BLACKLAWS, Air Fitter, EDWARD PATERSON, FAA/FX. 89636. H.M.S. Condor Royal Navy, 2nd February 1943. Age 29. Husband of Anna Blacklaws. Bay 4, Panel 4.

BURKE, Leading Airman, WILLIAM MAURICE, FAA FX. 705451. H.M.S. Condor Royal Navy, 31st July 1945. Age 19. Son of William M. and Alice M. Burke. Bay 6. Panel 1.

BURTON, Leading Airman, EDWARD CHARLES, FAA/FX. 705120. H.M.S. Condor Royal Navy, 31st July 1945. Age 21. Son of Charles Edward Coote Burton and Lizzie Burton, of Dagenham, Essex. Bay 6, Panel 1.

FORBES, Sub-Lieutenant (A), ANDREW SINCLAIR. H.M.S. Condor Royal Naval Volunteer Reserve. 30th July 1945. Bay 6, Panel 3.

FRASER, Sub-Lieutenant (A), GORDON ALLISON, H.M.S. Condor Royal Naval Volunteer Reserve. 14th September 1942. Age 20. Son of the Revd. Albert Edward Fraser, M.A., and Elizabeth Allison Fraser, of Solihull Rectory, Warwickshire. Bay 4, Panel 2.

GARGETT. Sub-Lieutenant (A), GERALD FREDERICK. H.M.S. Condor Royal Naval Volunteer Reserve. 15th August 1944. Age 22. Son of Frederick William and Helen Blanche Gargett, of Cottingham, Yorkshire. Bay 5, Panel 5.

GODFREY-FAUSSETT, Lieutenant, DAVID FREDERICK, D.S.C. twice Mentioned in Despatches, R.N. H.M.S. Condor Royal Navy, 11th March 1942. Age 28. Son of Captain Sir Bryan Godfrey-Faussett, G.C.V.O., C.M.G., R.N., and of Lady Godfrey-Faussett (nee Eugenie Dudley Ward) Bay 3, Panel 1.

HOWES, Chief Petty Officer Pilot, DONALD HARRY, FAA/FX. 96064. H.M.S. Condor Royal Navy, 8th November 1944. Age 22. Son of Harry and Jane Howes. Bay 5, Panel 1.

KELLOW, Leading Airman, GEORGE FREDERICK WILLIAM, FAA/FX. 112872. H.M.S. Condor. Royal Navy, 11th May 1944. Age 19. Son of Frederick George and Dolly Annie Kellow, of St. Marychurch, Torquay. Bay 5, Panel 2.

MARKLAND, Leading Airman. RONALD WILLIAM. FAA FX. 88404. H.M.S. Condor Royal Navy, 10th July 1942. Age 22. Son of Arthur Henry and Amy Bellingham Markland. Bay 3, Panel 2.

MARSHALL, Leading Airman, MICHAEL JOHN, FAA/FX. 96223. H.M.S. Condor Royal Navy, 15th August 1944. Age 20. Bay 5, Panel 2.

McCALLUM, Leading Airman, WILLIAM, FAA/FX. 97158. H.M.S. Condor Royal Navy, 10th July 1942. Age 21. Son of William and Ann Jane Caldwell Dunlop McCallum, of Riccarton, Ayrshire. Bay 3, Panel 2.

MEALING, Sub-Lieutenant (A), WILLIAM DOUGLAS, H.M.S. Condor Royal Naval Volunteer Reserve. 11th May 1944. Age 21. Son of William Herbert and Edith May Mealing, of Chester. Bay 5, Panel 6.

MICHELL, Sub-Lieutenant (A), LAWRENCE ARTHUR CHICHELEY, H.M.S. Condor Royal Naval Volunteer Reserve. 24th November 1941. Bay 2, Panel 7.

MITCHLEY, Leading Airman, GEORGE EDWARD, FAA/FX. 82875. H.M.S. Condor Royal Navy, 15th August 1944. Age 29. Bay 5, Panel 2.

OATES, Lieutenant, THOMAS HERBERT BEVERIDGE, H.M.S. Condor Royal Navy, 8th December 1941. Age 31. Son of John Val Oates and Nellie Oates. Polar Medal. Bay 1, Panel 6.

POWELL, Lieutenant (A), ALLEN CHARLES, H.M.S. "Condor" Royal Naval Volunteer Reserve. 9th November 1944. Son of James and Elizabeth Anne Powell, of Ponders End, Middlesex. Bay 5, Panel 4.

SMITH, Sub-Lieutenant (A), DUNCAN EDWARD, H.M.S. Condor Royal Naval Volunteer Reserve. 2nd October 1941. Age 21. Son of William Edward and Elizabeth Catherine Smith, of Nutley, Sussex. Bay 2, Panel 7.

SUTHERLAND, Acting Sub Lieutenant (A), JAMES DONALD, H.M.S. Condor Royal Naval Volunteer Reserve. 31st July 1945. Age 20. Son of Donald and Helen Sutherland, of Thurso, Caithness-shire. Bay 6, Panel 6.

THOMPSON, Sub-Lieutenant, RAYMOND CHARLES WILLIAM, H.M.S. Condor Royal Naval Volunteer Reserve. 7th June 1945. Age 22. Son of Charles Drummond Thompson and Minnie Thompson. Bay 6, Panel 5.

TILLARD, Lieutenant Commander, ARTHUR JAMES, H.M.S. Condor Royal Navy. 8th July 1941. Age 34. Bay 1, Panel 6.

TOWNEND, Sub-Lieutenant (A), RICHARD FRANK, H.M.S. Condor Royal Naval Volunteer Reserve. 9th August 1942. Age 24. Son of Herbert Patrick Victor and Lettice Joan Townend. Bay 4, Panel 2.

TREND, Leading Airman, EDWARD OLIVER DEANE, FAA FX. 112924, H.M.S. Condor Royal Navy, 11th May 1944. Age 21. Son of Edward Theophilus and Eleanor Deane Trend. Bay 5, Panel 3.

WADDY, Midshipman (A), ROGER LATHAM, H.M.S. Condor Royal Naval Volunteer Reserve, 19th July 1941. Bay 2, Panel 7.

WILLIAMS, Leading Airman, MICHAEL GEORGE OWEN, FAA FX. 112546, H.M.S. Condor Royal Navy. 8th November 1944. Age 18. Bay 5, Panel 3.

WRIGHT, Leading Airman, HUBERT, FAA FX. 606704, H.M.S. Condor Royal Navy. 8th November 1944. Age 29. Son of Walter and Lizzie Wright; husband of Muriel Louise Wright, of Handsworth, Yorkshire. Bay 5, Panel 3.

LEISTON CEMETERY - Suffolk

PACKMAN, Leading Airman, BERNARD HEWETT FX. 85252, H.M.S. Condor Royal Navy. 10th December 1941. Age 20. Son of Ernest and Winifred May Packman, of Leiston. Grave 670.

MERTHYR TYDFIL (CEFN) CEMETERY - Brecknockshire

DAVIES, Leading Airman, THOMAS ARTHUR, FX. 96168, H.M.S. Condor Royal Navy. 17th July 1943. Age 25. Son of George and Ada Gertrude Davies; husband of Beryl Margaret Davies, of Merthyr Tydfil, Glamorgan. Sec. 1. Uncons. Grave 7.

METHLICK CEMETERY - Aberdeenshire

MORRISON, Sub-Lieutenant (A), GEORGE CLARK, H.M.S. Condor Royal Naval Volunteer Reserve. 5th June 1942. Age 24. Son of Thomas and Catherine Burgess Morrison, of Methlick, M.A. (Aberdeen). Sec.1. Row 10. Grave 30.

NEWCASTLE-UPON-TYNE (ALL SAINTS) CEMETERY - Northumberland

COOPER, Ordinary Seaman, HENRY, P/JX 273042, H.M.S. Condor Royal Navy. 10th April 1942. Age 31. Son of James and Isabella Cooper, of Newcastle-on-Tyne; husband of Alice Cooper, of Shieldfield, Newcastle-on-Tyne. Sec. M. Cons. Grave 191.

War Graves, Western Cemetery, Arbroath

NORBURY (ST. THOMAS) CHURCHYARD - Cheshire

TUDGE. Petty Officer Airman, AIRMAN RICHARD, SR8144, H.M.S. Condor Royal Navy, 17th July 1943. Age 25, Son of John and Ethel Tudge, of Hazel Grove. Sec. F. Grave 254.

NOTTINGHAM CHURCH CEMETERY - Nottinghamshire

PIGGIN. Leading Airman, FRANK REDGATE FX, 85272, H.M.S. Condor Royal Navy, 10th December 1941. Age 19, Son of Frank and Sarah Rachel Piggin, of Nottingham. Rock Sec. Grave 6820.

PAUL (ST. PAUL DE LION) CHURCH CEMETERY - Cornwall

WRIGHT. Commander (Instructor), CECIL ERNEST, M B E, H.M.S. Condor Royal Navy, 27th April 1947. Age 54, Son of Joseph Bruce and Annie Wright, of Mousehole; husband of Eliza Jane Wright, of Mousehole. Upper part. Row H. Grave 5.

PERSHORE CEMETERY - Worcestershire

SEARLE. Leading Airman, NORMAN FREDERICK, FX77460, H.M.S. Condor Royal Navy, 11th August 1941. Age 20, Son of Henry William and Cecilia Maud Searle, of Holt Heath. North of church.

PORTSMOUTH (EASTNEY OR HIGHLAND RD) CEMETERY - Hampshire

COLES. Leading Airman, RONALD WALTER JAMES FX, 88499, H.M.S. Condor Royal Navy, 13th May 1942. Age 20, Son of Walter Constant Coles and Elizabeth Ada Coles, of Southsea. Sec. H. Row 11. Grave 33.

RHONDDA (TREALAW) CEMETERY - Glamorganshire

HOPKINS. Sub-Lieutenant (A), TREVOR, H.M.S. Condor Royal Naval Volunteer Reserve, 2nd February 1942, Age 25, Son of Thomas and Sarah Jane Hopkins, of Trealaw. Plot C. Grave 509.

ROCHDALE CREMATORIUM - Lancashire

RODGERS. Sub-Lieutenant (A), KEITH ASHWORTH, H.M.S. Condor Royal Naval Volunteer Reserve, 18th October 1945, Age 22, Son of Harry and Fay Rodgers, of Haslingden; husband of Beryl Rodgers, of Haslingden. Panel 6.

SHIPLEY (NAB WOOD) CEMETERY - Yorkshire

WATERHOUSE. Sub-Lieutenant (A), ARNOLD, H.M.S. Condor Royal Naval Volunteer Reserve, 27th February 1943, Age 21, Son of Allan Wilson Waterhouse and Annie Waterhouse, of Shipley. Sec. B. Grave 28.

SOUTHAMPTON CREMATORIUM - Hampshire

WATSON. Lieutenant (E), AULAY WILLIAM, M B E, H.M.S. Condor Royal Navy, 11th February 1946. Age 25, Son of Colonel William Douglas Watson and Kathleen Rose Watson, of Newton Tony, Wiltshire. Panel 6.

SOUTHEND-ON-SEA (SUTTON ROAD) CEMETERY - Essex

DUPERE. Lieutenant (A), CHARLES HENRY, H.M.S. Condor Royal Naval Volunteer Reserve, 13th May 1942, Age 31, Son of Mr. and Mrs. Hermon Dupere; husband of Ivy Addie Dupere, of Southend-on-Sea. Plot R. Grave 12109.

ST. STEPHEN'S-BY-SALTASH (ST. STEPHEN) CHURCHYARD - Cornwall

ASHTON, Leading Airman, GERALD JOHN FX. 90585. H.M.S. Condor Royal Navy. 12th November 1942. Age 19. Son of John Francis and Clare Ashton, of Saltash. Grave 3243.

STRENSALL (ST. MARY) CHURCHYARD - Yorkshire

LUNN, Sub-Lieutenant (A), DOUGLAS VERNON, H.M.S. Condor Royal New Zealand Naval Vol Reserve. 10th August 1943. Age 23. Son of Vernon Henry and Elsie Katherine Lunn; husband of Sarah Marjorie Lunn, of Strensall. Grave 48.

TWICKENHAM PAROCHIAL CEMETERY - Middlesex

FIELDING, Able Seaman, WILLIAM CORNELIUS. P J 35479. H.M.S. Condor Royal Navy. 9th July 1944. Age 45. Son of Cornelius John and Florence Elizabeth Fielding; husband of Ellen Elizabeth Fielding, of Twickenham. Also served in the 1914-18 War. Plot M. Row V. Class C. Grave 26.

UXBRIDGE (HILLINGDON) CEMETERY - Middlesex

KIRBY, Sub-Lieutenant (A), DONALD GEOFFREY, H.M.S. Condor Royal Naval Volunteer Reserve. 26th October 1943. Age 21. Son of Ernest Percy and Elise Kirby, of Hillingdon Heath Uxbridge. Row B.P. Grave

WALLASEY (RAKE LANE) CEMETERY - Cheshire

HARDY, Sub-Lieutenant (A), LESLIE THOMAS. H.M.S. Condor Royal Naval Volunteer Reserve. 10th March 1942. Age 21. Son of Thomas E. Hardy and Selina N. Hardy, of Wallasey. Sec. 13.G. Grave 152.

WANDSWORTH (STREATHAM) CEMETERY - London

GOMPERS. Petty Officer Wren, PAULINE MARY. 43752. H.M.S. Condor Women's Royal Naval Service. 27th July 1945. Age 23. Daughter of Henri R. Gompers and Marjorie C. Gompers, of Streatham. Block O. Grave 336.

WINDREW, Chief Petty Officer Airman, LEONARD STAFFEL JOHN FX. 80772. H.M.S. Condor Royal Navy. 29th March 1945. Age 30. Son of John William and Margaret Windrew; husband of Constance Theresa May Windrew. Block 17. Grave 326.

WAREHAM CEMETERY - Dorset

BASCOMBE, Stoker 1st Class. GEORGE. P K 17769. H.M.S. Condor Royal Navy. 8th August 1942. Age 47. Son of William and Mary Jane Bascombe; husband of Bessie A. Bascombe, of Wareham. Sec. C. Row. L. Grave 27.

WHITCHURCH (ST. MARY) CHURCHYARD - Glamorganshire

CRADOCK, Sub-Lieutenant (A), LEONARD FRANCIS, H.M.S. Condor Royal Naval Volunteer Reserve. 14th September 1942. Age 21. Right of Lych gate.

WYMERING (SS. PETER AND PAUL) CHURCHYARD - Hampshire

HOPE, Able Seaman. JOHN FREDERICK. P J 37187. H.M.S. Condor Royal Navy. 17th May 1946. Age 47. Son of John and Esther Hope. husband of Lily Florence Hope. of Cosham. Portsmouth.

9 (HMS CONDOR)   *Commonwealth War Graves Commission*

Casualties of H M S PEEWIT, WW 2.
From the Database of The Commonwealth War Graves Commission.

New Zealand

NEW ZEALAND NAVAL MEMORIAL, DEVONPORT, AUCKLAND

BROWNE. Petty Officer, AIRMAN BARRIE HAWTREY. 7778. H.M.S. Peewit Royal New Zealand Navy. 8th July 1945. Age 23. Son of Kenllin Abel Hawtrey and Millicent Brunt Browne, of Auckland City. Panel 3.

United Kingdom

ARBROATH WESTERN CEMETERY - Angus

BATTEN, Sub-Lieutenant (A), FREDERICK MONCRIEFF, H.M.S. Peewit Royal New Zealand Naval Vol Reserve. 5th December 1944. Age 22. Son of Sidney George and Janette Batten, of Paraparaumu, Wellington, New Zealand. Compt. D. North Border, Grave 26.

DRAKE, Sub-Lieutenant (A), JAMES WILLIAM, H.M.S. Peewit Royal New Zealand Naval Vol Reserve. 29th August 1944. Age 22. Son of James Edward Ralph Drake and of Vera Fenella Drake (nee Palmer), of Howick, Auckland, New Zealand. Compt. D. North Border, Grave 27.

IRVINE, Lieutenant (A), JAMES GRAHAM, H.M.S. "Peewit" Royal Naval Volunteer Reserve. 7th September 1944. Age 23. Son of James D. Irvine and Dorothy Irvine, of St. Margarets, Middlesex. Compt. D. North Border, Grave 25.

JUPP, Midshipman (A), ANTHONY DALLAS, H.M.S. Peewit Royal Naval Volunteer Reserve. 29th August 1944. Age 19. Son of William Dallas Lony Jupp and Cecil May Jupp, of Stafford. Compt. D. North Border, Grave 24.

MARSHALL, Sub-Lieutenant (A), JOHN, H.M.S. Peewit Royal Naval Volunteer Reserve. 28th March 1944. Age 21. Son of John Josephine Marshall, of Paisley, Renfrewshire. Compt. D. North Border, Grave 22.

MEDD, Lieut-Commander (A), PETER NESBITT, M B E, H.M.S. Peewit Royal Navy. 19th August 1944. Age 3. Son of Allan Nesbit Medd and Jane Adele Vaughan Medd, of Wonersh, Surrey. Compt. D. North Border, Grave 23.

PARKER, Sub-Lieutenant (A), HENRY KENNETH WISLHAM, H.M.S. Peewit Royal Naval Volunteer Reserve. 30th December 1944. Age 20. Son of Henry Parker, and of Elsie May Parker, of Montreal, Province of Quebec, Canada. Compt. D. North Border, Grave 28.

THRIFT, Leading Air Fitter, GEORGE CHARLES, FX77133. H.M.S. Peewit Royal Navy. 15th August 1944. Age 20. Son of Alfred John and Annie Edith Thrift, of Ventnor, Isle of Wight. Compt. D. North Border, Grave 36.

BASTON (ST. JOHN THE BAPTIST) CHURCH BURIAL GROUND - Lincolnshire

PELL, Marine, FOWLER, PO/X 125020. H.M.S. Peewit Royal Marines. 27th March 1946. Age 18. Son of Mr. and Mrs. John Thomas Pell, of Baston. Grave 401.

BURTON-UPON-TRENT CEMETERY - Staffordshire

COLSON, Leading Air Mechanic, EDWARD FX, 92832. H.M.S. Peewit Royal Navy. 28th July 1945. Age 22. Son of George and Edith Ellen Colson, of Burton-upon-Trent. Gen. Sec. Grave 5745.

CARDIFF (CATHAYS) CEMETERY - Glamorganshire

CLARKE, Paymaster Lieut-Commander, VIVIAN, R D, H.M.S. Peewit Royal Naval Reserve. 16th March 1944. Age 32. Son of William Henry and Lucy Maud Clarke, of Cardiff; husband of Elsa Dora Clarke, of Whitchurch. Sec. E.L. Grave 196.

DAGENHAM (CHADWELL HEATH) CEMETERY - Essex

WILKINSON, Able Seaman, WILLIAM EDWARD, P/JX324436. H.M.S. Peewit Royal Navy. 27th June 1947. Age 23. Sec. B. Grave 214.

DARLEY ABBEY (ST. MATTHEW) CHURCHYARD - Derbyshire

FLETCHER, Sub-Lieutenant (A), DEREK STUART, H.M.S. Peewit Royal Naval Volunteer Reserve. 26th April 1944. Son of Thomas and Norah Fletcher, of Derby. Grave 27.

DUNDEE CREMATORIUM - Angus

DRAPER, Assistant Steward, JOHN ERNEST, P/LX781932. H.M.S. Peewit Royal Navy. 19th June 1946. Age 18. Son of George Ernest and Ida Mary Draper, of Stocksbridge, Yorkshire.

EDINBURGH (MOUNT VERNON) R. C. CEMETERY - Edinburgh

EGAN, Wren, AGNES, 105568. H.M.S. Peewit Women's Royal Naval Service. 27th August 1946. Age 18. Daughter of Thomas and Isabella Egan, of Edinburgh. Sec. D. Grave 271.

EDINBURGH (WARRISTON) CREMATORIUM - Edinburgh

LANGWILL, Sub-Lieutenant (A), PETER GRAHAM WILSON, H.M.S. Peewit Royal Naval Volunteer Reserve. 26th November 1943. Age 19. Son of Lyndesay G. Langwill and Freda M. Langwill, of Edinburgh. Panel 2.

FELIXSTOWE NEW CEMETERY - Suffolk

OLSEN, Lieutenant (A), JOHN FERRABY, H.M.S. "Peewit" Royal Navy. 27th March 1946. Age 29. Son of Stanley Olsen and of Edith Olsen (nee Walsh); husband of Pamela Cecil Olsen. Block B. Sec. F. Grave 2.

LEE-ON-SOLENT MEMORIAL - Hampshire

MELLOWS, Sub-Lieutenant (A), JOHN WILLIAM MILES, H.M.S. Peewit Royal Naval Volunteer Reserve. 10th June 1944. Age 20. Son of William Ernest Valentine and Lilian Laura Mellows, of West Bridgford, Nottinghamshire. Bay 5, Panel 6.

WARNER, Sub-Lieutenant (A), ARCHIBALD CHARLES, H.M.S. Peewit Royal Naval Volunteer Reserve. 1st January 1945. Age 21. Son of Archibald Charles and Lily Eleanor Warner, of Gravesend, Kent. Bay 6, Panel 5.

WILLIAMS, Lieutenant (A), PETER HOWARD, H.M.S. "Peewit" Royal Naval Volunteer Reserve. 22nd November 1945. Age 29. Son of Stanley and Gertrude Williams; husband of Lavinia Elizabeth Williams. Bay 6, Panel 3.

TOTTENHAM AND WOOD GREEN CEMETERY - Middlesex

ELMSLIE, Marine, FREDERICK STANLEY, CH.24666. H.M.S. Peewit Royal Marines. 9th November 1944. Age 38. Son of George Elmslie, and of Elizabeth Elmslie, of Tottenham. Gen. Sec. Grave 4000.

The following are believed to have been attached to CONDOR at the time of their deaths - this, however, has not been confirmed.

Arbroath Eastern Cemetery , Arbroath and St. Vigeans.
MAIR, Sgt. (Pilot) James Irvine , R/92048. R.C.A.F. 404 Squadron. 16th June, 1942. Age 19. Son of William Alexander and Margaret Mair , of Victoria, British Columbia, Canada. Compt.V, Grave 1.
PELLATT, Sgt. (Air Bomber) Frederick James, 1800826. RA.F. (V.R.). 14th, August, 1943, Compt V.Grave 2.

Arbroath Western Cemetery, Arbroath and St. Vigeans.

BRAGG, Sub-Lieut. (A) Gerald Arthur, R.N. H.M.S. Daelalus. 23rd. October, 1940. Age 23. Son of Mr and Mrs. Arthur Cecil Bragg; husband of Joan Mary Kathleen Bragg , of Yapton, Sussex. Compt. D. North Border Grave 4.
BURNS, Wt. Offr. (Pilot) George Francis, 1255448. R.A.F. (V.R.), attd. 753 Sqdn., F.A.A. 27th July, 1942. Age 22 . Son of Robert George and Lilian May Burns, of Dagenham, Essex. Compt. D. North Border, Grave 34.
CHETTLE, Sub-Lieut. (A) Richard John, R.N.Z.N.V.R. H.M.S. Daedalus. 20th June, 1943. Age 24. Son of Arthur James Chettle and Violet Mary Chettle, of Christchurch, Canterbury, New Zealand. Compt.D. North Border, Grave 19.
EVES, P.O. Airman Herbert George, F.X.79983. R.N. H.M.S. Daedalus. 17th. November, 1940. Son of Percy Herbert and Henrietta Eves, of Upper Portslade, Sussex, Compt. D., North Border, Grave 48.
HANNAM,A.B. Kenneth Robert,5097. R.C.N. H.M.C.S. Niobe. 17th November, 1942. Age 24. Son of Leslie John and Evelyn L. Hannam, of Victoria, British Columbia, Canada. Compt. D. North Border, Grave 33.

HARE, Ldg. Airman James Charles, FX77594.R.N. H.M.S. Shark II. 30th. August ,1940. Age 20 Son of Arthur Charles Ravenstone Hare and Eleanor Hare, of Highgate, Middlesex. Compt. D. North Border, Grave 52.
HOLMES, Wing Cdr. (Pilot) William Tatham, 19053. R.A.F. 8th. February, 1941. Compt. D. North Border, Grave 7.
LAWLER, Sub Lieut.(A) Dennis Minter, R.N.V.R. H.M.S. Merlin. 25th. August, 1942. Age 26. Son of Maria Elizabeth Lawler , of Johannesburg, South Africa. Compt.D. North Border, Grave 16.
PIMLOTT, Supply Asst. Kenneth, P/MX.63613.R.N. H.M.S. St. Angelo. 17th November , 1940 . Compt. D. North Border , Grave 46.
PITTS,A.C.1. Harold George, 523122. R.A.F. attd.767 Sqdn. F.A.A. 21st. August, 1941. Age 31. Son of

William J. Pitts, and of Annie Pitts, of Baildon, Yorkshire. Compt. D. North Border, Grave 45.
SMITH,Ldg. Supply Asst. Richard Norman , P/MX 59637 . R.N. H.M.S. Daedalus. 17th. November, 1942. Age 19. Son of Charles Heath Smith and Florence Smith , of Gloucester. Compt. D. North Border, Grave 50.

Two other war graves, not part of the Commonwealth Commission, are in the Western Cemetery. These are also believed to have been attached to CONDOR :-
HEINE, R.A.C., Koninkriik Dir Netherlanden. 21st. May, 1943. Grave 21.
VAN DEN BRINK, M.I., Koninkriik Dir Netherlanden. 18th.May, 1945. Grave 29.